Special Report

Redefining the CSCE: Challenges and Opportunities in the New Europe

Edited by
Ian M. Cuthbertson

Institute for EastWest Studies
Finnish Institute of International Affairs

Copyright © 1992 by the Institute for EastWest Studies, New York

Distributed by Westview Press

      5500 Central Ave.
      Boulder, Colorado 80301
      (800)456-1995

Printed by   The Finnish Institute of International Affairs
      Pursimiehenkatu 8
      00150 Helsinki
      Finland
      Tel: (358) (0) 170 434
      Fax: (358) (0) 669 375

Library of Congress Cataloging-in-Publication Data

Redefining the CSCE : challenges and opportunities in the new Europe /
    edited by Ian M. Cuthbertson.
            p.   cm. -- (Special Report / Institute for EastWest Studies)
    Includes bibliographical references.
    ISBN 0-913449-33-4 (IEWS) : $12.85. -- ISBN 0-8133-8644-6 (Westview)
    : $12.85
        1. European cooperation. 2. Security, International.   3. Europe--
Military policy.   4. Europe--Foreign relations.   5. Conference on
Security and Cooperation in Europe (1990 : Helsinki, Finland)
I. Cuthbertson, Ian M., 1957- . II. Series: Special report
(Institute for EastWest Studies)
JX1393,C65R43   1992
327,1'7'094--dc20   92-18018
                                         CIP

To my father, James Alexander Cuthbertson,
for all he did to make this possible.

Dad,
you remain the most unique human being
I have had the privilege of knowing.

Contents

Foreword

Finland has a long and proud role in the CSCE process--it has been one of the basic elements of Finnish foreign policy, and Finland has worked hard for the process since its inception. From the beginning, Finland found the idea and goals of the CSCE valuable both for its own national interest and for European unity and security. The history of the CSCE has confirmed its importance, and its progress attests to the validity of the assumptions that inspired our thinking.

Over the past 20 years, Europe has experienced profound changes. As a result, many scholars now wonder whether the era of hegemonic wars is over. For the first time in the history of modern Europe, major geopolitical changes have taken place peacefully. This raises hopes that a true transformation has occurred, one that can become institutionalized, and it is to be hoped that we have passed a true historical watershed in which the specter of another general war has finally passed from the scene.

Yet it is important to question expectations for this lasting peace and the hope that it will endure solely through its own inertia. It is more important than ever to identify those policies that best perpetuate a lasting peace and generate timely, constructive ideas and proposals.

Scholars, policy specialists, and diplomats must maintain close contact with each other if viable approaches are to be found to the challenges that face the CSCE. Academic or diplomatic ivory towers should no longer exist. In fact, the arena of international relations is extremely well covered by the media. Therefore I am convinced that the kind of dialogue and debate that this volume represents is one of the best vehicles available to us for improving international cooperation as well as, in the final analysis, international peace.

Since the system of nation-states was established by the Treaty of Westphalia in 1648, European countries have been trying to build a security order that would ensure greater civility in their mutual relations. The CSCE represents the latest and most ambitious process to achieve this goal. Unlike past proposals for cementing international order, the CSCE strives for a community of democratic states through which a peaceful security order might be built.

This process is taking place at a critical juncture of European history. The Cold War confrontation has faded away and a new security order is emerging, but its shape has not taken on a clear definition. The Helsinki process provides both the vision and concrete means towards safeguarding the peaceful development of Europe. The CSCE has an indispensable responsibility to protect common values and to set common goals, but it cannot carry out its mission alone. As a catalyst, however, and a framework for action in cooperation with other existing organizations, the CSCE can be a powerful force.

The Charter of Paris constitutes a starting point for a peaceful order in Europe. It defines common and unifying values of freedom, human dignity and human rights, self-determination, and minority rights. Complementary actions, including the renunciation of force and adherence to the rule of law, are essential elements governing peaceful relations among states and nations. There is no choice but to build lasting stability, and it must be based on the concept of one continent. Furthermore, Europe must proceed from the recognition of the historic interdependence between Europe, the United States, and Canada.

With these factors in mind, it is necessary to explore some ideas for strengthening the CSCE in conflict prevention, crisis management, and the peaceful settlement of disputes. The CSCE must now acquire a greater scope for action. Its cooperative security architecture offers, as former German Foreign Minister

Hans-Dietrich Genscher stated in his farewell speech, "the possibility of safeguarding peace in Europe by other means than the obsolete principles of power politics, balance of power or the staking-out of spheres of interest." It is possible that the CSCE could develop into a regional arrangement of the kind envisaged in Chapter 8 of the United Nations Charter. This goal should be achieved gradually, but it is within sight. The legal and political consequences of this interesting idea need further elaboration and research.

The CSCE has been tested in the former Yugoslavia and in the Caucasus. We are all well aware of the flaws of the structures and institutions of the CSCE in coping with these challenges. However, we also see in these crises the needs that must be responded to, and a vision of what the CSCE can become. The CSCE, as a process that today connects 52 countries, could function most effectively *first* as an instrument of preventive diplomacy, and *second* as an instrument of crisis management. A peacekeeping role, should other measures fail, ought also to become an essential component of these endeavors.

While considering these issues, it is important to keep in mind the difference between conflict prevention and crisis management of issues purely political in nature, on the one hand, and the peaceful settlement of disputes, which entails international efforts to apply international law in a defined dispute. This difference became most evident during the recent discussions on the proposal to create a European Court of Conciliation and Arbitration. Some would like to strengthen the CSCE with legally binding elements such as this Court. But others argue that the uniqueness and strength of the process lie in its ability to use political persuasion in conjunction with, but distinct from, the former approach of preventive diplomacy. The basic purpose of this proposal to strengthen the CSCE merits our support. But there are still some questions to be raised. First, all the CSCE countries would not necessarily join such a legal institution, which could create awkward situations. Second, the difference between politically and legally binding commitments is not necessarily decisive in practice. Finally, another means to enhance the CSCE is peacekeeping. The CSCE without a peacekeeping capability under its guidance would be an institution without credibility in today's Europe. Without the capacity to act in crises, the CSCE would have a voice but no influence.

Europe is in the process of reorganizing militarily, politically, and economically. Existing components, organizations, and institutions should be mutually reinforcing. Lasting solutions can be found only in a cooperative fashion. What is needed is a stronger CSCE, and decisiveness is necessary for its creation. Increasingly, such decisiveness is being displayed.

Paavo Väyrynen
Minister for Foreign Affairs of Finland
Helsinki
May 1992

Editor's Acknowledgements

There are many people to acknowledge in a collective effort such as this. First of all, I would like to thank all the scholars and officials who took part in the conference on "Redefining the CSCE: Challenges and Opportunities in the New Europe," Helsinki, May 21-22, 1992. Their names are listed at the end of this volume. This meeting, cohosted by the Institute for EastWest Studies and the Finnish Institute of International Affairs and sponsored by the Ministry of Foreign Affairs of Finland, formed the basis for the book. I wish especially to thank the chairs, paper writers, and discussants at the meeting for doing so much to make it a success; without them the insights that came out of the discussion would never have emerged.

In addition, I wish to thank Tapani Vaahtoranta and Sari Okko of the FIIA, without whom the meeting would not have taken place and this volume would never have appeared. To Alpo Rusi goes the credit as the catalyst who made everything happen. My debt to Jeff Hoover for his organizational work on the meeting, his rapporteuring, and his editing skills as well is considerable, as it is to Adam Smith Albion for all his help. I wish to thank Richard Levitt, IEWS Publications Director, for his help with the manuscript, and his indulgence for my wilder flights of fancy. The same is true for Whit Vye, our graphic artist. To Rosalie Morales Kearns, IEWS Publications Editor, goes the lion's share of credit for making this work readable.

As Director of the Security Program at the Institute for EastWest Studies, I wish to thank George Perkovich of the W. Alton Jones Foundation, whose support of the CSCE Project at the Institute made this conference and publication possible, and also Fritz Moser and the Carnegie Corporation of New York for their support of the Security Program. Thanks also to the Ford

Foundation, the John D. and Catherine T. MacArthur Foundation, the Rockefeller Brothers Fund, the William and Flora Hewlett Foundation, and the Scherman Foundation for their continued support of the Institute's programs. On behalf of the Finnish Institute of International Affairs, I would like to thank Neste Corporation, Nokia-Group, Metra Corporation, Sanoma Corporation, the Confederation of Finnish Industries, and the Central Association of Finnish Forest Industries for their support.

List of Abbreviations

ATTU Atlantic-to-the-Urals

CC Consultative Committee

CEI Central European Initiative

CFE Conventional Armed Forces in Europe

CFSP Common Foreign and Security Policy

CIS Commonwealth of Independent States

CMEA Council for Mutual Economic Assistance

CPC Conflict Prevention Center

CSBM Confidence and security-building measure

CSCE Conference on Security and Cooperation in Europe

CSO Committee of Senior Officials

EAC Euro-Atlantic Community

EAS Euro-Atlantic Space

EBRD European Bank for Reconstruction and Development

EEA European Economic Area

EFTA European Free Trade Association

EPC European Political Cooperation

NACC North Atlantic Cooperation Council

NATO North Atlantic Treaty Organization

NGO Nongovernmental organization

ODIHR Office for Democratic Institutions and Human Rights

OECD Organization for Economic Cooperation and Development

START Strategic Arms Reductions Talks

WEU Western European Union

WTO Warsaw Treaty Organization

Introduction

Ian M. Cuthbertson
Adam Smith Albion

When Stalin asked "How many divisions does the Pope have?" he was implicitly asserting a "realist" approach towards political relations and international conduct, crudely maintaining that power, particularly military power, ultimately triumphs over principle. Yet the Conference on Security and Cooperation in Europe (CSCE), with no divisions at all, can be said to have been one of the major influences that helped bring about the end of Stalin's legacy of communist dictatorship, first in East Central Europe and then ultimately in the Soviet Union itself. If NATO provided the West's muscle, the CSCE provided Europe's conscience. It also turned out to be a more useful stick with which to beat the back of totalitarianism and repression than all the tanks and missiles at NATO's disposal during the 40 years of the Cold War. As Voltaire stated over 200 years ago, God is not always on the side of the big battalions--an observation Stalin would not have understood.

Although internal economic and political developments and an obvious moral bankruptcy ultimately toppled the Eastern bloc regimes, it was the standards of behavior set by the CSCE that brought into sharp relief the all-too-obvious shortcomings of these governments. Their flaws were perceived not only in Western states, but, more importantly, by their own citizens. In their struggles against the regimes that sought to control every aspect of their lives, East European dissidents, as weaponless as the CSCE itself, explicitly invoked the Ten Principles of the

1

Helsinki Final Act to which their governments were signatories. While the CSCE was originally conceived in the West to help humanize the East European tyrannies, in the end it helped indigenous actors in the East to bring them down.

It is also important to remember that it was not only in the human dimension that the CSCE process unmasked the facade behind which the communist governments of Europe tried to hide for so long. Initially through its regimes of confidence- and security-building measures (CSBMs), and later through the various sets of negotiations for conventional arms control and disarmament in Europe, the CSCE and its associated bodies dismantled piece by piece the justifications fabricated by Warsaw Pact governments, especially in the Soviet Union, for devoting a disproportionate share of their national wealth to the preservation of a massive numerical superiority over NATO's forces in Europe. The more that was revealed about both sides' capabilities and ultimately their intentions, the more impossibly extravagant such military expenditure was seen to be for such misdeveloped economies. If it was economic hardship that drove East Europeans out onto the streets to make their revolutions, the fact was that people became aware of the causes of the problems faced by East European economies largely due to the gradually increasing information flow that formed part of the CSCE. That information showed not only that many of the sacrifices East European citizens had been asked to make throughout the post-World War II era had been based on a faulty reading of the West's fundamental motivations and capacities, but also that, while they had pauperized themselves in the name of national security, the economic gap between East and West had continued to widen all the time.

A child of the Cold War, the CSCE is in many ways a

2

victim of its own success. It is being forced to undertake a deep self-examination of its role and structures, a necessary probe if it is to continue to grow into post-Cold War maturity. The broad and relatively unstructured mandate of the CSCE process, which gave it flexibility during the last two decades, is now seen by some as a liability. With antagonism between the two blocs dissipating, bloc discipline within the CSCE is disappearing in the West and has already vanished in the East. As the membership has grown from 35 to 52 (at the time of this writing), internal cohesion and shared sense of purpose, never strong characteristics in the CSCE at the best of times, have further dissipated; the political, economic, cultural, and conceptual fault lines among its members have been bared for all to see. In comparison, the European Community looks like a tight-knit partnership of 12 countries with clearly common interests and objectives, even after the "no" vote in the Danish referendum. NATO has maintained a clear security identity and weathered the loss of enemies by adding them as friends through the creation of the North Atlantic Cooperation Council (NACC), and it is increasingly asserting its role in peacekeeping and possibly also peacemaking. All the while, NATO has remained the court of last appeal for a Western Europe at first euphoric about developments in the East but increasingly uneasy about the instability crowding its borders.

But what of the CSCE? Do shared values for the 52 exist? Some critics of the CSCE maintain that a coherent set of principles, symbolically dubbed "European," is impossible if "Europe" extends from "Vancouver to Vladivostok," as James Baker has said. Others remark that principles may be agreed to, but become unrealizable among an unmanageably large and disparate CSCE membership committed to consensus voting, or even "consensus minus one." It is the perceived "unrealizability" of the CSCE's ideals in the postrevolutionary environment of 1992 that has led to a new discussion of "realism" in the context of the CSCE process. If it is to be credible, the CSCE must simultaneously redefine and focus its mission, and build institutions with the capabilities to match that mission. What we might term "new realism about the CSCE" underpins calls to strengthen the CSCE as an organization and to give it more coherence as a process.

What is the reality that the CSCE faces? In the last two years, the CSCE has welcomed 17 states as members, most of which are suffering from economic, political, and social instability, including ethnic strife and ecological disintegration. A few have a dimly remembered democratic tradition to fall back on; most do not. Some are ex-partners from the Europe before World War II; most are ex-enemies of the West from the Cold War era, and not a few are still at war today with either each other or themselves. Since stability and security are the basis for any form of development, the CSCE's efforts to fully integrate its new membership as equal partners has driven it to become once again preoccupied with security issues of Basket One. This is an area where the CSCE has a long, distinguished, and successful track record in defusing tension and confrontation; in revisiting this arena, the supporters of the process believe that it can once again play to its traditional strengths.

Under the old model of bloc-to-bloc confrontation in Europe, it was the East that originally sought from the CSCE recognition of the legitimacy of the national and political geography resulting from the division of Europe at Yalta. In exchange, they were ready to hold out the promise of an improved human rights record at home. When it became obvious that such a linkage was the price of Western involvement in the CSCE, for nearly 20 years the trade-off in priorities between the two military blocs worked, with the Warsaw Pact nations content to participate in a process that allowed them to act as equals with their richer and more populous neighbors to the West, especially a resurgent Germany. In turn, the NATO countries valued the CSCE as a forum that permitted them some right of legitimate concern and comment on the internal affairs of the totalitarian states across the Elbe. And finally, for the neutral and nonaligned (NNA) nations of Europe, the CSCE was a unique forum that allowed them to act as interlocutors between two power alliances, whose usual approach was to ignore their wishes and concerns. By providing such "good offices" to the process, the NNA gained a voice out of all proportion to their size and numbers.

However, the CSCE's state-based focus may be a major disadvantage in confronting postrevolutionary forms of insecurity that now face the states of Europe. Ironically, it is the West that is now seeking security through the CSCE, at a time when it feels it faces both actual and potential instability in the East. States in the region, however, are only rarely the actual originators of security threats in today's Europe. The dangers are not so much *from the East*, in the form of state-directed aggression, as *in the East*, in the form of possible ethnic clashes, civil strife, migration waves, nuclear disasters, etc. Not all governments of states east of the Oder represented at international forums such as the CSCE are necessarily in control of their territory, cities, or arsenals, or are even fully apprised of the situation on the ground at home. This fact alone explains much of the political and social instability that appears to stalk the continent. The states of Western Europe, whether members of NATO or the traditional neutrals, along with the United States and Canada, have therefore come to believe that CSBMs, such as military transparency or the type epitomized by the Open Skies Agreement, are reassuring supplements to the information coming out of capitals that may be out of touch with internal developments on their own territory. The days of the grand arms control treaties from the Atlantic to the Urals may be over, but the process that produced them still has considerable value.

Beyond this limited, though important, focus on physical security, the CSCE process has always emphasized the nonmilitary components of security, especially its human dimension. The wide consensus among theorists of political systems that democracies do not wage war on each other underpins (albeit often subconsciously) the CSCE's continued work on establishing democracy and the rule of law as perhaps the most important CSBM among the states of Europe--indeed, it may yet represent the best way of ensuring that states with longstanding and deep-seated quarrels with one another do not take to the battlefield to settle their disputes. This approach has worked well for Western Europe since 1945 (with the possible exception of the UK-Iceland "Cod War" in the mid-1970s), and the hope is that it will also work for the new democracies of East Central Europe and the Commonwealth of Independent States. A major addition to this work should be the CSCE Office of Democratic Institutions and Human Rights in Warsaw. Recognizing, however, the breadth of interests among its membership, the CSCE also established the Conflict Prevention Center in Vienna, with an interstate dispute settlement mechanism. To encourage coordination between the ODIHR in Warsaw and the CPC in Vienna--as both bodies would clearly be working towards a common goal--it has been suggested that they should not be geographically separated but housed together, or even joined to the Secretariat presently located in Prague. To strengthen the CPC, the creation of a stronger (legally empowered) Court of Arbitration and Conciliation is also being discussed.

These instruments work on an interstate basis. But until commitments to democratic practices are established vertically through societies as well as horizontally across states, there remains the danger of discrepancies between the governments that bind themselves by the Helsinki Final Act and the people who must agree to be bound and abide by these rules. There are rogue CSCE signatory governments that shrug off international commitments (relatively few), but there are also rogue peoples who refuse to obey the laws of the land (potentially many), ranging from maverick armies through ethnic secessionists to drug mafias. Confronted by a breakdown of order between or within states, the CSCE cannot hope to influence events unless there is a presence on the ground. Hence the voices urging for more CSCE rapporteur missions, good offices, and high-profile physical presence in Nagorno-Karabakh and Moldova.

The logic of the argument leads to a consideration of possible CSCE peacekeeping and peacemaking capabilities. The swing towards a "new realism about the CSCE" ends in the idea that perhaps the CSCE should have divisions after all. The West is beginning to show, however hesitantly, that it may indeed have the political will to muster soldiers for peacekeeping operations in the eastern reaches of Europe, and regional peacekeeping coordinated by the CSCE as a legitimizing umbrella organization is becoming a real possibility. In this regard, the countries of East Central Europe have a potential leadership role to play: alerting and mobilizing the West to the dangers facing them but that the West imagines itself shielded from by a resurrected cordon sanitaire. Much will depend on the development of the CSCE's relationship with NATO. The recent proposal by NATO that it make its materiel and expertise available for CSCE-sponsored peacekeeping is an intriguing idea, though many details remain obscure. Presumably a CSCE political mandate would overrule the North Atlantic Treaty's provision against out-of-area operations, and NATO would examine any application on its own merits and would always have power of refusal. In this way, at least on some occasions, the CSCE would have available the "muscle" it now so visibly lacks.

One advantage of the proposal is that the United States would be involved at both ends of the process, a fact that might increase the attraction of the CSCE for the US. One question mark is the EC (especially French) attitude regarding a role for the Western European Union in CSCE-sponsored peacekeeping. This is, however, a large question mark. Many believe that the future of the CSCE is inextricably bound to the modalities of its evolving relationship with the EC. As long as Western institutions jockey for position and influence, the CSCE as an organization or process is largely reduced to the role of spectator. But at a time when both the EC and NATO are attempting to stake out new turf in the security field, the states who do not sit at the table in either organization have discovered that only through the CSCE can they at least make their wishes and preferences known. A more vigorous EC role is the choice of many, but the wish to keep the US closely involved in European security issues is almost universal. Squaring this circle lies at the heart of the CSCE's problems in working out viable institutional arrangements with the other multilateral bodies crowding the European scene. It will not be easy, and at least for the time being the EC is still in the driver's seat, albeit precariously, with regard to both the nature and pace of future European-wide integration. However, the very exclusivity of the EC has had the unintended effect of boosting the CSCE, whose universality, although frequently debilitating, at least allows for the semblance of democracy rather than diktat.

At the beginning of this introduction, there was an implication of a connection of sorts between the CSCE and God. This was unintended. Many of the attributes of God are not shared by the CSCE, for it is neither perfect, nor immortal, nor the Ultimate Answer. This caveat needs restating, if only as a cruel reminder that the CSCE is not the panacea to all of Europe's ills that it seemed to be to many in the first rush of postrevolutionary enthusiasm. But it is a useful and needed organization, uniquely concentrated on a range of European security and cooperation issues. It is conceivable that the day will come when the CSCE will become coterminous with the EC, at which moment it will cease to exist. Until then, while the EC motors forward, the CSCE must turn inward to try to establish its principles throughout its vast domain. If there is a vision of God that approximates a vision of the CSCE, it is Aristotle's Unmoved Mover, which statically focuses inward in the act of contemplating its own perfection. In size, the CSCE is practically saturated (possible new members being Macedonia or Japan?). The general delineations of its mission will remain unchanged (CSBMs, democratization, the human dimension), despite some new challenges, such as the quest for clear definitions of group minority rights and responsibilities to supplement the individual human rights that have long been the CSCE's trademark issue. The important point is that--contrary to the predictions of critics of the CSCE--the revolutions in the East, the end of the Cold

War, and the drive throughout Europe for gradual economic and social integration have rendered the CSCE more, not less, necessary.

It is this heightened profile that the individual chapters of this volume seek to explore, while drawing some concrete conclusions on the CSCE's successes and failures and making recommendations for the future scope and activities of the CSCE in the rapidly changing Europe of today. The chapters in this volume are based on papers presented at a conference on "Redefining the CSCE: Challenges and Opportunities in the New Europe." The conference was held in Helsinki on May 21-22, 1992, and was cosponsored by the Institute for EastWest Studies and the Finnish Institute of International Affairs.

To open the book, Dr. Margarita Mathiopoulos, a Guest Professor for International Relations in the Law Department of Humboldt University, presents in a radical and controversial chapter a view of Europe in a debate where the challenges of drawing the continent together are underestimated and undue haste is displayed in trying to integrate the disparate states of the area. As an alternative to this rush to embrace the states of East Central Europe and the CIS in Western institutions, Dr. Mathiopoulos instead proposes, in "Washington, Brussels, Bonn: Alliances for the New Europe," a more gradualist approach, one in which the ability of the West to aid in the transition to democracy and market economy is not damaged by trying to do too much too quickly.

As an alternative to joining such Western organizations as NATO and the EC, Dr. Mathiopoulos proposes greater cooperation within and between the states of East Central Europe and the CIS, with Western aid and assistance but without full membership in Western institutions for these nations, leaving the

10

CSCE as the only forum where all European nations sit as equals. It is an approach that is sure to promote a great deal of discussion at a time when the disarray of Western institutions is becoming more and more obvious, and their failure to properly assist East Central Europe and the CIS all the more damaging. The question of whether these countries might be better off with lower aspirations thus becomes a fascinating one.

Dr. Mathiopoulos is of the opinion that it is impossible to consider creating one United States of Europe. A more realistic approach would be to set up three European houses: a transatlantic house, "based on NATO and the EC, enlarged to include the present EFTA states," an East European house, consisting of "Albania, the territory of the former Yugoslavia, the Baltic states, and the old CMEA countries with the exception of the republics of the former Soviet Union. This latter group, without the Baltic states, would form the third European structure, the house of the Commonwealth of Independent States."

Dr. Adam Daniel Rotfeld, Director of the Stockholm International Peace Research Institute (SIPRI), opens his chapter, "CSCE: Continuity and Change," by stressing the fact that threats to European security today are entirely different from those that emanated from Cold War antagonism. Therefore, he proposes that the CSCE establish "a new catalogue of principles" that would legitimize intervention to defuse threats to "common values" as defined by the CSCE. Dr. Rotfeld hypothesizes that political and legal maneuvering will eventually replace the emphasis on military issues that has characterized post-World War II European security. He challenges the CSCE to become involved in this sort of transformation, which should also lead to a shift in focus from national security to cooperative security.

11

Dr. Alpo Rusi of the Finnish Ministry for Foreign Affairs notes in his chapter, "Is This the Chance for a New Euro-Atlantic Alliance?" that "the revolutionary events of 1989-1991 were ... symptoms of both longer-term, historical processes and shorter-term, accidental factors." He argues that a "qualitative transformation" is occurring in the international security system; "this process has its roots in the progress of economic and political modernization influencing the world system and has become gradually a decisive factor." He adds that "the final condition of the realization of the modern world system is macropolitical 'maturity.'"

Dr. Rusi believes that European unity has now become a real possibility. "Unity without stability is not, however, possible in the long run," and stability is "increasingly a function of the Euro-Atlantic relationship." The new Euro-Atlantic community should continue "the original spirit of the Anglo-American special relationship, with new conditions and new participants." Dr. Rusi observes that "the relationship between security, democracy, and the free market constitutes a basis for a more peace-prone international development in the long run."

In his chapter, "The Future Relationship and Division of Responsibilities Between the EC and the CSCE," Dr. Fraser Cameron, Foreign Policy Adviser to the European Commission, points out that the EC has taken a "keen interest" in cooperating on the CSCE even prior to the 1975 Helsinki Conference. Over the years, it has developed a regular consultation mechanism within the framework of European Political Cooperation. It has not always been possible to reach consensus, Dr. Cameron notes, but the trend has always been toward closer Community cooperation. The Paris summit confirmed the EC's growing involvement in the CSCE, and the Community continues to play an active role in the Helsinki follow-up meetings.

Dr. Cameron emphasizes that the Maastricht Treaty provided a major boost for the EC's efforts to establish a European security identity, and he suggests that the agreement on a common foreign and security policy was a reflection of the Community's growing weight and influence on the world stage. In his view, the nature of the security problems facing Europe has changed dramatically since 1989, and now requires a "multifaceted approach" to security. As the leading exponent of "soft security," the Community is thus well equipped to maintain and develop its security role in the continent.

In his chapter "Does the US Have a Role in the Future European Security System?" Dr. Charles Kegley, Jr., of the Department of Government and International Affairs of the University of South Carolina, critically examines current US policy regarding the future of European security against the backdrop of emergent conditions of multipolarity, the constraints presented by the relative decline of the US, and the resurgence of isolationist sentiments in US public opinion. Dr. Kegley conducts a comparative analysis of the costs and benefits to the US of alternate frameworks for contributing to European security in the new order. In particular, he focuses on the prospects for embedding US participation in and through the United Nations, the European Community, NATO, and the CSCE (as well as the web of networks with which these are linked). He argues that a strengthened CSCE affords the US the greatest opportunity to play a continuing and constructive role, while pointing out that the potential for the CSCE to perform a central security function has not as yet been recognized by US policy makers.

Dr. Kegley recommends that to realign US policy and preserve US engagement, the US needs to be given greater incentives to strengthen the CSCE's collective security capabilities. For this, he believes that a new Concert of Europe, within the structure of the reinvigorated CSCE, may be required.

Dr. Oleg N. Bykov, Deputy Director of the Institute of World Economy, examines "The Role of the Commonwealth of Independent States in the New European Security System." Dr. Bykov believes that "their current predicaments notwithstanding, the Soviet Union's successors, the Russian leadership in particular, remain deeply committed to the strengthening of European security." They view security as "vital to their objectives of surmounting the tremendous domestic difficulties and making the process of democratic reform irreversible." However, he points out that post-Soviet policies have been beset with limitations and inhibitions. "The recently recovered sovereignty has put the former Soviet republics in an entirely new geopolitical context," Dr. Bykov adds. "Each is in search of a new foreign policy and security identity. Some tend to gravitate westward, while others seem to be east- or south-bound, with Russia itself apparently torn between Europe and Asia."

But urgent common security interests require cooperation in managing the awesome military capabilities built and deployed over the decades of confrontation. Dr. Bykov points out that although they are "submerged in internal turmoil," Russia and other former union republics "have nevertheless been moving to intensify their participation" in the various European security institutions and structures. "While engaging the people in even more vigorous participation in the so-called Helsinki process," the leaders now seek a "new European security architecture in which the CSCE interacts with NATO, the European Community, the Western European Union, the Council of Europe, and other institutions."

14

Dr. Bykov describes the stakes as enormous. If Russia and the other new states "make the transition to a new political and economic system, the next century is likely to be marked by peace and prosperity. If they fail, Europe and the entire world will have to face unpredictable threats to security."

Dealing with the "New Democracies in East Central Europe: Expectations for the EC and the CSCE," Dr. Andrej Cima of the Foreign Ministry of the CSFR emphasizes in his chapter that the political changes in East Central Europe profoundly changed the "political environment in which the CSCE, the EC, and other European and transatlantic institutions operated." The postcommunist leadership of the countries of the region are pursuing in these organizations completely different policies than those of their predecessors, Dr. Cima notes. They are seeking aid for their domestic programs of economic and social transformation as well as new security guarantees. As a result, the CSCE is being severely tested as a framework for political and economic stability. The East Central European countries identify it with the building of a cooperative, all-European security system following the dismantling of the WTO.

Dr. Cima points out that the EC meeting in Maastricht recognized the possibility of trouble ahead. Leaders of the Twelve reaffirmed their schedule for deeper economic integration and attempted to accelerate political integration with new emphasis on common defense policy. Dr. Cima also notes that it is impossible to assume that macroeconomic stability has been achieved in most East Central European countries. With the economic recession at hand, the transition to market economy may be seriously hampered and political stability may be undermined in East Central Europe. In order to offer the necessary political and economic support, international

15

institutions need to act in a coordinated way. Dr. Cima's conclusion is that this coordination of the activities of the multilateral institutions, especially in the security field, could be ensured through regular consultations on an expert level.

In his chapter "The Future of the CSCE: The Needs of East Central Europe," Dr. Andrzej Karkoszka of the Polish Institute of International Affairs focuses on the specific expectations of the East Central European states from the next stage of the CSCE process; these expectations are shaped by the geopolitical as well as the present economic and social situation around and within these states. The East Central European nations are currently sandwiched between the affluent and militarily powerful West and the inherently unstable, economically backward but militarily still very dangerous states of the East. Faced with this predicament, the East Central European states need to find the most practical ways to secure their economic and social development on the one hand and preserve the long-term stability of the areas surrounding them to the east and south on the other.

Dr. Karkoszka goes on to argue that East Central European societies and governments have focused their energies and attention on internal factors, and are only now transforming their attitudes to the outside world, seeing an urgent need to integrate themselves as closely as possible with existing European organizations and institutions, of which the EC is the most successful and attractive. The CSCE process is very important in this respect, not only because of its primary role in establishing general political, legal, social, and other norms, but also because of its unique democratic, comprehensive, and universal character.

Dr. Karkoszka lists and discusses a number of future challenges confronting the CSCE, as seen from the vantage point of East Central Europe. These challenges are the preservation of stability or, in other words, the prevention of instability in the eastern and southern regions of Europe; conflict resolution and peacekeeping; further progress in restraining military capabilities in Europe through arms control, disarmament, and confidence-building measures; and coping with nonmilitary threats, particularly environmental destruction.

Of all these tasks, Dr. Karkoszka believes the CSCE is well-prepared to handle only a few, notably in the area of security and confidence building. In all the other cases, especially in conflict prevention and resolution, the CSCE's resources and abilities are very limited and need to be expanded. The East Central European states see this requirement as crucial to the further effectiveness of the CSCE.

"The Future of Institutionalization: The CSCE Example" forms the subject for the chapter of Dr. Heinz Gärtner, a senior research fellow at the Austrian Institute for International Affairs. Dr. Gärtner reminds us that "CSCE institutions and mechanisms consist of rules, norms, and principles" and are "based on the expectation that governments comply with them and their rules of procedure." However, "no matter how much the CSCE process influences the foreign policy of the participating states, the process itself and its new institutions alone are not sufficient to uphold CSCE norms and principles." Dr. Gärtner shows how the Yugoslav crisis has "raised the question of what the CSCE should do in the case of violations of its norms and principles." He suggests that "means of coercion appear to be necessary to take action against defecting states." Meanwhile, he believes that the CSCE process "will continue to be characterized by the tension between coercion and accommodation."

According to Dr. Gärtner, "neither the CSCE nor any

other pan-European security system is a panacea that can resolve all Europe's security problems," and trying to create "a pan-European security system that would provide enduring and effective security under current conditions would overburden the CSCE institutions and mechanisms." He suggests that the question of which regimes and institutions will lead European security is to a large extent resolvable only by determining who will dominate these regimes and institutions, rather than the nature of the institutions themselves.

In his thoughtful paper, "The Challenges of Helsinki II," Dr. Michael R. Lucas, a senior researcher at the World Policy Institute, shows how a political, economic, and "security architecture of European and Euro-Atlantic institutions is rapidly evolving" but is being confronted with daunting challenges. The ongoing fighting in Yugoslavia and the disintegration of the Soviet Union have, he believes, underlined the need to expand, politically upgrade, and streamline CSCE crisis prevention and crisis resolution machinery. The proposals for setting up within the CSCE a Forum for Security Cooperation, a regional, United Nations-type security council, and various other executive and coordinating organs are to be seen as important in this context, Dr. Lucas notes. One critical element is that the new framework must embrace all CSCE states as equal participants and target cooperative and collective security goals. With this objective in mind, NATO, the North Atlantic Cooperation Council, and the CSCE must work closely together to promote extensive programs of East-West security cooperation, disarmament, and confidence building.

Dr. Lucas emphasizes that the Yugoslav crisis has starkly underlined the relationship between human dimension issues, such as the protection of minority rights, and international security. Thus, the CSCE agenda must expand to include a "CSCE codex of minority rights" and effective implementation procedures; CSCE mechanisms of dispute mediation and settlement, the setting up of forms of compulsory arbitration, and the meshing of CSCE instruments into those of other European institutions; and the enlargement of the CSCE's powers for sanctioning states that "grossly violate human dimension and other basic principles of the CSCE."

In summing up, Dr. Lucas considers that "while the CSCE and the Euro-Atlantic system as a whole face daunting tasks," if these and other suggestions are implemented, "there are many reasons to be optimistic concerning the chances for their achieving qualitatively new forms of security in the EAS [Euro-Atlantic Space] and globally in the coming years."

Not all the recommendations put forward by the authors in this volume will be put into effect. Some are beyond the scope of the political accommodation that the CSCE's current structure of state membership can easily handle, and in some cases the various viewpoints contained in this book contradict one another. This is less important, however, than the general agreement shared by the authors and participants in the conference: that the CSCE can and should play the pivotal role in shaping the future security architecture of Europe. No other European body approaches its universality or history of accommodating disparate approaches. While its approach to issues, oblique rather than head-on, does not promise quick or necessarily smooth solutions to the problems that confront Europe, its kind of gradualist progress can lay a firm foundation for a cooperative system of collective security in Europe, a goal that the populations of all CSCE states continue to view as the best guarantee of their own safety and security.

Part I
21-91

International
System
Change in
Europe and
the CSCE

1

Washington, Brussels, Bonn: Alliances for the New Europe

Margarita Mathiopoulos

Is the 20th Century Going to Start All Over Again?

Europe longed for the end of the Cold War, an end to communist oppression, the division of the continent, the arms race, and the constant military threat; it longed to overcome the major European crisis. On December 2, 1989, a few days after the Berlin Wall came down, the presidents of the United States and the Soviet Union, George Bush and Mikhail Gorbachev, met on the Mediterranean island of Malta. The US and the Soviet Union had controlled Europe since the continent was carved up into spheres of influence at Yalta in 1945, and the two countries had been the dominant superpowers in a bipolar world. Now, 44 years later in Malta, the world realized that the two great powers were now spectators on the sidelines of European events. Europe was becoming emancipated, and people and nations were taking their destinies into their own hands, setting the scene for the resurrection of the Old World. Speeches and statements by leading politicians from both East and West were imbued with unfamiliar optimism. This mood reached its high point in Paris on November 21, 1990, when the Warsaw Pact and NATO signed a nonaggression agreement as the basis for future political coexistence. The effusive document stated that: "The signatories solemnly declare that, in the *new era* of European relations, they are no longer adversaries, and will build new partnerships and extend to each other the hand of friendship."

On the same day, all of the then 34 participating states in the CSCE signed the Charter of Paris for a New Europe. In the same exuberant tone, it was announced that "the age of confrontation and division in Europe has ended ... Europe is liberating itself from the legacy of the past. The courage of men and women, the strength of the will of the peoples, and the power of the ideas in the Helsinki Final Act have opened a *new era* of democracy, peace and unity."

Europe was blinded by the euphoria of the turnaround in events in Central and Eastern Europe. The understandably high hopes for a better future clouded vision and hid reality. A stable power system that had lasted four decades had been destroyed, revealing that there was no European structure to replace it. Soon after, members of the Warsaw Pact--in Paris still a contracting partner--settled the conditions for the organization's demise, and one year later the Soviet Union itself ceased to exist. The Gulf War and the civil war in Yugoslavia came as drastic reminders that any optimism about a new age of peace was premature. Once again, the hopes of "peace in our time" were dashed. The end of Marxism-Leninism and the fall of the Berlin Wall did not mark the end of history but a new beginning, bringing great opportunities as well as great risks.

Furthermore, the old rule that anyone seeking to exploit opportunities must first be aware of the risks remains in force. It is important therefore to identify the risks if we are to avoid them.

The disintegration of great empires in world history has invariably led to bloodshed. This was true not only of the collapse of the Roman Empire, but also of the end of the Empire of Charles V, the Ottoman Empire, the Hapsburg regime, and the British Empire. Why should the fall of the Soviet Empire be an exception? Nothing suggests it will, and the hitherto largely peaceful character of the revolutions in Central and Eastern Europe and the process of dissolution in the Soviet Union should not be allowed to obscure the issue.

For all our hopes that the present Eastern upheavals will be free of violence, the outlook is not optimistic. Free elections are no guarantee of peaceful coexistence within or between ethnic groups. It is highly likely that the civil war in Yugoslavia is merely the prelude to a series of battles that will shake Europe in future. Post-World War II fixed borders in Eastern Europe can no longer be taken for granted, and since 1990, old states have vanished, and dozens of new ones have been born. Long thought under control, ancient destructive nationalist forces are emerging, and the West has had little success in its attempts--using both a stick and a carrot--to halt this growth. Religious disputes, ethnic tensions, the resurgence of old nationality conflicts, the jealousies of power politics, and a litany of economic and social problems abound--it would take a miracle to find a peaceful solution to many problems in Europe today.

An added danger is that, unlike the situation in Yugoslavia, many of these conflicts are concentrated in territories with stockpiles of sophisticated nuclear arms. No one knows who really has control over some 27,000 nuclear warheads in the CIS arsenal and how effective that control might be in case of emergency. The dangers of nuclear proliferation or the spread of nuclear know-how with the migration of nuclear scientists point to further potential trouble spots. The resulting instability, the poverty and hardship in large sections of these countries' populations--90% of the inhabitants of Moscow are living below subsistence level and, according to ILO estimates, a further 15 million people are due to be out of work in the CIS by the end of 1992--and the low level (relative to expectations) of assistance from the West are likely to generate a spirit of disillusionment with democracy and the market economy and prepare the ground for new authoritarian solutions.

The virus of destructive nationalism threatens to spread to Western Europe. Since the EC has lost its protective screen--the Iron Curtain--it is increasingly facing problems that it was never intended or designed to solve. Nationalist groups in major countries are struggling in different ways and with varying levels of intensity to gain greater autonomy and recognition of a separate and distinct identity.

This question of how the EC will deal with these forces will become all the more urgent the larger the EC grows geographically, for extension will inevitably be at the expense of depth and consolidation. Twenty or more EC states cannot be "governed" the same way, using the same procedures as 12. The Maastricht accord and the road to a currency and social union and a political union, are now the targets of political and popular attack of a severity that was quite inconceivable to most commentators at the end of the 1980s. The electoral successes of the radical right in various European countries are due, at least in part, to growing anti-EC feeling. Many people are afraid of trading in their national identity for a faceless Euro-authority that is not thought to be subject to the same democratic controls as national governments.

Until recently, conventional wisdom maintained that developments in East and West were taking divergent courses: integration in the West, disintegration in the East. Today, there is less of such talk. Maastricht cannot be made "irreversible" simply by invoking its name. Rather, the debate on the nature and consequences of the agreement, an exchange of views absent from most EC countries before their signature of the treaty, is now taking place against a backdrop of greater concern about the postwar loss of national sovereignty and the benefits, both long-term and short-term, to be gained from such a surrender.

Furthermore, the discussions are being staged against a background of frightening crises in less developed countries (LDCs). Although the end of the Cold War has helped defuse prolonged conflicts in the southern hemisphere, new potential conflicts include the debt crisis, the risks of ecological disaster from the destruction of the rain forests, the world's advancing deserts, the population explosion, and growing technological gaps.

There are now some 170 states in the world, but around 3,000 distinct national groups. Without a bipolar division of the globe, there is a growing risk that hitherto repressed tensions will be discharged and generate new waves of refugees. When the High Commission for Refugees at the UN was set up in 1951, there were 2 million politically persecuted people in the world; today, there are 17 million refugees. Complaints of xenophobic tendencies in Europe are rising despite the fact that only a small percentage of all migrants ever reach Europe. The more usual case is for refugees to move from one poor country to another.

These developments are taking place at a time when the world's richest country, the United States, is increasingly withdrawing into itself. The Cold War left the Soviet Union prostrate, but it drained the US as well. It was an impressive feat when the US President in 1991 united much of the world behind him in what may have been the last great effort of its kind, and fought a successful war against a well-armed aggressor state. On

27

March 6, 1991, immediately after the liberation of Kuwait, George Bush announced before the US Congress a new world order based on freedom and human dignity. Just one year later, Theo Sommer in the newspaper *Die Zeit* noted the rapid failure of this vision in a headline: "New world--new disorder." Indeed, Saddam Hussein is still in office and busy rebuilding that power. The Middle East conflict is as intractable as ever, and the security system in the region, for which optimistic prophets had already conjured up a sort of ersatz CSCE, has proved to be a mirage. With a continuing budget deficit, an education system viewed as inadequate, the social misery of the lower classes, a rise in drug abuse and violent crimes, and a general lack of self-confidence brought about in large measure by a loss of faith in politics and politicians, the US has withdrawn.

George Bush has refrained from further remarks on the new world order and has told Americans that he will from now on make domestic rather than foreign affairs his first priority. And even though many commentators in Europe have found it hard to conceal their "schadenfreude" in the face of such a rapid reversal of fortune, developments in the US affect everyone. Is the richest country in the world about to abandon its global responsibilities? Is the United States going to leave Europe to the Europeans? Will America's imagination, enterprise, and huge resources be absent from attempts to rehabilitate Eastern Europe and Russia, and save the south? Who could fill the vacuum of values, economic strength, and military security if the new US were to revert to isolationism?

These issues loom so much larger against the background of a generally poor global economic situation. Recession is advancing everywhere, with growing budget deficits, rising interest rates, less liquid capital, and similar dire economic trends. The threat of trade wars and protectionism and the trend toward concentrating on one's own national problems--in view of the limited resources available--suggest that it will be impossible for the world to use the opportunities offered by the end of the East-West conflict. The ballyhooed peace dividend has disappeared without a trace, and if it exists, it is obviously being spent first on the home front, not on combating global problems. Neither the US nor Japan is showing a willingness to play an appropriately major role in solving the crises in the south and in Central and Eastern Europe. In Western Europe, especially in Germany, there is much good will available to offer assistance. But resources are limited there as well, and there is a threat of overextension. Are the West's problem-solving capacity and crisis management mechanisms impotent when faced with these new challenges?

On the basis of the scenarios described above, Germany, Europe, and the US will have to set some important courses in the future. It will be crucial that the Bonn-Brussels-Washington relationship continue to work and endure.

Konrad Adenauer called again and again for "the opposites between nation-states in Europe to disappear in the course of time" (June 11, 1961). This basic realization, which defined West German foreign policy over four decades, must continue to apply. After the end of the Cold War, we must seize this opportunity and finally overcome nationalist and racist patterns of behavior. Democratic values and the inviolability of human dignity, not "blood and soil" theories, must become central structural principles all over Europe. Only if it is possible to hold on firmly to such a European vision based on freedom, and not be misled by short-term shifts in the popular mood, will we be able to meet the major challenges brought by the years 1989-1990.

First, we will succeed in dealing with resurgent nationalism in Central and Eastern Europe only if the Germans, French, British, and other Western Europeans can unconditionally accept this principle. The supranational European message will gain in credibility only if West Europeans practice what they preach.

Second, a US presence in Europe--political, economic, and military--will continue to be of elementary importance. The area of the former Soviet Union, with its major stocks of nuclear weapons, will be a source of incalculable risks for a long time. To date, we have had no reason to assume that Europeans will in the near future be able to find a counterforce to match the potential danger this involves. That being so, US soldiers should go on being cordially welcomed in Europe. Economically and technologically, Europeans by themselves would not in the long run have a chance of competing with Japan. The US and the EC must join forces more effectively than in the past if they are to face the ongoing challenge from the economic potential present in East Asia.

A strong US military and economic presence in Europe can also act as a safety net for Europeans against the growth of German power. This is a very important principle. The US commitment in Europe is an indispensable factor for stability. After World War I it was sorely missed when the US retreated into isolationism. After World War II, by contrast, the US presence on the continent underpinned a long period of peace and stability. There can be no European security without the Atlantic link. Quite the contrary: it is now in Europe's interest to extend the Atlantic contacts and enlarge them to include Central and Eastern Europe and the former Soviet republics. There, people look up to the US with great expectations; we need only think of Poland in this respect. For Americans--unlike the Germans--Central and Eastern Europe are "grudge-free" zones. The opportunity this brings is one that the US, faced with huge problems of its own, has not yet recognized or been able to exploit.

Also at stake is the maintenance of America's cultural, intellectual, and political influence. The idea of human rights and democracy embedded in institutions based on a separation of powers comes from the US Declaration of Independence, the most important political document of modern times, which also forms the nucleus of freedom in Europe.

To some, however, this American dream is already a myth. Commentators point to a variety of domestic problems to show that the US was worn out by the Cold War. Yet, although no one, and certainly not US citizens themselves, wish to play down the problems of the United States, it is also true that though the US giant may be ailing, its condition is not yet terminal. The US remains a young, dynamic nation, enjoying regular transfusions of talent and skills from immigrants from all over the world. The US still has a role to play in shaping the post-Cold War world.

To prove this thesis, one need only examine the existing and functioning supranational institutions and their roles as safety anchors for European security. Specifically, both the EC and NATO must be strengthened. Yet at present, the opposite is happening. Anyone yielding to calls for a rapid extension of these institutions to include Central and Eastern Europe is undermining their power by weakening their ability to function. The two institutions will have the power of attraction only if they

31

offer depth and coherence, two attributes that will be lost if they are enlarged too quickly. This is not in the interest of the Central and East European countries either. Customized association treaties and political and military ties are better ways to take account of the interests and needs of Eastern countries than airy pledges of early full collaboration. Anyone promising to both deepen and extend the EC and NATO at the same time is simply being disingenuous.

Supranational European institutions instead of renationalization, preservation of and extensions to transatlantic ties instead of an American "secession," a deepening of NATO and EC as safety anchors, instead of premature extensions and dilution--these are the foundations for a responsible foreign policy in a peaceful Europe.

In this respect, we must give up the idea of *one common European house*. That would be an unmanageable structure. If everybody is allied with everybody, then nobody is allied with anybody. Ideas of "one world" have always proved to be dangerous illusions: from Woodrow Wilson in 1919, who wanted to make the world "safe for democracy," through Franklin D. Roosevelt, who developed the concept of "one world" in the final years of World War II, all the way to the illusions of the Paris CSCE summit or the Bush concept of a "new world order." Contrasts and conflicts remain; eternal peace is still far off.

For *one* European house, nationalism is just too strong, the contrasts in our interests too stark, the economic and social homogeneity too weak, and the geographical area too great. Such a concept is doomed to failure. At best, the consequence would be a loose customs union, although even that hardly seems possible in view of the great economic divide.

A transatlantic house, for example, could be based on

NATO and the EC, enlarged to include the present EFTA states. The second building could be called the East European house; it would consist of Albania, the territory of the former Yugoslavia, the Baltic states, and the old CMEA countries with the exception of the republics of the former Soviet Union. This latter group, without the Baltic states, would form the third European structure: the house of the Commonwealth of Independent States (CIS).

In this way, we would have three more or less manageable units with political and geographical compositions that can be explained by previous cooperation between these nations. Such an architecture would require that the West have the courage to tell the states of Central and Eastern Europe the truth: EC membership is not an option in the foreseeable future. Such a message might be acceptable if there were enough brisk contacts between the houses, and if serious help were given by the Western group. The CSCE would have to continue as the bond between the three supranational organizations, and the North Atlantic Cooperation Council would provide a security-policy link. Finally, a number of bilateral agreements are conceivable: from association treaties between individual states and the EC, all the way to the setting up of certain regional cooperation zones based on historical ties, which--in a multilateral setting--would connect the various "apartments" of one house with the "apartments" of the other two. The object of this construction, therefore, is not to promote competition and conflicts between the three supranational units, but, on the contrary, to avoid disputes by having a network of interrelationships.

33

The Transatlantic House

The transatlantic building rests on the pillars of established organizations: the EC, NATO, and the Western European Union. The European Community, including the EFTA countries, must offer the clear prospect of real political union to supplement the Single European Market and the economic and currency union. The European Parliament must be given political clout. It must be able to elect the members of the Commission, the European government, or at least the President of the Commission, who could then appoint and dismiss the commissioners. As in national parliaments, the European Parliament must be given monitoring functions, rights of initiative, etc. It must become the nucleus of a European government system.

What is at stake today is no longer a confederation of various nation-states. What is needed is a European federal state, a federation, whose members surrender real power. To this end, it will be necessary to work out and adopt a European constitution or treaty. In addition to this further evolution of the EC, great importance must be attached to economic cooperation between North America and Europe. The transatlantic links must not be allowed to wither into a series of trade wars. Instead, huge internal markets for Western Europe and America need to be created. Going beyond GATT rules, a common market for services and labor is needed. It will be difficult, but maybe a good start lies with clearly formulating the goal.

Still, the transatlantic house has not merely an economic floor, but a security level as well. In this respect, NATO, with its integrated command structure, is and remains the crucial pillar. After the end of the Cold War, NATO will undoubtedly become more European, but it will also continue to link the US and Canada with Europe. Its main object will still be to deter potential invasion and counter any external pressure on the alliance or on its individual members. The military and nonmilitary components of security policy--precautionary action, crisis management, and arms control--are all part of the package. These functions must interlock to form an organic whole in peace, crisis, and war, but without appearing to pose any threat outside the alliance. The alliance remains a defensive organization; it will go on needing nuclear weapons as political insurance, though at a much lower level than in the past. Against the background of the uncertainty in the East and the frightful risk of the proliferation of nuclear weapons or nuclear know-how, the transatlantic house must maintain a credible deterrent capacity and effective armed forces. Only in this manner can the transatlantic house make its stabilizing influence felt in Central and Eastern Europe as well.

The EC summit at Maastricht expressed a wish that a course be set toward developing a joint foreign and security policy in a political union. As a forum for the envisaged "European defense identity," we have the WEU, in which France and Germany play roles and which could act as a bridge between NATO and the EC. In the runup to the various Maastricht agreements, there was a good deal of political controversy about the relationship between NATO and the WEU. The US, the UK, and the Netherlands, in particular, feared that Germany and France would push ahead with the WEU to render NATO superfluous eventually. Although the US had repeatedly affirmed its support in principle for a European pillar inside NATO, Washington's response to the attempt to revive the WEU in the runup to the Maastricht summit was definitely negative. The US feared that it might one day be confronted with an inflexible European "bloc" inside NATO. The military alliance, Washington felt, ought not to be a forum for European-Atlantic disputes. In this way, the White House feared, the US might be ousted from Europe and the WEU might evolve to become the pivotal military organization instead of NATO.

Ways must be found to ensure that the WEU does not weaken but rather strengthens NATO. One option might be to use WEU structures for the future deployment of multinational European troops outside the NATO alliance area.

But in this regard it is important to note that if Germans are to remain alliance-worthy in Europe, they must take the steps needed to clarify their situation. In terms of a Bundeswehr contribution to a multinational force within the scope of the WEU or a UN mandate, Germany can no longer afford to obfuscate in this matter, hiding behind constitutional smokescreens.

The East European House

The East European house is based very much on the tradition of cooperation between the former CMEA states. The spokesman of the Executive Board of Deutsche Bank, Hilma Kopper, was correct in pointing out in spring 1992 that it had been a mistake to dissolve the CMEA as an economic organization. The one-sided look toward the West and the neglect or scrapping of established economic relations in Central and Eastern Europe has only helped make a disastrous economic situation worse. It was understandable and legitimate for the Baltic states and Hungary, Poland, or the CSFR to seek closer links with the EC after their liberation. In some cases, association agreements have already been concluded, and others will follow.

But, going beyond that, the states located between the transatlantic and the CIS houses should also attempt to revive their manifold contacts and interrelationships and develop the prospect for something like a common market. They should be coming closer together at political, military, and cultural levels and to find their main mission there instead of launching into new national feuds.

On the other hand, this approach could be said to rob these states of West European perspectives, depriving them of the most important glimmer of hope in their hour of economic hardship. But such an objection overstates the case. As stated earlier, full EC membership is inconceivable in the foreseeable future, unless at the price of dispensing with a properly functioning and effective EC. At present, the countries of East Central Europe are the victims of a dangerous delusion. It is better to tell these countries the unvarnished truth now and say: "Join together; take the same route that Western Europeans once took with the Rome treaties. Don't pin your faith only on the Big Brother in the West; build your own European home. It may take longer, but it will be your own place."

In addition to an amalgamation in Central and Eastern Europe and bilateral association treaties with Brussels, it might be possible to make more use of a further instrument: specific agreements signed between individual members of the transatlantic house and Central and East European states to foster local and regional cooperation.

One approach, for example, might be the Pentagonale (subsequently expanded with the addition of Poland to become the Hexagonale). In May 1990, the governments of Italy, Austria, Hungary, Yugoslavia, and the CSFR met at Bratislava. Building on previous contacts, these states--this was before the civil war in Yugoslavia--developed some courageous plans. The Italian Foreign Minister Gianni De Michelis vowed that the area between Prague, Vienna, Budapest, Belgrade, and Rome would eventually be one of the world's richest regions. Extensions to road and rail networks, a joint communication satellite, boundary-crossing natural parks and other projects were resolved. A division of function was agreed: Austria was to be in charge of the environment, Italy of traffic, Hungary of the promotion of small and medium-sized business, the then Yugoslavia of telecommunications, and the CSFR of culture. There was talk of a "region of small and medium-sized nations between Germany and Russia."

When the Pentagonale states met for the third time in July 1990 in Venice, Bulgaria and Romania were on hand as observers. This showed that cooperation between Central and East European states--in close collaboration with one or two Western powers--can definitely prove an attractive proposition. When the breakup of Yugoslavia is complete, there is no reason an attempt should not be made to imbue the Pentagonale with new life, to extend the Danube-Adria cooperation to include Romania and Bulgaria as well.

In the same way, there might be special cooperation between Hungarians, Poles, Czechoslovaks--the "Visegrad troika" --and Germans in border regions, or the creation of an international Hanseatic region in the Baltic, including Kaliningrad, although this latter idea would only be tolerable if it were possible to dispel any trace of national ambitions on the part of Germans with regard to Kaliningrad. Other examples of such regional amalgamation might be in the relations between Finland and Estonia. Indeed, Scandinavian countries could make substantial efforts at an institutional level on behalf of other

Baltic states, and there might be regular twinning processes between West European and East European states. Finally, in addition to twinning with the EC and EFTA, this might also be a way to bring the US, Canada, and even Japan into the picture. Each of them could focus on one or the other region and, in this way, help promote development in the house of the East European countries. The stronger and more successful such coordinated initiatives are, the less will be the pressure in these countries to march on Brussels tomorrow.

The CIS House

The third European house would be formed by the states of the former Soviet Union, although without the Baltic countries. Even before the disintegration of the USSR, there was a vision of a new union, a federation of independent republics on the territory of the former Soviet empire. The military in particular favored an amalgamation of sovereign states on the NATO pattern. It is of crucial importance for stability and peace in Europe that the CIS should survive as an organization of countries with headquarters in Moscow capable of performing certain tasks--in defense policy, in the control of both nuclear weapons and the nuclear industry, and perhaps in economic and financial policy as well. Most CIS countries are likely to realize that they can hardly survive on their own. It has always been tempting to make Moscow or Russian domination responsible for the misery in Ukraine, Georgia, and Tajikistan, so the strengthening of the CIS confederation and the maintenance of certain central functions in Moscow will be the most difficult task for European construction work. There is the risk that the Islamic republics in the south will turn away from Moscow and extend their relations to Ankara, Baghdad, or Teheran. The risk that such processes may involve a proliferation of the tactical nuclear weapons located in these territories can hardly be overrated. This prospect alone would justify any attempt to support the CIS and encourage it to continue along its present course.

What was said about the East European house applies here as well: in addition to the desired deepening of cooperation between the member states, it will be necessary for the West and the countries of Central and Eastern Europe as well to agree on a division of functions and set up regional priorities for their involvement. Only by concentrating efforts in this manner will it be possible to recognize the elites in the new states, offer them perspectives, and build confidence. The overriding goal must be to establish a wide range of efficient neighborhood contacts between the various apartments in the three houses.

The CSCE and the North Atlantic Cooperation Council

In addition to such bilateral relations or the formation of "inter-apartmental" links, there is the possibility of institutionalized cooperation between all tenants in the three houses. This is true of the NACC, for instance. Instead of the full NATO membership aspired to by many states in the former Warsaw Pact, there is now a deeper liaison between the alliance and Central and East European states. In this way, NATO has taken account of the view that "our own security is indivisibly bound up with the security of all other states in Europe." The NACC will have its long-term impact on the promotion of a mutual insurance between European nations. A comprehensive liaison program covers numerous consultations for strengthening confidence and transparency, forming armed forces, and discussing defense doctrines, administrative questions concerning defense burdens in the various economies, and arms conversions. Conferences and seminars have been organized; there are invitations to attend military exercises and a brisk exchange of information on troop strengths and military material. In this way, the NACC could make an essential contribution toward the evolution of a sense of security throughout Europe.

The chief instruments, however, are offered by the CSCE. This is one of the most successful institutions in the history of diplomacy. Proposed originally by the Soviet Union instead of a peace treaty in an attempt to cement the postwar order and status quo in Europe, the Helsinki Final Act in 1975, with its human rights principle and humanitarian "third basket," provided the spark for the brush fire of liberation movements across Eastern Europe that finally led to the end of division on the continent. Originally, it included 35 European states. Following the disintegration of the Soviet Union and Yugoslavia, it now has 52 members. There can be no doubt that its ability to act has suffered as a result.

All the same, the CSCE can continue to be an important discussion forum for all of Europe, the US, and Canada. In January 1992, the CSCE foreign ministers in Prague resolved to abolish the unanimity rule, which had often paralyzed the organization, regarding issues of serious violations of human rights, and to condemn such occurrences. It is conceivable that the CSCE instruments for punishing violations of the principles behind the CSCE Final Act and the Charter of Paris will be further extended--all the way to the creation of CSCE blue helmets who can be deployed as a "European UN" on crisis-containing and peacekeeping missions.

In the future, too, the CSCE will be of great importance in coming to grips with change in Europe. In addition to the human rights question, this is still true of the security-policy dialogue, the continuation of agreements on confidence-building and disarmament in Europe, and diplomatic consultations to avoid crises and engage in troubleshooting. An economic forum has been set up in Prague with the aim of pushing ahead with market economy reforms and strengthening cooperation in business, ecology, and research.

The CSCE process has now become institutionalized; it has acquired a bureaucracy of its own, a permanent Secretariat, a Conflict Prevention Center, and an Office for Free Elections, which have started work. Many may consider the costs of this gigantic diplomatic process to be excessive and the results obtained to be negligible. But the CSCE, in its own unique way, does contribute to the networking of Western, Central, and Eastern Europe, as well as the CIS. In this way, it creates contacts, knowledge, and confidence. To surrender or even underestimate the value of this instrument, when taken in concert with the other tools available, would be a mistake. It seems not only to survive but also flourish in the new European security structure. How it interacts with the other actors in this structure will, to the largest extent, determine its future viability and longevity.

2

CSCE: Continuity and Change

Adam Daniel Rotfeld

Introduction

For some time now, the discussion about the future of the CSCE has focused on the role of and relations between the new European institutions and security structures.[1] In the past, however, the approach to the CSCE process differed in a number of important ways.[2]

First, the process initiated at Helsinki and the decisions adopted within its framework were of a political rather than legal character.

Second, the follow-up meetings were supposed to make sure that the Helsinki process was continuous without institutionalizing the process or creating organizational structures.[3]

Third, the CSCE process assumed an above- or non-bloc character, the conference being attended exclusively by states, and not organizations or military alliances.[4]

Fourth, the democratic character of the process was assured by two rules of procedure to the effect that: (a) "all States participating in the Conference shall do as sovereign and independent States and in conditions of full equality;"[5] and (b) "decisions of the Conference shall be taken by consensus."[6]

Fifth, the pan-European character of the Helsinki process was determined by the following elements: (a) all European states (except Albania) and the United States and Canada participated in the CSCE; and (b) all provisions concerned security and cooperation in Europe.[7]

Sixth, the CSCE provisions are comprehensive in scope (three "baskets"), referring to all areas of interstate relations; however, the participating states attached the greatest weight to the "human dimension of the CSCE"--human rights and Basket Three. Military security aspects of the Helsinki process (except CSBMs) were not a matter of central importance; likewise the issue of a European system of peaceful settlement of disputes did not go beyond academic considerations.[8]

Seventh, the cornerstone of the Helsinki process has been the "decalogue of principles," agreed upon and included in the Helsinki Final Act. At the same time it was agreed that all the principles set forth in the Helsinki Act are of "primary importance and, accordingly, they will be equally and unreservedly applied, each of them being interpreted taking into account the others."[9]

And, last but not least, the Final Act was treated as a confirmation of the balance of interests of the three groups of states--members of the two political-military groupings (NATO and the WTO) and the neutral and nonaligned group. These interests, in some simplification, boiled down to the East striving for legitimization and corroboration of the territorial and political status quo through the so-called territorial principles (inviolability of frontiers, territorial integrity) as well as the tenets of sovereign equality and nonintervention in internal affairs, and the West seeking expansion of individual rights and freedoms and liberalization of the system in the East. The former endeavors found their expression in three principles--respect for human rights and fundamental freedoms, including the freedom of thought, conscience, religion, or belief (VII), equal rights and self-determination of peoples (VIII) and cooperation among states (IX). Accordingly, the Western states believed that they succeeded in having the Declaration of Principles confirm, for example, that not only governments, institutions, and organizations, but also "persons have a relevant and positive role to play in contributing toward the achievement of these aims of their cooperation."[10]

In sum, in the policies of NATO states and the United States in particular, the CSCE was an instrument of public diplomacy rather than an important part of their security policy. Postulates were aimed at the "other side." Until 1990, the CSCE provisions were never intended to play a serious role in ensuring national security.

The end of the Cold War, the disappearance of the division into East and West, and the acceptance of a system of common values have thoroughly changed the perspective, functions, and place of the CSCE process. The provisions adopted in Helsinki, Madrid, and Vienna had staked out the framework and limits of confrontation. Now, expectations connected with the Helsinki process are entirely different. The situation has undergone such a transformation that both the fundamental aims and assumptions as well as the means of their realization call for a thorough reappraisal and change.

The first attempts to readapt the process to the changed environment and undertake new tasks were made at the summit meeting in Paris.

The Charter of Paris for a New Europe adopted by the CSCE heads of state or government in November 1990 announced new principles for the post-Cold War European system:

- steadfast commitment to democracy based on human rights and fundamental freedoms;
- prosperity through economic liberty and social justice;
- equal security for all the countries.[11]

One can ask the following questions: to what extent are these principles being realized? What are the possible new risks? To what extent are the Paris decisions and the new security structures set up on their basis adequate to meet the new challenges that Europe faces?

Principles and Realities

The authors of the documents negotiated in Vienna in 1989-1990 and signed in Paris in 1990 were guided by the assumptions and political philosophy that breathed life into the European multilateral process initiated almost 20 years ago in Helsinki.[12] The Europe of those years was part of the world divided by two political, economic, military, and ideological blocs. Relations between the two opposing groupings were marked by mutual mistrust and suspicion, tension, and confrontation. The Helsinki Final Act formulated aims for the signatory states in the sphere of security so as to gradually reduce tensions and overcome divisions. The Helsinki Act postulated, inter alia, the following:

- The need to continue efforts to make detente a lasting, continuing, all-embracing process that was universal in scope (implementation of CSCE results was to be a significant contribution to this process).

- Solidarity among nations and the common pursuit of goals set out in the CSCE documents were to lead to developing better and closer relations between them in all fields, and thus "to overcom[e] the confrontation stemming from the character of their past relations, and to better mutual understanding."

- The search--fully taking account of their individuality and diversity of their positions and views--for possibilities of joining their efforts with a view to overcoming distrust and increasing confidence, solving the problems that separate them, and cooperating in the interest of humanity.

The list of tasks agreed in Helsinki was naturally much longer. It is worth remembering that the predominant conviction --expressed both in documents and in declarations by the participants of the negotiations--was that the bipolar world and the separate sociopolitical systems were of durable character. It was a time when the aim was to liberalize the communist system ("socialism with a human face" as proclaimed by the leaders of the Prague Spring) rather than overthrow it. In essence, a possibility of radical transformation of the autocratic and one-party system into a democratic and pluralist one was not given a thought in the states ruled by the communists. The form of the rule could at most undergo some favorable evolution: in return for limited freedoms of citizens and expanding the rule of law in the East, the Western states consented to recognition of the political-territorial status quo that took shape in the wake of World War II. In this context, of key importance for East European governments in the CSCE process were the territorial principles (inviolability of frontiers, territorial integrity) and nonintervention in domestic affairs, thus legitimizing the one-party forms of rule.[13] The East European states considered the principle of sovereign equality as the commitment to "respect each other's political, social, economic and cultural systems as well as its right to determine its laws and regulations." The sovereign rights, then, were interpreted as if the CSCE commitments were addressed to governments, not to nations.

In turn, in Western policies the process initiated in Helsinki (and continued in Belgrade, Madrid, and Vienna) was supposed to contribute to a sui generis humanization of totalitarian, one-party, and undemocratic governments in Eastern Europe. The CSCE process was perceived in the West as a tool to legitimize the emphasis on domestic developments in communist-ruled states. Relevant demands contained in CSCE documents were directly aimed at the states of the then Warsaw Pact, for the purpose of increasing the movement of people, information, and ideas. With time, the provisions (in the Madrid and Vienna concluding documents)[14] took on the character of very detailed instructions on how to safeguard the freedoms of conscience, belief, speech, and association, the right to emigration, and respect for individual liberties. In this regard, the Charter of Paris for a New Europe is the crowning moment of the process of inclusion in the catalogue of international commitments of provisions of a political nature regarding the respect for individual freedoms, the democratization of internal systems, and the rule of law. For the first time, it was stated that "democratic government is based on the will of the people, expressed regularly through free and fair elections.... Democracy, with its representative and pluralist character, entails accountability to the electorate, the obligation of public authorities to comply with the law and justice administered impartially. No one will be above the law."

In this way, international recognition was given to the internal changes that--starting with the establishment of the Solidarity popular movement in Poland in 1980--led almost 10 years later, through peaceful transformation, to the giving away of power by communist parties across Central and Eastern Europe. The adoption of the Paris document closed a specific chapter in the history of the CSCE process but did not change the essence of the process itself. The era of confrontation and division of Europe has ended, reads the Charter of Paris. The signatories declared that "the Ten Principles of the Final Act will guide us towards this ambitious future, just as they have lighted our way towards better relations for the past fifteen years." It now seems legitimate to question whether the ten principles of the Final Act as they stand can really guide us into the future. The new commitments covered human rights and the consolidation of the rule of law and democratic institutions. It was decided in Paris that a number of new CSCE structures and institutions should be established, among them a Council of Foreign Ministers, a Committee of Senior Officials (CSO), the Conflict Prevention Center in Vienna, as well as the CSCE Secretariat in Prague.[15] Regular summit meetings are also envisaged. The "human dimension" of the CSCE was reflected in the decision to convene meetings of experts on national minorities (Geneva, July 1-19, 1991) and on strengthening democratic institutions (Oslo, November 4-15, 1991). In this context, one should also see the results of two successive meetings on the human dimension of the CSCE (Copenhagen, June 5-29, 1990; Moscow, September 10-October 4, 1991). Consequently, the CSCE Human Dimension Committee was called into being, and under the Paris Charter, the Office for Free Election was set up in Warsaw, the latter being recently turned into an Office for Democratic Institutions and Human Rights with expanded functions.[16]

All these meetings, conferences, institutions, and offices are supposed to adjust the CSCE process to new conditions. Only two years ago these kinds of decisions would have meant a revolutionary change. However, in the light of the transformation that has taken place in Europe, and particularly after the breakup of the Soviet Union and the departure from the political stage of the Soviet communist party, it seems that a thorough rethinking and reassessment is needed of not only specific solutions and institutions, but, first and foremost, the basic premises of the whole political philosophy that underlie the multilateral process initiated almost two decades ago at Helsinki. It is worthwhile to ponder if in the new situation the European process is still to define rules and determine the framework within which the processes of domestic transformation in individual countries and relations between states should take place. If repressive systems and large-scale violation of human rights have given way to governments that have declared their readiness to abide by the universal values of the democratic world, then one should consider whether the principles and norms negotiated in the antagonistically divided Europe of the Cold War era can fulfil their task in an entirely different environment.

It would be, of course, naive to equate the end of the bipolar world with the extinction of divisions. Europe from the Atlantic to the Urals is still being torn by conflicts, although quite different from those of the past. Those are neither ideological antagonisms nor rivalries between the two military blocs. The new contradictions result from the economic collapse of the East European countries, differences in their development and associated disintegration, and growing ethnic and national conflicts in postcommunist Europe. On the other side of the former divide--west of the Oder River--accelerating integration processes are taking place, accompanied, quite unexpectedly, by the sense of threat of a different kind: rightist-nationalist, racist, and fascist trends (Le Pen in France, Haider in Austria, the Los Angeles riots, etc) that are reviving and gaining in popularity. In a nutshell, one can note that Europe is still divided de facto, although less and less formally, into the group of affluent and prosperous states with assured external security, and the group of postcommunist states, including the post-Soviet ones, whose situation is in shambles, economically, socially, and in security terms, since they have been deprived of former guarantees and have not obtained the new ones.

A New European Agenda

The new international environment and radical changes have brought to the forefront the need to rethink anew the whole concept of the multilateral CSCE process. In other words, the expectations connected with Helsinki II do not amount to streamlining the existing mechanisms but rather to reinterpreting the old and elaborating some new principles, norms, and procedures. They should meet the challenges and needs of the future, not of the past. That is why, in the search for a European security system, one should start from a different point of departure:

- The end of the Cold War means that a new system will not organize one group of states against another; nor will it, as it had in the 1970s and the 1980s, determine the framework of rivalry between antagonistic blocs.

51

- The need and the role of mediating actors played so far by the neutral and nonaligned (NNA) countries is fading away.

- A need to create a new cooperative security system is entering the European agenda. NATO is the only military-political structure that passed the test throughout its 40-year history, but none of the non-NATO CSCE participating states considers it an overarching alternative to new structures.

- The preservation of the present situation in the longer term would lead to menacing developments that would get out of control. The civil war in Yugoslavia helped demonstrate the simple fact that in the world of interrelationships, the border is blurred between what was formerly considered a domestic conflict and what today constitutes a matter of warranted concern and intervention on the part of the international community. That conflict also revealed the inadequacy of existing structures to handle new tasks, e.g., the prevention and settlement of such conflicts.

- The relationship between NATO and the CSCE will be decisive for the future of the Helsinki process. An accession of the group of former WTO states to NATO would be tantamount to a thorough change of character of the organization. However, the arguments raised to warrant NATO countries' restraint do not reflect their real motives: prior to the failed coup in the Soviet Union, they usually insisted that accession of Poland, Czechoslovakia, and Hungary to the Atlantic Alliance would unnecessarily provoke the USSR. However, everything changed after August 21, 1991. The establishment of a new structure--the North Atlantic Cooperation Council,[17] is an important step towards the institutionalization of a new type of security system in Europe.

- The new architecture of European security consists of the following: the CSCE process and institutions formed within its framework;[18] "European Security Identity" ("which might in time lead to a common defense"[19]); the Western European Union and its links with the new European Union and with NATO;[20] and various attempts to establish new structures east of the Oder River. An example of such initiatives was the Pentagonale Group (later expanded to the "Hexagonale" grouping), the undertaking that had been wrecked by the armed conflict in Yugoslavia before it took deeper roots. Another example is the triangular cooperation of Poland, Czechoslovakia, and Hungary. The transitory character of this undertaking found expression in their leaders' statement to the effect that: "The principal task set by Poland, Czechoslovakia, and Hungary is a full-range integration into the European political, economic and juridical as well as security system."[21]

- Finally, all the abovementioned institutions (and the others not mentioned here, like the Council of Europe in Strasbourg) proved to be inefficient or even helpless in the face of the swelling wave of new conflicts, tension, and threats. One of the possible explanations of this phenomenon is that the main source of those threats is not exactly that the balance of forces between military blocs has been upset that one of the major powers was getting the upper hand, but rather the downright collapse of the one-party totalitarian system, which constituted a component part of and point of reference for constructing the security mechanisms of the Western democracies. The lack of democratic institutions and deep-rooted democratic political culture in postcommunist states means that an economic

53

collapse in those countries (the scope of which would be much greater than that of the Great Crisis of 1929) would trigger off enormous social as well as national and religious conflicts. Existing international institutions and mechanisms are unable in their present form to fulfill their preventive function vis-a-vis uncontrollable conflicts of a domestic character. Nor are they suitable for defusing crisis situations when they have spilled over into open conflict.

New Members, New Dimensions, New Institutions

The CSCE structures created in 1990-1991 illustrate the desire to adapt available instruments to meet new challenges.[22] However, many of these structures have been overtaken by events. By decision of the second meeting of the CSCE Council of Ministers for Foreign Affairs in Prague on January 30-31, 1992,[23] the status of participating CSCE states was accorded to Armenia, Azerbaijan, Belarus, Kazakhstan, Kyrgyzstan, Moldova, Tajikistan, Turkmenistan, Ukraine, and Uzbekistan, (following Estonia, Latvia, and Lithuania, which had already been accepted).[24] Immediately after the dissolution of the Soviet Union and the formation of the CIS, the Ministry of Foreign Affairs of the Russian Federation announced that the USSR's membership in the United Nations and all its institutions and organizations, as well as its participation in all treaties, conventions, and negotiations, would be continued by the Russian Federation as the successor state.[25] This move was not contested by any state.

Enlarging the number of participants of the CSCE process has also been accompanied by a considerable expansion of tasks. The new CSCE concept of security and stability includes human rights and political, military, economic, and environmental factors. An important new role of the Helsinki process consists in fostering democratic development and fully integrating participating states into the network of shared CSCE values.

The Document on Further Development of CSCE Institutions and Structures defined new guidelines for the negotiation at the Helsinki Follow-Up Meeting that began in March 1992.[26] It was agreed that the efficiency of the institutions established in 1991 should be enhanced. To this end, the Committee of Senior Officials will act as the agent of the Council of Ministers in taking appropriate decisions (between meetings of the CSCE Council). Therefore, the CSO will meet more regularly, at least once every three months. The facilities of the CSCE communications network will be made available to the Chairman-in-Office of the CSO "for transmission of urgent messages related to the work of the Committee."[27]

The tasks in the human dimension of security, which "remains a key function of the CSCE," were also broadly expanded.[28] Regarding the task of crisis management, the intentions resemble academic parlance (e.g., "to study possibilities for improving") more than concrete political and organizational decisions. Hopefully, actions will be backed by instruments tested both in theory and practice: fact-finding and rapporteur missions, monitoring, good offices, counselling and conciliation, dispute settlement, but also peacekeeping activities in Europe. The tasks entrusted to the Conflict Prevention Center remain in blatant disproportion to the means and capabilities available for carrying them out.

The meeting of the CSCE Council of Ministers in Prague was attended by officials of the United Nations and the UN Economic Commission, and by representatives of the heads of a number of international institutions and organizations: NATO, the WEU, the Council of Europe, the OECD, and the European Bank for Reconstruction and Development. Until 1991, all conferences and meetings were held in accordance with the Helsinki Final Recommendations of 1973, outside military alliances.[29] Hence, the participation of NATO and WEU representatives means a substantial change of and a new approach to the role of these institutions in the pan-European process. What is important is that the Prague Document determined for the first time the rules of cooperation with such organizations as NATO, the EC, the WEU, the Council of Europe, the OECD, the EBRD, the European Investment Bank, and other European and transatlantic organizations. As a result, these institutions and organizations are seen as compatible and not competitive with the CSCE. There is no doubt that the one area in which the CSCE role is not challenged is the human dimension of relations between states. The meetings in Copenhagen, Moscow, Geneva, and Oslo gave the human dimension of security an institutional shape.

The same cannot yet be said about military aspects of security. The decisions contained in the Vienna documents concerning CSBMs and those in the 1990 CFE treaty concerning conventional force reductions reflect significant progress; however, they are not adequate to the new political-military realities of a post-Cold War Europe.

A qualitatively new approach is also required in the areas of crisis management and conflict prevention. The Prague Document asserts only "the need to strengthen the capacity of the CSCE to contribute ... to a peaceful solution of problems involving national minorities which could lead to tensions and conflict--both within and between States--including possibilities for 'early warning' and the 'need for further development of the CSCE's capability for conflict prevention, crisis management and peaceful settlement of disputes.'[30] This is how the tasks and the mandate of the Helsinki Follow-Up Meeting have been formulated.

The CSCE's admission of all the former Soviet republics gives institutional scope to a new security area from Vancouver to Vladivostok. The CSCE decisions already apply not only to Europe ("from the Atlantic to the Urals") and North America (the United States and Canada), but also to the states of Central Asia. Such a significant expansion of geographic scope and the inclusion of new participating states necessitate a differentiation of tasks and expectations connected with the implementation of the provisions already adopted and those yet to be negotiated. States that have emerged as a result of the collapse of the Soviet Union are at a crossroads--facing difficult choices about how to proceed with their development. Their acceptance as participating states in the CSCE process was contingent upon the commitment of each of them to accept "in their entirety all commitments and responsibilities" contained in the CSCE documents.[31] Indeed, they declared their determination to act in accordance with these provisions. Specific commitments were made regarding the Vienna Document 1990 requirements on CSBMs and the prompt ratification of the 1990 CFE treaty.

To implement these commitments, it was agreed in Prague that the governments of the newly admitted states will invite a rapporteur mission (arranged by the Chairman of the Council of Ministers of the CSCE) to visit and will fully facilitate its activities.[32] This mission will report back to the CSCE on progress towards full implementation of CSCE commitments in those states and will provide assistance towards that objective.

57

The procedures adopted within the CSCE and the established institutions and structures ought, on the one hand, to facilitate a stabilization of democracy and the rule of law in the post-totalitarian states, and, on the other hand, help prevent the Central Asian participants from sliding into Islamic fundamentalism. It is also envisaged that informal consultations under the direction of the CSO Chairman should take place at Helsinki during the follow-up meeting in order to establish the modalities for a program of coordinated support to recently admitted states, through which appropriate diplomatic, academic, legal, and administrative expertise and advice on CSCE matters could be made available.[33]

A clear tendency has developed in the CSCE process to make specific and binding decisions, as well as general recommendations, and to apply multilateral mechanisms and procedures to monitor implementation of those decisions. Thus, the possibility exists to shape a common system based on both declared and implemented values. An important step along the road towards making the system more viable is the understanding reached in Prague, which makes possible a departure from consensus decision making in cases of clear and gross violations of CSCE commitments regarding human rights, democracy, and the rule of law.[34]

Conclusion

The changes in Europe confirm the fact that menaces today are of an utterly different character compared to those of the Cold War period. They no longer arise from the supremacy of one bloc or from the aggressive policies pursued by one of the great powers. The new threats result from the domestic plight that was bequeathed to new democratic states in Central Europe and Asia, both in economic terms and in terms of national and interethnic conflict. The main challenge for the future is uncertainty and its related risks.[35]

The search for a new security system in Europe must take account of mechanisms for preventing both external aggression and aggression directed by a state against its own society. Consequently, a new catalogue of principles should embrace-- along with CSCE Principle VI (nonintervention in internal affairs)--a principle of legitimized interventionism to fend off a threat to common values. Proposals for a new political and legal regulation in this area deserve careful attention on the part of not only experts in international law but also political decision makers.[36] It is of utmost importance to match the words in the declaration on equal security with concrete actions: to reduce in equal measure the levels of armaments in both East and West to diminished external threats, and to establish common institutions in the area of military security. The shaping of these institutions should by no means be subject to ready-made blueprints or theoretical concepts but, as a starting-point, must take into account the different and heterogeneous situations in various parts of Europe, and the territory stretching from Vancouver to Vladivostok. This presupposes a need for a thorough transformation of not only the CSCE but also NATO and other Western institutions, and the possibility of cooperation between the new democratic states and the Western organizations with a view to future full membership for them in these structures.

NATO, the WEU, the EC, the Council of Europe, and other multinational organizations should get involved to an increasing degree in the multilateral CSCE process. One cannot exclude the possibility of membership of some Central European

59

states in Western organizations such as the EC and NATO. An improvement in mutual relations between NATO and the CSCE was heralded by the Rome decisions of the NATO summit meeting on November 7-8, 1991. It was agreed that, as a result of the Paris summit meeting, the CSCE process now included new institutional arrangements and "provide[d] a contractual framework for consultation and cooperation that can play a constructive role, complementary to that of NATO and the process of European integration, in preserving peace."[37] The Rome NATO document clearly staked out the role of the CSCE process in "the Alliance's new strategic concept."

The potential of dialogue and cooperation within all of Europe must be fully developed in order to help defuse crises and prevent conflicts, since NATO's security is inseparably linked to that of all other states in Europe. To this end, NATO will have to support the role of the CSCE process and its institutions. Other bodies, including the European Community, the Western European Union, and the United Nations may also have an important role to play.[38]

The main result of the CSCE summit meeting should be the establishment of a CSCE Forum for Security Cooperation. For East European states, the significance of such a body consists chiefly in handling the problems of preventing and resolving conflicts; for West European states, which abound in these types of institution, the new forum will likely be a useful instrument to deal with developments in Europe. The task of the new Security Forum will be to complete and expand the old arms control agenda and address new dangers and opportunities.[39]

Political rather than military factors will play an increasing role in maintaining security. Clearly, the threat of armed aggression between states has substantially diminished.

Whereas the sources of instability are of a political and economic, and not military, character, new means and mechanisms must focus on political, ethnic, and economic problems, rather than on military ones. This applies both to the CSCE and NATO,[40] as well as other organizations. The aim is not to form one all-embracing security institution but the effective operation of the "interlocking system of institutions."[41] The starting points in building a new system in the military field are multilateral agreements (on CSBMs, the CFE treaty, the CPC and its emergency mechanisms, the Treaty on Open Skies, and the regulations concerning arms transfers and nonproliferation). The foundations of the new system will be, among others, the already agreed principles: openness and transparency of military activities, restraint from threatening activities, limitation of armed forces, and a permanent dialogue on security. One of the ways of consolidating the new security order might be the conclusion of a General Treaty on Security and Cooperation in Europe.

Until recently, security, as a rule, was seen as tantamount to arms control. Now it seems that the period of grand agreements and treaties (like START or CFE) is a thing of the past. In the years to come the most important thing will be conflict prevention. Accordingly, the main role will be accorded not to arms control but rather to a new organization and new principles of a peaceful order. The tasks that had been entrusted to the CSCE 20 years ago were fulfilled in part or have become irrelevant. The new regime of security in and for Europe will probably combine the concept of a European directorate (or a European Security Council)[42] with the participation of the three Western powers (US, UK, and France) as well as Germany and Russia, and an appropriate role for NATO, the EC, and the WEU.

Today we already know that even in the best possible

new international system, conflicts will not disappear. Rather, they are becoming more numerous; and while they do not pose a direct threat of world war, they are still dangerous to overall stability. The new peaceful order must be based to a greater degree on effective political and legal instruments rather than on military deterrence. In the future, that regime is likely to cover a comprehensive ban on weapons of mass destruction, combined with a conventional weapons nonproliferation regime and an efficient system of peacekeeping activities.[43] New dimensions of the CSCE process can and should promote the shifting of the center of gravity from national security to a cooperative system of security--pan-European and global.

Changes, by their very nature, are inevitably accompanied by instability. The transitional period we are living in may last a relatively long time. Old threats have faded away but at the same time the sense of stability has disappeared, too. At present there is quite a widespread conviction that the bipolar system created in the wake of World War II will be replaced by an equally stable and at the same time less costly international structure. This is wishful thinking that reflects needs and hopes as opposed to a clear political program. In effect, a gap has appeared between the sought-after "world order" or "new security order in Europe" and actual realities.

There exits, too, a gap between the expectations connected with the CSCE and the capabilities of the process itself. In the past, this process was overestimated in the East and underrated in the West. Today we face the reverse situation. Nevertheless, analyzing the negotiations and actions undertaken hitherto within the framework of the Helsinki process, one can draw some general conclusions:

- First, the norms and procedures agreed 20 years ago are suitable only in a limited measure for the new situation.

- Second, the main features of the CSCE have changed, and those constituting its drawbacks have been altered to a considerable degree; nonetheless the process does not meet the new expectations. For instance, treaties are being negotiated within its framework that are binding on the basis of international law; consensus is already not always observed and the adopted decisions are of obligatory character; an increasingly important role is played by military questions; a number of institutions and structures have been established to ensure proper monitoring and the effectiveness of the decisions adopted. All in all, however, the CSCE is neither an alliance nor a security organization.

- Third, the role of the Helsinki process is recognized as that of a forum for ongoing and future negotiations concerning arms control and the dialogue on military security. However, in the changed situation, the need for negotiating grand treaties on arms control is not of primary significance.

- Fourth, the role of the CSCE in ensuring security will be determined by whether NATO and its structures will make use of the CSCE in peacekeeping activities and solving conflict and crisis situations.

In sum, the significance of the Helsinki process will be determined to a great extent not by the establishment of new structures and institutions but rather by the efficient use and adaptation to the new circumstances of this already existing, well-functioning, trusted organization to which the participating states have delegated some of their competence. As a matter of fact, the role of structures and institutions dealing with security problems is determined not by bodies and tasks entrusted to them but rather by the states' readiness to make use of those bodies. The CSCE institutions are not an exception to this rule.

Notes

1. See more on this in A.D. Rotfeld, "New Security Structures in Europe: Concepts, Proposals, and Decisions," in *SIPRI Yearbook 1991: World Armaments and Disarmament* (Oxford: Oxford University Press, 1991), pp. 585-615; and A.D. Rotfeld, "European Security in Transition," in *SIPRI Yearbook 1992: World Armaments and Disarmament* (Oxford: Oxford University Press, 1992), pp. 563-82.

2. See more on this in L. Acimovic, *Problems of Security and Cooperation in Europe* (Alphen aan den Rijn: Sijthoff and Noordhoff, 1981), pp. 139-72; A.D. Rotfeld, *Europejski system bezpieczenstwa in statu nascendi* (Warsaw: PISM, 1990), pp. 85-108; and S. Lehne, *The Vienna Meeting of the CSCE 1986-1989: A Turning Point in East-West Relations* (Vienna: Austrian Institute for International Affairs, 1991), pp. 3-15.

3. A.D. Rotfeld, "Follow-up to the Conference: Forms of Cooperation after the CSCE," in *CSCE--A Polish View* (Warsaw: PWIN, 1976), pp. 221-70.

4. Rules of Procedure--Recommendation 65, in *Final Recommendations of the Helsinki Consultations* (Helsinki, 1973).

5. Ibid.

6. Ibid.

7. Likewise the zone of CSBM application covered "the whole of Europe as well as the adjoining sea area and air space." See Concluding Document of the Madrid Meeting 1980, Madrid, Sept. 6, 1983, in *From Helsinki to Madrid: CSCE Documents 1973-1983*, ed. A.D. Rotfeld (Warsaw: PISM, 1983), p. 285.

8. This is demonstrated in the CSCE documents and outcomes of the expert meetings in Montreux (1978) and Athens (1984). For the text of the reports see *From Helsinki to Madrid*.

9. Ibid., p. 121.

10. Ibid., p. 120.

11. Charter of Paris for a New Europe, CSCE Paris Summit, Nov. 19-21, 1990, p. 13.

12. Stefan Lehne, *The CSCE in the 1990's: Common European House or Potemkin Village?* (Vienna: Austrian Institute for International Affairs, 1991).

13. For the most part it failed to be noticed that East European signatories of the CSCE Final Act gave more prominence to their functions as party leaders (Leonid Brezhnev, Edward Gierek) that determined their real positions in their own countries rather than state functions. Illustrative of this is the situation where the Soviet delegation at Helsinki, being unsure whether the Western representatives would accept Leonid Brezhnev in his capacity of CPSU General Secretary in the CSCE Final Act, presented him at first as the chairman of the USSR delegation to Stage III of the CSCE. It was not until Edward Gierek's presentation as the Polish party chief met with no reservation that the Soviet delegation demanded that the title of CPSU General Secretary be appended to the name of Leonid Brezhnev.

14. For more on this see Rotfeld, *Europejski system bezpieczenstwa*.

15. See Rotfeld, "New Security Structures in Europe."

16. The relevant decisions were adopted during the course of the Prague meeting of the Council of Foreign Minsters of the CSCE (Jan. 30-31, 1991).

17. Final Communique issued by the Foreign Ministers of NATO states, Dec. 19, 1991, and NACC Statement on dialogue, partnership, and cooperation, Dec. 20, 1991. *Atlantic News*, no. 2328 (Annex I & II).

18. Rotfeld, *Europejski system bezpieczenstwa*, p. 6.

19. Final Communique, Annex I, p. 3.

20. Declaration of the Member States of Western European Union which are also members of the European Union on the role of WEU and its relations with the European Union and with the Atlantic Alliance. Annex V. European Council, Maastricht, Dec. 9-10, 1991. Presidency Conclusions, Maastricht, Dec. 11, 1991, pp. 29-33.

21. The document (the Cracow Declaration, Oct. 6, 1991) adopted at the end of the meeting of Lech Walesa (Poland), Vaclav Havel (CSFR), and Jozsef Antall (Hungary) was preceded by similar declarations of intention issued in Bratislava (1990) and Visegrad (1991).

22. See Rotfeld, *Europejski system bezpieczenstwa*, pp. 612-15.

23. The decision was preceded by the recommendation of the sixth meeting of the CSCE Committee of Senior Officials that the states interested in accession to the CSCE forward a letter in which they state that they would undertake to adopt the Helsinki Final Act, the Charter of Paris for a New Europe, and all other documents of the CSCE. See *Journal*, no. 1 (Prague), (Jan. 27, 1992). They also agreed (a) to apply all the provisions of the Vienna Document on CSBMs; and (b) to "an understanding that the geographic scope of its application should be revised as soon as possible in order to ensure full effect of the rules of transparency, predictability and conflict prevention" on their territories. The specific provisions will be included in the Vienna Document 1992. The governments of the new states also recognized the requirement for "prompt entry into force of the Treaty on Conventional Armed Forces in Europe." See "Draft letter of Accession to the CSCE," *Journal*, no. 1 (Prague) (Jan. 27, 1992), annex 2. The letters of accession are published in "Second Meeting of the CSCE Council of Ministers, Prague," *Journal*, no. 1 (Jan. 30, 1992).

24. Georgia, the last post-Soviet state to join the CSCE, joined on March 24, 1992 during the Helsinki Follow-Up Meeting.

25. Russia sent notes to this effect to the UN and the Conference on Disarmament on Dec. 24 and 27, 1991, respectively, and to all diplomatic missions in Moscow (Jan. 12, 1992).

26. See Prague Document on Further Development of CSCE Institutions and Structures, CSCE/2-C/2 Dec. (Jan. 30, 1992).

27. Ibid.

28. Ibid.

29. Recommendation 65, *Final Recommendation of the Helsinki Consultations* (Helsinki, June 8, 1973).

30. Summary of Conclusions, Prague Meeting of the CSCE Council, Jan. 30-31, 1992.

31. See "Second Meeting of the CSCE Council of Ministers, Prague."

32. Ibid. A relevant identical formula is contained in the letters of all foreign ministers of the newly admitted states addressed to the Chairman-in-Office of the CSCE Council of Ministers, Jiři Dienstbier, Foreign Minster of the Czech and Slovak Federal Republic.

33. See Summary of Conclusions, Prague Meeting of the CSCE Council, Jan. 30-31, 1992, para. 19, p. 8.

34. See Prague Document on Further Development of CSCE Institutions and Structures, especially section 4, para. 16. The Romanian delegation made an interpretative statement to the effect that "the conditions and modalities of implementing this procedure ... should try to prevent the risks that resorting to it might become a stimulus for those who may be tempted to use the issues of human rights, including in particular the rights of persons belonging to minorities, as a substitute for promoting a revisionist policy, through incitation from outside of tensions, unrest and even conflicts in another country." An example of the new practice is the suspension of Yugoslavia as a CSCE participant. *International Herald Tribune*, May 13, 1992.

35. In NATO documents the term "threats" is being replaced by "risks" and "uncertainties." See "The Alliance's New Strategic Concept, Agreed by the Heads of the State and Government participating in the Meeting of the North Atlantic Council in Rome on 7-8 Nov. 1991," *NATO Review*, no. 6 (December 1991), pp. 25-32.

36. L.F. Damrosch, "Politics Across Borders: Nonintervention and Non-forcible Influence Over Domestic Affairs," *American Journal of International Law*, no. 1 (1989); R. Bierzanek, "Ingerencja w sprawy wewnetrzne innych panstw," *Sprawy Miedzynarodowe*, no. 12 (1991).

37. See Prague Document on Further Development of CSCE Institutions and Structures, para. 5.

38. Ibid., para. 34.

39. See *An Arms Control Strategy for CSCE-Helsinki 1992* (Santa Monica: RAND, 1992).

40. "The Alliance stands ready to make its own collective experience available to CSCE and will seek to establish an appropriate relationship with the CSCE." See "Final Communique issued by the North Atlantic Council Meeting in Ministerial Session, 19th December 1991," *Atlantic News*, no. 2382 (Dec. 21, 1991), p. 3.

41. See statement by Krzysztof Skubiszewski, Minster of Foreign Affairs of the Republic of Poland, at the meeting of the CSCE Council of Minsters in Prague, Jan. 30, 1992.

42. J. Goodby, "Commonwealth and Concert: Organizing Principles of Post-containment Order in Europe," *The Washington Quarterly*, Summer 1991.

43. H. Weston Burns, "Law and Alternative Security: Towards a Just World Peace," in *Alternative Security: Living Without Nuclear Deterrence* (Boulder: Westview, 1991), pp. 78-107.

3

Is This the Chance for a New Euro-Atlantic Alliance?

Alpo Rusi

"If communism is dead, then anticommunism is dead, too."
--Irving Kristol

The Revolution of 1989-1991 in Perspective

The collapse of the communist regimes in East Central Europe and the former Soviet Union opened up a debate about the future of the international system. The revolutionary events of 1989-1991 were, however, symptoms of both longer-term, historical processes and shorter-term, accidental factors. For Europe a new era has begun. European unity has become a real possibility for the first time in the history of the continent.

Unity without stability is not, however, possible in the long run. The history of the European security complex consists of an array of repeating political arrangements that have never lasted more than about 25 to 40 years. The traditional European security order (a multipolar system based on the balance of power) collapsed after World War II and was "overlaid" by the two superpowers. The local--European--security relations had ceased to operate. After the events of 1989-1991, this security complex has also collapsed. The present and transitory system is, however, by definition a political process that should be replaced by another, more fixed, political process. It is clear that the post-World War II security complex is also intertwined with emerging security structures, with stability in Europe now increasingly a function of the Euro-Atlantic relationship. In fact, Europe's unity may become a reality only within the framework of that community--within the Euro-Atlantic as well as within the global framework.

The post-Cold War international system will be in a state of flux for years. There is no consensus among observers as to what extent the basic nature of the international system has really changed. On the one hand, it has been questioned whether the transition from Yalta (1945) to Malta (1989) constituted a qualitative step toward a more stable world peace. Skeptics stress that whereas at Yalta they divided Europe, at Malta they divided the whole world, or most of it. This view insists that the post-Cold War order is, in fact, an even more dangerous and unjust place to live compared with the one dominated by the two superpowers. On the other hand, there exists another view that argues that nothing has changed as such although the Cold War is over. The basic nature of the international system remains the same although its dominant powers may be replaced by new rivals.[1]

This chapter tries first of all to make an argument that there is a qualitative transformation taking place in the system. This process has its roots in the progress of economic and political modernization influencing the world system and has become gradually a decisive factor forging international relations. In brief, modernization derives from long-term systemic change. In the short term, the process encourages transformation from a world order based on strategic stability as well as diplomatic relations between the former Soviet Union and the United States to an order dominated by the Euro-Atlantic community. This chapter also tries to clarify these two aspects, and makes a related argument that the final condition of the realization of the modern world system is macropolitical "maturity."

The spread of democratic values combined with an economic boom created a special relationship between the US and United Kingdom in the early 19th century. This relationship constituted the core of the globalization of the modernization process. It widened in size and scope, evolving into NATO in the late 1940s. Following the end of the Cold War, this original transatlantic alliance has gradually been turning into a Euro-Atlantic security community in which geographic area and function are to a certain extent different compared with its original focus.

The transformation of the transatlantic alliance to the Euro-Atlantic security community began in the years 1989-1991 when a new Europe was declared and defined in the CSCE Paris Charter in 1990. As a result of this Charter, and in particular as a result of the final collapse of the Soviet Union, the system of modern states is becoming one founded on shared democratic values. The global crisis of authoritarianism ended and led to the spread of liberal democracy, which constitutes the dramatic turning point in the history of the modernization of the international system. In the present situation one could assume that the time may be ripe to modify post-World War II Western "realism" with a "forgotten tradition," which by definition means "the specific Anglo-American tradition" in thinking about international relations. According to this older tradition, a democratic republic could transcend the logic of power politics, itself be a "uniquely virtuous nation," and have a civilizing impact on international relations.[2]

For the states that have not been members of the Atlantic organizations, like the neutrals and the new democracies in the East, the profoundly changed geostrategic landscape of Europe is both challenging and demanding. It is in the interest of every citizen and European state to promote the changes that are overcoming the remnants of the political and economic division in Europe, and its evolving new security architecture should be developed accordingly. The CSCE process will play a crucial role in this respect. However, the transatlantic alliance could be transformed to a new Euro-Atlantic community as the core of this architecture. This development should not hinder the further development of the European Community initially into the European Union. The existence and further development of the Euro-Atlantic community could, in fact, guarantee a stable security order and thus facilitate the peaceful development of the European union primarily as a civil entity in international affairs.

The Modern World System in Progress

This chapter emphasizes the role of the macropolitical phenomenon from authoritarian rule to democracy as a decisive factor in the process of modernization and formation of a stable world order. The emergence of the Euro-Atlantic security community is but a logical repercussion of this development.

In 1795, Immanuel Kant suggested that peace among nations might come about as a result of three things: 1) the increasing destructiveness of war; 2) the spread of republican governments; and 3) the growth of commerce and trade. In the short run over two centuries, Kant was wrong. Extensive trade and enormous destructive military capability did not prevent Europe from destroying itself in the First and Second World Wars.[3] But perhaps a century and a half was too short to test the validity of Kant's prescriptions. Unlike in 1914, when many leaders and their citizens glorified and even desired war, the threat of nuclear annihilation, the slow spread of market economies and democratic values, and the progress of modernization have made a large-scale war between nations far less attractive in the post-World War II era.[4]

The origins of the current world system date back to the late 15th century or, in fact, to the "long sixteenth century" running from about 1450 to 1640, when Europe started expanding across the globe, enhancing the demand, as one observer put it, "for organizations that would be capable of operating on such a scale. All the basic organization types of modern society--the modern state, modern corporate enterprise, modern science--were shaped by it and benefitted greatly from it."[5] Consequently, Europe created a world economy that transcended the boundaries of any given political structure.[6] From the middle of the 17th century onwards, modern capitalism and the emergent modern state were, as Max Weber states, assimilated to the form of an "alliance" within the framework of a new nation-state.[7]

The new international order based on the system of modern nation-states never prevented, however, the outbreak of war. The Peace of Westphalia of 1648 included some elements of stability, but "did little to reduce the incidence of war," as Kalevi J. Holsti has noted.[8] The upshot of this development was that states were "not subject to international moral requirements because they represent separate and discrete political orders with no common authority among them."[9] The real turning point in this respect first took place at the end of the 18th century and became more evident in the following century.

From a Special Relationship to a Euro-Atlantic Community

The French Revolution heralded the destruction of the *ancien regime* in Europe in the 1780s. In this sense, political modernity was conceived during that decade. But the actual birth of political modernity, delayed by the long and destructive gestation period formed by the Napoleonic Wars, could begin in full measure, as Paul Johnson has observed, only when peace came and immense new resources in finance, management, science, and technology, which were now available, could be put to constructive purpose. This development took place from 1815 until 1830.[10]

During these 15 years, political and economic modernity expanded decisively, primarily in Western Europe and the US, but also in many other areas worldwide. Unfortunately, Russia, although expanding fast, was also developing the fatal fissures in its society that were to engulf the country in the immense tragedies of the 20th century. In China and Japan, the seeds of future catastrophe were also becoming apparent.[11]

With respect to the evolution of the international system as such, the emergence of "a special relationship" between the UK and the US in 1815 constituted a landmark. It resulted from the Treaty of Ghent, "which proved to be one of the most durable and decisive in world history," as one observer has noted. Indeed, it became the peace treaty between the UK and the US.[12] In the years to come, the logic of the special relationship proved to be powerful: the human and material interaction started rapidly expanding across the ocean after 1815. A great economic boom created a solid basis for the new Anglo-American community. The ruling political parties in both countries promoted, as Robert Kelley stated, "an interdependent world of peace and order."[13]

The special relationship grew gradually to a transatlantic strategic alliance that first existed in full scale during World War I. The US commitment to European defense after World War II was possible in large part because of this "special relationship" between the two English-speaking democracies. There remained the indestructible relationship of common heritage and common values and traditions, a common cause in peace and security. Furthermore, through NATO, the Anglo-American relationship had evolved into a strategic alliance.[14]

The Cold War vanished primarily as a result of the expansion of modernity in East Central Europe and the former Soviet Union. Now it is important to proceed with the "aftercare" of the Cold War. It seems evident that the US will remain committed to Europe both through NATO and the CSCE--indeed, through the evolving Euro-Atlantic community for decades to come. Since history also suggests that global conflict is more likely when the US withdraws from world affairs, the further evolution of the Euro-Atlantic community in security terms should be undertaken as a necessity. Once again, this should take place in compliance with the emergence of "an ever closer union between the peoples of Europe" in the form of the European union.[15]

The Emergence of the Euro-Atlantic Community

On June 18, 1991, in his speech in Berlin, US Secretary of State James Baker stated that "our objective is both a Europe whole and free, and a Euro-Atlantic community that extends east from Vancouver to Vladivostok." In his speech, Baker attempted to go beyond the vision of a new European architecture that he had presented about a year before.[16] The concept of the Euro-Atlantic community constituted a final stage of modernization that had its origins in the Anglo-American relationship. Baker noted that "our structures need to promote Euro-Atlantic political and economic values, the ideals of the Enlightenment." Now a historical opportunity has emerged to bring the Euro-Atlantic values and to widen cooperation geographically eastward.

Modernization and integration have gone together. This has been the main feature of development in the post-World War II Europe. In the early 1950s, the so-called Schumann Plan proposed to integrate the economy and political future of West Germany with its neighbors by locking its coal and steel industries--the key heavy industries--into a common framework. In the decades following, the West European economy became each year less and less an interdependent group of national economies and more and more an integrated economy.

During the 1980s, integration became a means for the EC countries to respond to economic and technological competition from the US and Japan. Consequently, the structure of the European international economy become more "European." Finally, the EC emerged as the core regional organization in Europe, with which all the other countries were deepening their relations. Furthermore, the recent agreement between the EC and EFTA, if ratified by all 19 nations involved, will create a unified market of 380 million Europeans, by far the largest and wealthiest in the world.[17]

From the point of view of the Euro-Atlantic community, NATO, the EC, and the CSCE play key roles; yet the key players ensuring European stability in the immediate future will remain nation-states, especially the US, Germany, and Russia.

Undoubtedly, the strength of the Euro-Atlantic community depends on cooperation between the EC and the US. In brief, the new Euro-Atlantic community should build upon the original spirit of the Anglo-American special relationship, with new conditions and new participants.[18]

The Geostrategic Landscape of the Post-Divisional Europe

Although the international system is undergoing a qualitative transformation, it is questionable to what extent its basic nature will change. We should attempt to think of international relations primarily "as living matter, like any organism sometimes developing in natural balance, at other times afflicted with disease or disturbed by extraneous elements." Therefore, as George F. Kennan has stated, "artificial tampering with natural--'mechanical,' 'legalistic,' or 'universalistic'--solutions to problems of foreign policy are odious, almost perverse." Furthermore, Anders Stephanson has commented, "Nature (or the real) in this particular domain is power, embodied in a series of states with differing interests. The reality of power might, rather as with sex, be passed over in embarrassed silence, but ultimately it would demand its due."[19]

Even in Kantian terms, the "eternal peace" will be nothing but a process based on temporary political settlements conditioned by systemic changes as well as accidental factors. The qualitative aspect derives primarily from the withering of the role of hegemonic war as a decisive instrument of change in international relations. Hegemonic war, not war as such, has lost its historical impetus. The revolutions of 1989-1991 constituted a historical testimony of this evolution.[20]

The Cold War was primarily an ideological war. The political East is withering and returning to Europe and embracing democracy. German unification and Russian disintegration are symbols of this process. The European states as a whole are seeking a new political and security order. Any new security arrangement should be built, however, on the achievements of the existing ones; on the basis of *acquis securite*. Europe after the end of the superpower confrontation should be a new Europe in partnership with the one remaining superpower. This is necessary because the ending of the Cold War has removed the basic structure of European stability, even if, in fact, this was nothing but "metastability." Now the task is to create "real stability" based primarily on the common values and principles approved in the Paris Charter, but based first of all on the cooperative security behavior of the democratic states.

The problem is that a new Europe seems likely to be based primarily on solutions that are "mechanical" (integration), "legalistic" (the CSCE), as well as "universalistic" (the CSCE as a regional security system of the UN). Does this concept match the reality that is the precondition for any possibility to create a stable world order?

Although the "organic nature" of international relations will remain, Europe's security order is now "afflicted with disease" (ethnic conflicts, border disputes), and also in the future will continue to be "disturbed by extraneous elements" (the breakup of Russia and the threat of immigration from the poor South). However, the process of modernization is the key to demilitarizing both the "disease" as well as "the extraneous elements" afflicting Europe. History has confirmed Woodrow Wilson's hypothesis that democracies do not go to war against each other. In Europe, the old "metastability" should be replaced gradually with a more realistic and stable security complex. Thus both Barry Buzan and Ole Waever have stated that "the EC project is not possible without an overall stability of the European security order (and vice versa)."[21] It seems likely, therefore, that any stable security order in Europe cannot be purely "European" in nature.

Threats to the Euro-Atlantic Community

It would be misleading to assume, however, that the further emergence and evolution of the Euro-Atlantic community could be taken for granted. There are at least four threats to the realization of this international enterprise:

1. The possible withdrawal of the US from the global scene and from Europe in particular. Especially in the US, a political view that favors total withdrawal from Europe may become popular. "Withdrawal of the Red Army from Europe would remove.... the military instrument of Marxist restoration. If Moscow will get out, we will get out," stated US Republican presidential candidate Patrick J. Buchanan. Also, the collapse of the Uruguay Round and the deepening economic recession would place enormous strain on Europe's relationship with the US and Japan.[22]

2. The possible breakup of Russia may endanger both an accelerated European integration and the emergence of a new Euro-Atlantic community. After the failed coup in Moscow, a total "Soviet" military withdrawal from East Central Europe and the Baltic states is looming on the horizon. Both the US and "Europe" bear great responsibility to prevent the sort of Russian

breakup that would lead to a return of authoritarianism in the Kremlin.

3. The emergence of a new military-political superpower in the form of European union. It is also evident that the concept of "European integration" is still very much evolving. In brief, the question is whether a "fortress Europe" will supersede an open "union model" as the driving force of European integration. If the former concept prevails, the Euro-Atlantic community may face fatal flaws. Europe would be left alone to cope with "a new Russian question," and old rivalries inside Europe could easily emerge, at least between Russia and a "unified Europe."[23]

4. The renationalization of Germany. Germany is now the largest European state, with the exception of Russia. Its population is almost 40% larger than that of France. It also has the strongest and most dynamic economy on the continent, and is the third largest economy in the world. The internal political development of Germany, as well as its relations with its neighbors, will have a profound, even determining, influence on the direction of European affairs. Should Germany begin to go its own way, the "renationalization" of Germany could bring both European integration and the future of the Euro-Atlantic community to a definitive end.[24]

The Structures and Functions of the Euro-Atlantic Community

The political and structural transformation of Europe amounts to a revolutionary but uneven change, manifesting and creating new asymmetries and inequalities in the domestic and external capabilities of countries and in the political structure of the all-European system. This is inevitable, as the object of the emerging common policies and institutions is a *transitory system*. In the new order, there is a built-in idea that system change will continue, affecting not only the states and societies undergoing political and economic transition, but also the political structure of international society.

Managing and facilitating peaceful change in such a situation will be a demanding task for international cooperation. The problems of weak states (i.e., the new democracies) that are struggling with deficient cohesion, identity, or legitimacy will be confronted. Their strengthening will have to be an integral part of the construction of a new mature and stable international security order. These ambitions are not likely to be fully satisfied by, for example, the relatively weak structure and limited security services provided by the CSCE. But as Kari Möttölä notes, "no shortcut to an EC or NATO membership kind of solution to the security problem is in the offing, either, for outsiders."[25] New solutions are needed to cope with the transitory problems of the emerging European security order.

The question is, then, whether this is the chance for the new Euro-Atlantic community. The Euro-Atlantic community is by definition a community of democratic states linked in a historical process. If so, it should be based on the achievements of the transatlantic relationship, *acquis transatlantic*. This deduction draws from the need to promote the process of modernization worldwide as the core of a future system to ensure international peace. The evolving Euro-Atlantic community constitutes the basic framework for this process. Moreover, the forms and means for the Euro-Atlantic community do, to a large extent, already exist and they need only to be developed within existing organizations like the CSCE, the EC,

NATO, the WEU, and the NACC.

In the shorter term, the basic problem is the division of labor among organizations. Major differences of opinion exist between the key players, such as the US and France, on how best to evaluate the "realities" of the Europe of the early 1990s. The perception of realities has an impact on the question of how to solve the problem of division of labor between the existing organizations. It is possible, however, to envisage a solution based on the evolving Euro-Atlantic community. In political terms, one could consider it a compromise formula between the US and France, although it would in principle reject any final Europeanization of European defense or political identity. In this model, the CSCE would provide the political framework, and vision, for its 52 members.

The Charter of Paris comes closest to being the peace settlement of the Cold War division of Europe and the covenant for a future unified Europe. The Charter codifies, in an exhaustive manner, the norms to be included in the new community of values, although it is weak in providing tools for their implementation. The document defines only initial guidelines for the institutional structure of the new European order and claims no monopoly for the CSCE in its architecture and functioning. Despite this, one merit of the CSCE is precisely that it brings together by loose institutional means these 52 diverse states. The CSCE is a kind of "standing conference" coping with twists of "organic reality." Accordingly, the participating states redefine the role of this political process constantly. One could assume that it could become a regional security arrangement in compliance with Chapter 8 of the UN Charter. At the very least, the CSCE should function as the key political organization for a new security order for Europe. This is because "unlike in the aftermath of earlier major wars in the present century, the post-Cold War rearrangement of international relations is not a once-for-all or definite event but a complex and even eclectic political process," as one prominent Finnish scholar has noted.[26]

As long as the CSCE remains a nonlegal and cooperative security arrangement, it will not provide security guarantees or collective security in other forms. The role of the CSCE will be to regulate its relations with military alliances providing collective defense, on the one hand, and the UN providing collective security, on the other. Changing the CSCE into an institution for collective security would create what many have called "a European UN." It would also raise the possibility, as Kari Möttölä noted, "of the CSCE taking over the functions of the military alliance in the long run and making the whole of Europe a zone of equal security."[27]

This option contains one particular problem: would it lead to the "Europeanization" of European defense? If so, the fear of recreating a 1939-style European security arrangement for the year 2000 would be justifiably real. If, on the other hand, the CSCE security blueprint were based on maintaining the Euro-Atlantic community, such fears would be assuaged. In order to strengthen the Euro-Atlantic community as the core of a new security order, one has to distinguish between military-political and security issues in the broadest terms. The establishment of the NACC is a case in point. It focuses entirely on military-political issues.[28] And its work is largely related to the "aftercare" of the Cold War. According to the program presented by NATO, the practical work of the NACC will focus on supporting the implementation of the Treaty on Conventional Arms Forces in Europe, reforming armed forces in Europe, reforming armed forces in accordance with the principles of defensive doctrine, as well as the conversion of the defense industry.[29] The NACC was an immediate response to the immediate security concerns of the new democracies in East Central Europe. As such, some of its functions may well overlap with some of the activities of the CSCE. Yet the most threatening situation would result from an "underlapping" of organizational capabilities in the field of the "aftercare" of the Cold War.

The traditional Euroneutrals have welcomed the foundation of the NACC. The Foreign Minister of Finland, Paavo Väyrynen, has made a proposal that the Nordic countries could help the Baltic states with projects similar to those contained in the NACC's mandate.[30] The NACC has proved to be a correct response to crucial security concerns in a number of European states. The NACC should be considered, then, an innovative solution for military-political concerns within the framework of the Euro-Atlantic community. Consequently, from the Nordic point of view, a total Europeanization of the European defense postulate is not helpful. Western Europe and Scandinavia alone forming an EC defense bloc would deepen, not solve, the security problems in Europe. Neither a purely "European" nor a purely "transatlantic" concept can provide a flexible and politically realistic security structure for post-divisional Europe. The concept of "Euro-Atlanticism" could emerge as a compromise formula for this search. The question is less about "mechanical synthesis" than about theoretical wisdom. The problem is no longer whether Europe should be more independent vis-a-vis Russia or the US. The question is perhaps more about a solution "for the construction of a global system through Europe," as Maurice Bertrand has proposed.[31]

However, we need to go beyond this and replace

"Europe" with the "Euro-Atlantic community." The European union through the EC should develop its identity, not as an emerging superpower, but rather as a new type of international entity. This is not contradictory to the goals of the Treaty of Maastricht in terms of *politique finalite*, but would avoid any repetition of historical mistakes.

We live in a world of increasing economic, ecological, and political interdependence. The Europe of nation-states will gradually give way to the Europe of regions. The political and economic driving force in Europe will be the EC. The CSCE will remain a political stabilizer for the whole Euro-Atlantic community, which itself will gradually strengthen its responsibilities as its military and political core are further defined.[32]

Theory in Perspective

To sum up, the argument of this chapter that the spread of liberal democracy is the final stage of the process of modernity could imply a mode of international behavior that transcends the logic of power politics. However, such a thesis can only be proved in the long run. Empirical studies have, however, indicated that democracies are less likely to fight wars with each other. Jack S. Levy has noted that "this absence of war between democratic states comes as close as anything we have to an empirical law in international relations."[33]

It is important, however, to realize that modernity does not solve the dilemma of war and conflict as such. Democracies are more "peaceful" when in an environment of other democracies. But, unless a secure environment is present (through fortuitous geography or through "free riding" in an alliance), there seems to be less historical evidence for the emergence of long-term, stable democracies. In the foreseeable future, capacities are still needed to balance threats and guarantee security; if security is not present, then democracy cannot be nurtured. At the very least, we need to consider whether or not democracy is "security dependent." If so, then we need to find ways to balance threats and capacities in new ways-- by abating threats that confront nascent democracies.[34]

There has never existed a permanently stable order inside the democratic community of nations, either. On the one hand, the racial riots in Los Angeles in 1992, inside the Euro-Atlantic community, indicate that the democratic society tolerates a good deal of internal insecurity. On the other hand, some of the attributes of sociopolitical modernity can also advance without coalescing into a democratic polity. This was especially true during the early days of Mikhail Gorbachev in the former Soviet Union.

It is crucial to note, however, that the relationship between security, democracy, and the free market constitutes a basis for a more peace-prone international development in the long run. If so, the political core of this development can be the further evolution of the Euro-Atlantic community, a "zone of civility" in international relations.[35]

Notes

This paper is drawn from a book-length study in progress dealing with the influence of "modernity" (economic, democratic, other related phenomena) on international relations.

1. I am not going to discuss this debate in detail, but I will note that I refer to such articles as Johan Galtung, "Geopolitical Transformations and the World Economy" (forthcoming) and a number of articles such as Lloyd C. Gardner, "Old Wine in New Bottles: How the Cold War Became the Long Peace," *The Long Postwar Peace; Contending Explanations and Projections*, ed. Charles W. Kegley, Jr. (New York: Harper Collins, 1991), pp. 125-46.

2. Here I would like to refer first to Daniel Deydney, "States and Republics in the Emergent Global Greater Synthesis," a think piece for the "Whither the State?" workshop at the University of California, August 1991; and to Francis Fukuyama, who makes this argument in his article "Liberal Democracy as a Global Phenomenon," *PS-- Political Science and Politics* 24, no. 4 (1991), pp. 659-64. I have also drawn from Ole Waever, "Territory, Authority, and Identity: The Late 20th Century Emergence of Neo-Medieval Political Structures in Europe" (Paper presented at the first general conference of EUPRA, The European Peace Research Association, Florence, Nov. 8-10, 1991).

3. See Michael Doyle, "Kant, Liberal Legacies and Foreign Affairs," *Philosophy and Public Affairs* 12, nos. 3 and 4.

4. George Modelski, *Principles of World Politics* (New York: Free Press, 1972), p. 37.

5. I have dealt with this perspective, although tentatively, in *After the Cold War: Europe's New Political Architecture* (New York: St. Martin's Press, 1991). My analysis simplifies the development of a democratic state. Basically, I agree that the historical conditions surrounding the rise of democracy have been complex and varied. I would like to argue, however, that the trend is there. See Robert Dahl, *Democracy and its Critics* (New Haven: Yale University Press, 1989), and D. Held, "Democracy, the Nation-State and the Global System," *Political Theory Today*, ed. D. Held (Cambridge: The Policy Press, 1991).

6. Regarding the emergence of a world economy, see Immanuel Wallerstein, *The Modern World System: Capitalist Agriculture and the Origins of the European World-Economy in the Sixteenth Century* (New York: Academic Press, 1974). See also Aristide R. Zolberg, "Origins of the Modern World System: A Missing Link," in *World Politics* (1981), pp. 253-81, who states that Wallerstein makes a systematic error throughout his book by neglecting the political structures and processes.

7. Max Weber, *General Economic History* (London: Allen & Unwin, 1923).

8. See Kalevi J. Holsti, *Peace and War: Armed Conflicts and International Order 1648-1989* (Cambridge: Cambridge University Press, 1991). See also A. Cassese, *International Law in a Divided World* (Oxford: Clarendon Press, 1986), pp. 396-99.

9. See C. Beitz, *Political Theory and International Relations* (Princeton: Princeton University Press, 1979), p. 25.

10. With respect to the concept of modernity, I have drawn greatly from two books: Paul Johnson, *The Birth of the Modern* (New York: HarperCollins, 1991) and Stuart Hall and Bram Gieben, *Formations of Modernity* (Cambridge: The Policy Press in Association with the Open University, 1991).

11. Johnson, *The Birth of the Modern*, p. xvii.

12. Ibid., p. 34.

13. See Robert Kelley, *The Transatlantic Persuasion: The Liberal-Democratic Mind in the Age of Gladstone* (New York: Knopf, 1969), pp. 3-7.

14. With respect to the origins of NATO, see, for example, Don Cook, *Forging the Alliance 1945 to 1950* (London: Secker & Warburg, 1989), pp. 1-23, which makes the argument about the political nature of the alliance. The particular reason for the establishment of NATO was to "contain" Soviet military and ideological power.

15. The debate about the role of NATO is one of the hottest items in the field of international relations. This chapter has drawn, for example, from the following sources: Stephen M. Walt, "Alliances in Theory and Practice: What Lies Ahead?," in *The Global Agenda: Issues and Perspectives*, ed. Charles W. Kegley and Eugene R. Wittkopf (New York: McGraw-Hill, 1991), pp. 189-97.

16. James Baker, "The Euro-Atlantic Architecture: From West to East," address to the Aspen Institute Berlin, June 18, 1991.

17. With respect to the political economy of Europe, see William Wallace, *The Transformation of Western Europe* (London: Pinter, 1990).

18. Regarding the debate concerning the meaning of a new Euro-Atlantic community see, for example, Henry Kissinger, "The Atlantic Alliance Needs Renewal in a Changed World," *International Herald Tribune*, March 2, 1992, p. 5.

19. Anders Stephanson, *Kennan and the Art of Foreign Policy* (Cambridge: Harvard University Press, 1989), p. 176. I have dealt with the "organic nature" of international relations in *After the Cold War*.

20. I have dealt with the problem of war in international relations in, for example, my review of Holsti, *Peace and War*, and *The Long Postwar Peace*, ed. Charles W. Kegley, Jr. (New York: HarperCollins, 1991). The review of both books was published in *Helsingin Sanomat*, March 3, 1992.

21. See Holsti, *Peace and War*, p. 5. I have drawn here from Barry Buzan and Ole Waever, "Framing Nordic Security: European Scenarios for the 1990s and Beyond," in *European Security: Nordic Perspectives and Options*, ed. Jan Oberg (London: Pinter, 1992).

22. Patrick J. Buchanan, "America First--and Second, and Third," *National Interest* 19 (Spring 1990), p. 79. For a scholarly argument for the withdrawal, see Stephen D. Keasner, "Realist Praxis: Neo-Isolationism and Structural Change," in *Journal of International Affairs*, no. 1 (1991), pp. 143-60.

23. There is an active debate going on in Europe about the future of the EC on the basis of the Maastricht Treaty approved by the leaders of the Twelve on December 9, 1991. A new kind of international entity is emerging on the basis of this treaty. It will most probably take a decade to create European Union, although such a Union will be established formally on January 1, 1993. At the same time, the EC will widen with a number of new members, consisting primarily of the advanced EFTA countries. Regarding this debate, see Craig Whitney, "Three Months After Maastricht, Europe Finds Itself Bogged in a Slump," *International Herald Tribune*, March 30, 1992; and Richard von Weizsäcker, "Maastricht als Historische Chance Begreifen," *Frankfurter Allgemeine Zeitung*, April 13, 1992. With respect to the problems of

European integration in political and security policy terms, see, for example, Maurice Bertrand, "European Integration in a World Perspective," *Europe in the Making* (Southampton: International Social Science Journal, UNESCO, 1992), pp. 69-77.

24. See Alan Sweedler, "Role of the US in Future European Security: Implications for *Northern Europe and the Baltic,"* in *New European Security Architecture,* ed. STETE-Finnish Committee for European Security (Helsinki: Parafix, 1992), pp. 77-88.

25. Kari Möttölä, "Prospects for Cooperative Security in Europe" (Paper presented at the international seminar on "The CSCE and the New Europe," Helsinki, April 3-4, 1992).

26. Kari Möttölä, "Prospects for Cooperative Security in Europe." See also James Goodby, "Commonwealth and Concert: Organizing Principles of Post-Containment Order in Europe," *Washington Quarterly* (Summer 1991).

27. Möttölä, "Prospects for Cooperative Security in Europe."

28. An interview entitled "Security Has to be Redefined," with John Kornblum, US Ambassador to the Helsinki CSCE Follow-Up Meeting, in *Helsingin Sanomat,* April 16, 1992.

29. With respect to the functions and goals of the NACC, see "Work Plan for Dialogue, Partnership and Cooperation," (report issued at the meeting of the NACC held at NATO Headquarters, Brussels, March 10, 1992).

30. Paavo Väyrynen, "Nordic Security in a New Europe," address at the Stockholm Försvarshögskolan, March 12, 1992.

31. Bertrand, "European Integration in a World Perspective."

32. Concerning the nature of the Maastricht Treaty as a catalyst of decentralization of Community policy and institutions, see the report by Belmont European Centre, "The New Treaty on European Union; Volume 2: Legal and Political Analyses," Feb. 26, 1992. With respect to the scenarios for Europe beyond the Cold War, see in particular Adrian Hyde-Price, *European Security Beyond the Cold War* (London: Royal Institute of International Affairs, 1991), pp. 189-207.

33. I am very grateful to Dr. Daniel N. Nelson and Kari Möttölä for their views and comments on earlier versions of my chapter, which contributed in particular to the final part of the text. See Jack Levy, "The Causes of War: A Review of Theories and Evidence," in *Behavior, Society, and Nuclear War*, vol. 1, ed. Philip E. Tetlock, Jo L. Husbands, Robert Jervis, Paul C. Stern, Charles Tilly (New York: Oxford University Press, 1989).

34. See also David A. Lake, "Powerful Pacifists: Democratic States and War," *American Political Science Review* 86, no. 1 (March 1992), pp. 24-37.

35. Kalevi J. Holsti, "A 'Zone of Civility' in European Diplomatic Relations? The CSCE and Conflict Resolution" (Paper presented at the annual meeting of the International Studies Association, Atlanta, March 31-April 4, 1992).

Part II
93-145

Alphabet Soup: CSCE, NATO, EC

4

The Future Relationship and Division of Responsibilities Between the EC and the CSCE

Fraser Cameron

EC Involvement in the CSCE

Any discussion of the future relationship between the EC and the CSCE needs to begin with a review of EC involvement in the CSCE process. In the early 1970s, the CSCE was an attractive field of cooperation for the EC countries' newly established EPC (European Political Cooperation) machinery. European security and cooperation was an area of common interest to all EC countries and satisfied the basic requirements for political cooperation. While arms control, disarmament, and confidence-building measures were to be coordinated within NATO, the nonmilitary character of EC consultations on CSCE suited the capacity of the Davignon machinery, and the CSCE became a regular item on EPC agendas in the preparatory phase for the 1975 Helsinki Conference.

Although the CSCE was based on the principles of sovereignty and equality among the participating states, the EC indicated at an early stage that it would act as a group and be bound by CSCE commitments. The Community's identity was most forcefully expressed through Basket Two (economic cooperation) and to a lesser extent Basket Three (human rights) of the CSCE's activities. There was never an EC delegation in the CSCE, and the Community as such cannot make proposals, but the negotiations in the second basket, for example, were conducted by Commission officials, who are included in the national delegation of the country holding the presidency of the Community. The Helsinki Final Act and other CSCE acts and declarations are adopted not only by the individual EC countries, but also on behalf of the Community by the presidency. Initially some CSCE participating states, particularly the Soviet Union, opposed this collective behavior on the part of the EC states, but gradually the opposition lapsed, partly as a result of changes in Soviet foreign policy brought about by perestroika and partly as a result of the Commission's close involvement in the 1990 CSCE Bonn Conference on Economic Cooperation.

From Helsinki to Helsinki

As mentioned above, the EC played a significant role before and during Helsinki I. The initial success of the Community's coordinating machinery, however, was not repeated in all subsequent follow-up meetings. The EC was handicapped by its exclusion of defense questions from EPC--only political and economic aspects of security came within its consideration--and thus was unable to coordinate, for example, arms control proposals. In the stages of heightened East-West tension, it was the US that played the most prominent role on the Western side. The early meetings in Belgrade, Montreux, Malta, Madrid, and Stockholm were painful experiences, with the two opposing blocs approaching the CSCE from completely different perspectives and refusing to agree on anything of substance.

The Community did make an impact at Venice in 1984 and at the Vienna Follow-up Meeting, when the CSCE agreed to, *inter alia*, increase economic and environmental cooperation. The

1989 Sofia meeting on the environment saw a further increase in EC cooperation, but it was really the Bonn meeting of April 1990 that established the Community in the CSCE driving seat. The Bonn Document, in which participating states committed themselves to multiparty democracy, the rule of law, respect for human rights, and the introduction of market economies, was based almost entirely on a Community draft prepared by the EC Commission. Participants also noted that international economic cooperation and domestic reform were interdependent, and they acknowledged that more competitive conditions would enable reforming countries to participate to a greater extent in the international economic and financial system. By establishing criteria for giving assistance, the Bonn conclusions were a reflection of the Community's interest in promoting the transformation of centrally planned states to market economies. The Bonn conclusions covered most of the essential Basket Two issues: business conditions, economic information, property rights, economic policies, energy, environment, investment, and monetary and financial questions.

The Paris summit in November 1990 was the next important milestone for the CSCE and for the Community. In June 1990, the Dublin European Council had stated that the Community should continue to play a leading and active role in the CSCE. Member states were instructed to increase cooperation and seek common positions. At the summit, EC President Jacques Delors signed the Paris Charter along with other heads of state and government, thus confirming the Community's increased status in the CSCE.

The Paris summit was also important in establishing the institutionalization of the CSCE, with agreement to hold summits every two years and annual meetings of foreign ministers. In addition, the summit agreed to establish a small secretariat in Prague, a Conflict Prevention Center in Vienna, an Office for Free Elections in Warsaw, and an increased parliamentary input into the CSCE.

Despite good intentions, there was limited EC cooperation in the 1991 CSCE meetings held in Valleta, Cracow, Geneva, and Moscow. However, the Berlin Council of Foreign Ministers meeting in June 1991 formally approved the Community's convening of a peace conference on Yugoslavia and approved the sending of EC monitors to that country. Four CSCE countries (Sweden, Canada, Poland, and Czechoslovakia) also sent monitors. The recognition of the EC's role in crisis management in Yugoslavia was a clear indication that the Community was becoming the principal actor in the CSCE process. At regular meetings of the Committee of Senior Officials (CSO), the Community reported on the latest developments in Yugoslavia and received CSCE recognition and approval for its efforts.

Proposals for Change

The opening session of the 1992 review conference in Helsinki, attended by foreign ministers, witnessed a number of proposals for strengthening the CSCE by the Community and its member states. The French government was keen to give the CSCE a legal basis and put forward proposals to establish an arbitration and conciliation body. The German government was interested in the establishment of a multinational force, the "green helmets," both for peacekeeping operations and for environmental protection. The Belgian government proposed that the CSCE should become a collective regional security instrument under chapter 8 of the UN Charter. The Dutch government put forward proposals to create a High Commissioner for Minorities within the CSCE. Other proposals from EC member states were also put forward, reflecting the interest in further strengthening the CSCE machinery.

The European Commission has consistently pressed the member states of the Community to coordinate CSCE positions more closely, but EPC works on the consensus principle, and understandably it has not always been easy to achieve unanimity. The Commission has itself proposed a number of areas to further develop CSCE cooperation, including science and technology (a number of Community research programs have already been opened up to participants from Central and Eastern Europe); telecommunications (where the Community is actively promoting trans-European networks); the environment (increasing importance of trans-boundary cooperation); transport (improving infrastructures, reducing environmental repercussions, and increasing safety); human resources (several Community initiatives on education and vocational training); energy (support for implementation of the Energy Charter); regional cooperation; and economic cooperation (building on the Bonn conclusions to overcome trade obstacles, improve standardization and arbitration procedures, promote commercial services, etc.). The Commission has also drawn attention to the relationship between all three baskets, the importance of Mediterranean cooperation, and the need to ensure the effective functioning of CSCE institutions.

The EC's Growing Security Identity

The Community has a particular responsibility for European stability and security. There are two main trends apparent in Europe today: the trend towards integration, as exemplified by the European Community; and the trend towards disintegration, as exemplified by what is happening in the former Soviet Union and Yugoslavia. The EC, which is for the East Europeans the image of success, has a particular responsibility to prevent the extension of insular nationalism across Europe and to provide an anchor of stability for the entire continent.

The Maastricht Treaty laid down firm guidelines for the development of a European security identity. This is not a new idea. It was integral to the concept of European integration that was put forward in the early 1950s but foundered in the abortive plans for a European Defense Community in 1954. In the first instance, EPC is to be transformed into Common Foreign and Security Policy (CFSP), which is designed to reinforce the Community's identity on the world stage. One of the principal instruments will be "common action" in areas where the Community, or rather the European Union, decides to act together. Policy decisions in these areas will remain subject to unanimity (except in defined aspects of implementation), but will be binding on all member states. The CFSP now covers all areas of security, the old military caveat having been dropped. The Western European Union is to operate as the defense arm of the Union, and in due course this may lead to a common defense policy. The CFSP will be reviewed in 1996, two years before the expiration of the WEU Treaty. There is already widespread support for the incorporation of the WEU into the EC.

Maastricht aside, the Community has developed into a significant actor on the European security stage. Mention has already been made of the EC monitor mission and peace conference for Yugoslavia. The EC's crucial role vis-a-vis the former Soviet Union and the states of East Central Europe should also be noted. The Community is by far the largest provider of economic, financial, and technical assistance to these countries both within and without the G-24 aid program that the European Commission coordinates.

The Community has also negotiated association agreements with Poland, Hungary, and the Czech and Slovak Federal Republic; is about to negotiate similar accords with Bulgaria and Romania; has signed trade and cooperation agreements with the Baltic states; and is preparing similar accords with Albania. Interim agreements are being prepared for the states of the former Soviet Union and Yugoslavia.

A political and security dialogue, with the involvement of the WEU, is foreseen between the EC and the countries with which it has concluded association agreements.

With its new Mediterranean program, the EC is also the largest provider of assistance in the region, using a mixture of economic, financial, and technical instruments to promote development.

Finally, the establishment of the EC Humanitarian Aid Office is another indication of the Community's growing role as the main provider of soft security, principally but not exclusively in the European region.

Furthermore, by its successful pooling of sovereignty even in sensitive areas, particularly in the area of national security, the EC has demonstrated a new way to order political relations between states. The Community model has become a magnet for all European states, not least because of its contribution to European security. Arguably the EC has become the most important confidence-building measure in the history of Europe.

New Security Problems

Since the revolutions in East Central Europe in 1989, the European landscape has changed profoundly. The collapse of communism and the resulting problems have led to a very different environment in which European states must assess their security needs. Although uncertainty and unpredictability are the most prominent characteristics of the current situation, it is important to retain a balanced perspective. The stability and certainty of yesterday meant ruthless oppression for 400 million people. The old system was an unjust, unsound, and precarious form of stability. There are new problems in the world today, but they are the price of a gigantic move forward in the direction of freedom.

Security must also be seen in a wider context. States have ceased to be the exclusive source of threats to their neighbors, as Chernobyl reminds us all too clearly. A multifaceted approach is required, embracing military, political, economic, social, environmental, and cultural factors.

European security is now threatened by a host of related problems:

- the problem of nuclear (and chemical) proliferation;

- the resurfacing of nationalism, racialism, and ethnic disputes, with the consequent potential for armed conflict, of which Yugoslavia is the most tragic, but not the only, example;

- the mistreatment of minorities and the possible mass movement of people;

- the threat of social unrest resulting from frustrated economic and social expectations;

- the problem of adapting and restructuring armed forces and defense industries to the new conditions.

These are among the most prominent issues that the CSCE must confront. But are the participating states ready to go beyond pledges of cooperation and adherence to fundamental values and agree to invest the CSCE with the full array of means to assure implementation of commitments undertaken and provide for security in the whole of Europe? Or is it true, as Ambassador Pertti Torstila of Finland has stated, that governments exhibit a persistent lack of trust in the CSCE and its possibilities to manage current or prospective European problems and conflicts? If this is true, then how adequately and responsively can other institutions provide security for all of Europe? Is the best of all possible worlds to be found through the much-employed but little understood term "interlocking institutions"? Or are responses to future turmoil more likely to involve--and perhaps risk--ad hoc endeavors entailing overlap among all organizations?

Future Security Architecture

There is no consensus on how best to reduce the present "alphabet soup" of institutions that have a security role--NATO and the NACC, the EC and the WEU, the CSCE. Depending on how broadly security is defined, one could even add further institutions such as the OECD, the UN Economic Commission for Europe, the EBRD, and even the Council of Europe.

103

The 1991 Prague meeting of the CSCE Council of Foreign Ministers called for "multi-faceted forms of cooperation" and a close relationship among European, transatlantic, and other international institutions and organizations. Helsinki is unlikely to resolve all the problems of institutional overlap, particularly if the plans to establish a permanent CSCE Security Forum in addition to the agreed Economic Forum are carried out. Only in the human dimension is there acceptance of a clear working relationship and division of responsibility between the CSCE and the Council of Europe.

All institutions have had to adapt to the changed situation in Europe. NATO has added a third pillar to its policy of deterrence and dialogue--cooperation with its former adversaries in the East. The North Atlantic Cooperation Council was established by the Rome NATO summit in November 1991 to create a forum for discussion and assistance between NATO and the former Warsaw Pact states.

In the turmoil surrounding the collapse of the Soviet Union at the end of 1991, there was little time for a proper discussion of the merits of including all CIS states within the NACC (the same mistake was made by the CSCE). Accordingly, both the NACC and the CSCE have become unwieldy organizations, partly because of their size but also because of their continuing adherence to the unanimity principle, which allows one participant to block developments by withholding consensus. However, at least in the CSCE, this is changing with the move to consensus minus one on some issues.

While the NACC may have a role to play in promoting a modern security culture, it also runs the risk of creating serious misunderstandings, as NATO cannot grant the primary wish of several of the countries of the former communist bloc, namely, membership in NATO. The NACC also risks introducing confusion into the original concept of the Alliance. An alliance must be based on shared values, clearly expressed, understood, and approved by the general public in each member state. This has existed between North America and Western Europe for a long time. But it is highly doubtful whether such shared values extend across the board from Vancouver to Vladivostok.

While in the short term NATO remains the only organization able to provide hard security in Europe, doubts remain about its long-term viability. These doubts stem from the possibility of changes in US congressional opinion, the inability of the Alliance to operate "out of area," and its loss of raison d'etre on the European continent with the disappearance of the military threat from the Warsaw Pact. Some have suggested that a solution to this latter problem would be closer ties with the CSCE and indeed a role for NATO (and/or the WEU) as the security arm of the CSCE in Basket One issues. But in the absence of consensus it is difficult to imagine how this idea could be realized. Nor is there support within NATO to extend membership in the alliance to the former WTO states. NATO cannot be at the same time a protector of Armenia against Azerbaijan and protector of Azerbaijan against Armenia.

The concept of concentric circles of security has been advanced, with the EC constituting the "hard core," surrounded by the members of EFTA in the EEA (European Economic Area), the East European countries in their association agreements, and then the outer ring of ex-Soviet republics. NATO, the NACC, and the CSCE could also fit in this pattern on the condition that these are homogeneous groups that could build circles together. As mentioned above, there must be serious doubts about the shared values of such groups. Indeed, the countries of East Central

Europe are trying to distance themselves from the ex-Soviet republics (and even from each other) in their race to establish the closest ties with the Community and other Western institutions.

Because of its size and mandate, the CSCE can claim to play a unique role in the new security architecture. The CSCE is currently evolving from an ad hoc process, rooted in the old confrontation between the blocs and concentrating on a limited area where agreement was possible, towards a structured system of political consultation among participating states, with its own institutions and mechanisms, involving cooperation at all levels aimed at ensuring security and stability in its widest sense.

The CSCE is also transforming itself from an essentially Euro-Atlantic forum into an institution encompassing a number of Asian states. The full impact of this extension of membership is unclear, and it is difficult to see the logic of the present membership that includes Uzbekistan but excludes Japan.

A number of important questions remain to be answered. How can the CSCE strengthen its existing functions? Is there likely to be a consensus to provide appropriate resources for the CSCE? What progress can be expected in the CSCE's capacity to safeguard human rights or protect minorities? Can we expect agreement on sanctions based on the principle of "consensus minus one" or minus two or three? What are the prospects for establishing ground rules for fact-finding and rapporteur missions? Or the establishment of an "early warning" system? At present one would have to be skeptical about the likelihood of agreement being reached at Helsinki to give the CSCE real teeth.

In contrast, the Community and its member states have shown the way forward in certain areas, e.g., the Yugoslav crisis. The EC's prominent role in Yugoslavia may be viewed as a precursor of common action. Despite the Community's many mistakes, the fact remains that it is regarded by all sides as the key to any long-term solution to the Balkan imbroglio. The EC also anticipated some proposals put before the CSCE, for example, the appointment of the Badinter Arbitration Commission on Yugoslavia. The results of the Badinter Commission were accepted by the EC and led to subsequent political and economic moves, notably recognition of some Yugoslav republics and sanctions against other republics.

The EC has been at the forefront of new ideas to strengthen the CSCE. But not all areas fall within the Community's competence, and hence there is no coordinated EC position, for example, on CFE and CSBMs. There are, however, positions of EC member states, not always coordinated, on a potential CSCE peacekeeping role, the establishment of a conciliation and arbitration body, and proposals to beef up the Conflict Prevention Center.

Future EC-CSCE Division of Responsibilities

The key words for CSCE in the coming years will be "security and stability," understood in the comprehensive concept outlined above. There is a growing call to devise a new security architecture for the whole of Europe that is able to cope with new threats, such as racial, ethnic, and religious tensions, violations of human and minority rights, nuclear and other environmental damage, and putative civil wars. The main role of the CSCE after Helsinki will be conflict prevention, crisis management, and peacekeeping. The military negotiations for arms control, disarmament, and CSBMs will continue.

The issue of respect for human rights, the rule of law, and democratic structures is no longer an area of confrontation

107

between the blocs, but rather an essential area for cooperation between participating states. The question of economic cooperation has to be seen in a similar light. The degree of political commitment to market economies and the extent of practical steps for their implementation has already attained a level that makes it doubtful whether there will be a need for new and meaningful commitments after Helsinki. What will be important is to ensure that participating states adhere to existing commitments.

The enlargement of the Community is likely to further increase its influence on the world stage and in the CSCE in particular. Assuming that all EFTA countries were to join the Community in the mid-1990s, the EC would represent a bloc of 19 states out of the current 52 CSCE members. With over one-third of CSCE participants belonging to the EC, the European Union will inevitably play a highly important if not dominant role in the CSCE.

Obviously, however, much will depend on the cohesiveness of the EC operating within CFSP. But there has been growing recognition that no single state, no matter how large, can achieve its aims more successfully by operating on its own than by working within a larger group. The concept of national sovereignty has lost its meaning in many areas, but foreign and security policy remains a highly sensitive domain, and progress towards automatic and genuine cooperation will take time.

What then will be the division of responsibilities between the EC and the CSCE? An enlarged and strengthened EC is likely to serve as the driving force within the CSCE. It is difficult to imagine the necessary consensus being obtained within the CSCE to ensure a significant increase in its very limited present powers, and hence it will be important to ensure that existing CSCE principles and commitments are upheld and maintained. A judicious carrot and stick approach will be required from Western states and institutions. The EC has already introduced the principle of conditionality, based on CSCE principles, to its range of agreements with other European countries.

But although the EC is the principal example of European integration at work, it does not seek a monopoly of tasks. These must be shared between existing institutions on the basis of suitability, skills, track record, and transparency. In short, it will be important to examine problems on a case-by-case basis to decide which institution or ad hoc group is best suited to lead.

Although a significant extension of CSCE powers is unlikely in the near future, this does not mean that efforts to strengthen the CSCE should cease. It took many years to win acceptance of the present modest status, and it may take many more before participating states are willing to move further. But meanwhile, the CSCE has a full agenda and should concentrate on the following priority areas:

- compliance with existing commitments (under threat of sanctions?);

- arms control (completing unfinished business and moving towards the lowest level of armaments);

- preventive diplomacy (maintaining pressure to uphold human and minority rights and seeking to move forward on monitoring and control mechanisms).

Relations between the Community and the CSCE have developed in a way that has been of overall benefit to both. The

CSCE has profited to a considerable extent from initiatives taken by the Community, while the EC has accepted CSCE principles in establishing conditions for new relationships with states to the east. EC policy towards the CSCE is now moving on to a higher plane as a result of the Maastricht decisions on CFSP. The future development of both the EC and the CSCE should be viewed as complementary and not competitive or conflictual.

5

Does the US Have a Role in the Future European Security System?

Charles W. Kegley, Jr.

With the collapse of the Soviet Union, the United States is without military rival and in many respects has achieved its "unipolar moment."[1] Fifty years after Henry Luce heralded the "American Century," the US is not just stronger than anyone--it is stronger than *everyone*.

Having claimed credit, with questionable justification, for "winning" the Cold War, however, US policy makers now confront the equally daunting task of managing the peace. They must heal socioeconomic hemorrhages at home while helping shape the emergent global order. Essential to this latter task is the establishment of a *modus vivendi* with Europe--including both US allies and former adversaries who are coalescing into a cohesive bloc.

Along the way, US leaders must relinquish their static Cold War conceptions and the institutional frameworks they dictated, which are profoundly ill-suited to the challenge at hand. The shift from a bipolar, ideological clash of wills to a multipolar, consensual balance of power is among the most sudden and dramatic global transformations ever to face the US. To keep pace, its response must be equally rapid and far-reaching.

No strict guidelines yet discipline this reappraisal, for the post-World War II foreign policy consensus about America's global purpose in the world has splintered.[2] Bereft of a shared vision, US leaders are left with no organizing principle around which to structure foreign policy. They are intellectually unarmed, with only the elastic concept of the "national interest" to shape their assumptions. In simpler times, following the national interest--"the one guiding star, one standard for thought, one rule for action"[3]--was relatively easy. National interests can be readily defined when threats are transparent and the public is in agreement about the need to meet them.

But today that answer begs the question. Contemporary threats, although more ambiguous than a nuclear-tipped Soviet empire, are many. They include an array of vexing challenges, both international and internal, ranging from the ever-present specter of war in the sphere of high politics to economic stagnation and environmental decay in the sphere of low politics. Trend is not destiny, but if present trends continue, the future will likely be shaped by these and other influences:

- continued turmoil among the independent republics of the former Soviet Union;

- the widening dispersion of political, economic, and military power, and a diminished capacity to estimate states' relative overall "strength" and degree of convergent interests;[4]

- the erosion of US influence relative to other great powers, particularly Germany and a unifying Europe;

- the rise of powerful trade blocs that are internally cohesive but prone to intensely competitive beggar-thy-neighbor postures toward one another;

- the resurgence of hypernationalism alongside the vigorous pursuit of independence by minority nationalities in Europe and the former Soviet republics;

- a new wave of national disintegration and the end to the integrity of many current borders that the 1975 Helsinki accords sought to cement;

- the growing interdependence of states in response to both economic linkages and environmental threats such as global warming, deforestation, the pollution of the oceans, and deterioration of the atmosphere.

These threats collectively will exert enormous pressure on the US to pay increasing attention to many nonmilitary dangers. "Geo-economics"[5] could replace geopolitics because "the distinction between high politics (vital interests affecting national security) and low politics (petty questions of economic dispute and rivalry among states) may be disappearing, [and] low politics may be becoming high politics."[6]

Because the Cold War is barely over, it is too early to know which of the many countervailing integrative and disintegrative trends unfolding in world affairs will dominate.[7] Current patterns pull in both directions, rendering doubly complex the *consistent* formulation and implementation of policy.

Abraham Lincoln once noted, "If we could first know where we are and whither we are tending, we could better judge what to do, and how to do it." Today, great uncertainty prevails about where we are and the direction in which we are headed. As President Bush correctly noted at the NATO summit in November 1991, "the enemy is no longer the Soviet Union.... The enemy is uncertainty.... The enemy is unpredictability." As a result, judging what to do, how to do it, and the vision that should guide US conduct abroad presents a formidable challenge.

The scope for unilateral action--by the US or any other

major power--has diminished considerably. Addressing shared threats without the cooperation of others will be increasingly difficult. US foreign policy makers must adapt to these new realities without the certainties and degrees of freedom of the past. At issue is whether the new global order warrants radical revision of prevailing definitions of US national interests, particularly vis-a-vis Europe, the region that has historically served as the fulcrum of US geostrategy. For the purpose of this examination, we can best recommend policy adaptations by first taking cognizance of 1) the constraints on the range of viable choices facing US policy makers; and 2) the alternate ways in which the emergent security environment in Europe is best characterized.

Constraints on the Range of US Choice

The supreme irony of this historical watershed is that US paramountcy and its emergent relative decline have coincided. A world dominated by one power--a Pax Americana--could vanish in the blink of an eye. The US may be "first" in the international hierarchy of military power, but that status could quickly erode, and even now no longer translates into a capacity to exercise proportionate political influence. In its "unipolar moment" the US is more constrained than it was when a widely perceived "clear and present danger" existed.

As noted above, the range of US choice is constrained by the murkier multipolar world that now exists and the relative decline of the US economy, both of which have propelled neo-isolationalism within the US public and some elite circles. These twin developments require individual attention.

114

Multipolarity

As Deputy Secretary of State Lawrence Eagleburger wrote in 1989, "We are now moving into.... a world in which power and influence [are] diffused among a multiplicity of states--[a] multipolar world." This will transform the world, and pose new threats that the US must confront.

A multipolar system of relatively equal powers, similar to the classical European balance-of-power system, is likely to consist of the US, Russia, Japan, perhaps China, and both Germany and the European Community (EC). In this multipolar system, we can expect the major powers to fear each other and align with or oppose each other in particular issue areas, as interests dictate. If history sets a precedent, behind the diplomatic smiles and handshakes, one-time allies will grow apart and formerly "specialized" relationships will dissolve.[8] For example, the alignment of the US with Germany and the EC can be expected to weaken and competition increase. Under conditions of multipolarity, there are no permanent allies; alliances are based on short-term convergences of interest--they are marriages of convenience.

Multipolarity also presages the potential alignment of former adversaries. The US and the remnants of the Soviet Union find themselves exhausted at the end of the Cold War and united in their mutual fears of the EC, Germany, and Japan. As a result they have become, as Russian strategist Peter Gladkov observes, "natural" allies, given their mutual need to balance the ascendant power of these "new" superpowers.

If the US wants to play a meaningful role, its responsibilities could greatly exceed those that consumed it during the Cold War. Under multipolarity, disorder is likely:

As the world becomes more multipolar--with economic leverage and even political-military power being more widely dispersed among nations--it isn't necessarily becoming a safer, gentler globe. And as nations become more interdependent, they aren't necessarily becoming more cooperative.

[There] is every reason to believe that the world of the 1990s will be less predictable and in many ways more unstable than the world of the last several decades.... It is rather basic. So long as there were only two great powers, like two big battleships clumsily and cautiously circling each other, confrontations--or accidents--were easier to avoid. Now, with the global lake more crowded with ships of varying sizes, fueled by different ambitions and piloted with different degrees of navigational skill, the odds of collisions become far greater.[9]

US Declinism

To a growing number of Americans, the passing of the Cold War requires that external challenges be subordinated to domestic problems. This neo-isolationist mood is animated by the belief that US national interests call for putting the national economy ahead of military preparedness and external interventionism. To an increasing number of US citizens, "The problem.... today is not new challengers for hegemony; it is the new challenge of transnational interdependence."[10] The US public is acutely aware that the next war will be fought on the economic, rather than the military, battlefield. Accordingly, US public opinion recently has riveted attention on the vision articulated by Walter Lippmann, who in 1943 observed that "foreign policy consists of bringing into balance.... the nation's commitments and the nation's power."[11] Coping with the "Lippmann gap"[12] is perhaps more vital a concern today than it was a half-century ago. As the US has become "more ordinary, more like the others, and increasingly subject to unaccustomed constraints, the central question now is how to manage domestic and foreign affairs to bring about a sustainable foreign policy."[13]

Historian Paul Kennedy intensified concern over the perceived "decline" of US influence with his comparative historical analysis, *The Rise and Fall of the Great Powers.* "Although the United States is at present still in a class of its own economically and perhaps even militarily," Kennedy wrote,

> it cannot avoid confronting the two great tests which challenge the longevity of every major power that occupies the "number one" position in world affairs: whether it can preserve a reasonable balance between the nation's perceived defense requirements and the means it possesses to maintain those commitments; and whether.... it can preserve the technological and economic bases of its power from relative erosion in the face of ever-shifting patterns of global production.[14]

America's economic position relative to others has steadily eroded since its zenith at the end of World War II.

"Today's greatest threat to the liberal Pax Americana is not from [abroad] but from the financial disorder of the United States."[15] For the world's strongest military power, the capacity to lead has declined in association with staggering US debt, education and health crises, and the demise of the country's internal infrastructure.[16] This decaying infrastructure and fiscal indebtedness necessitate a reversal of entrenched budgetary priorities through defense conversion--a reordering that also commands revision of Cold War assumptions about the means to the exercise of US influence abroad. US military might, the country's one area of unquestioned preponderance, has lost much of its potency as a component of national strength. US leaders must accept the fact that the power to destroy is not necessarily the power to persuade if they are to guide US foreign relations into the next century.

Setting Priorities

The prevention of disorder will be the preeminent challenge of the new era in world politics. Stability is a *sine qua non* at any time, for without peace, other national interests such as prosperity and the promotion of democracy cannot be served. However tempting, an isolationistic US retreat from European security affairs could create a power vacuum at a dangerously turbulent phase in history and the kind of uncertainty from which wars have sprung throughout history. As with the 1823 Monroe Doctrine, which sought to position US foreign policy in light of the post-Napoleonic balance-of-power system in Europe, the US must again define the kind of balancer role it will play in the fluid new European system. The question, accordingly, is not one of *ends*--whether the US should be involved; it is more a question of *means*--how to harness the available institutional machinery through which US involvement can best contribute to the stability in Europe that is in all states' interests.

There is no choice but for US leaders to make the maintenance of European peace a top foreign policy priority. How, then, can the US maximize its ability to realize this goal?

Any accounting of the trade-offs among options must be guided by appreciation of the relative advantages and disadvantages associated with each alternative. For this, we can predict that the US pursuit of its goals will be directed toward strategies perceived to:

118

- most promote US power, position, and primacy, and enhance the capacity of the US to exercise influence;

- advance the core liberal principles at the foundation of US foreign policy since 1787, including support for democracy, human rights, free markets, and international law;[17]

- reduce the risks of "accidental war" and of diplomatic crises that could inflame smoldering European rivalries;

- build a security arrangement that hastens disarmament and inhibits pursuit of rearmament;

- ensure US solvency by balancing commitments against resources;

- maintain support from actors in Europe whose interests might be compromised by the policy paths taken.

If they are to avoid being inundated by cascading developments, US policy makers must make difficult choices about how best to strengthen US ties to the constellation of layered and complementary European security organizations created to preserve regional stability. This means resisting the temptation to reject collective security in favor of a unilateral policeman role, and engaging in collaborative arrangements to keep the peace.

Security Architectures

The alternative frameworks on which the US may focus are arrayed on a continuum of varying size, composition, and purpose, with diverse interrelationships among them. The common European home is congested with a network of linked institutions. On one end of this scale is the universal, multifunctional United Nations. Nested within it is the Conference on Security and Cooperation in Europe. Paralleling it is the European Community and its variegated, nascent security structures. Also to be reconciled is the role of NATO--a security alliance that has recently shifted toward a more comprehensive security organization, the North Atlantic Cooperation Council (NACC), which includes the former members of the Warsaw Pact.

Besides this menagerie of multilateralism is the continuing possibility of unilateral initiatives, as well as such "backdoor" bilateral ties as the proposed Franco-German security corps, a "new Rapallo" of Russo-German entente, or the Russian-American defense condominium envisioned by Fred Charles Iklé[18] and others. For the US, each of these separate but overlapping institutional forms of association presents some opportunity for US promotion of European security. Given this division of labor and authority, US leaders must decide which structure(s) can best advance this purpose.

The Setting For Choice

There is danger that the US will seek to retrofit old policies onto the new realities. The temptation to retain old visions is understandably powerful. In retrospect, the international simplicities of the bipolar era had a certain appeal:

the world was divided; Europe was divided; Germany was divided. Stability within the Eastern and Western blocs was essential, and generally maintained. But now the Cold War is over, and these simplifying realities have given way to a clouded European landscape. The dizzying end of the Cold War has been likened to waking up from a long sleep--with a headache![19]

To manage these changes, we must recognize that Europe is in such a state of flux that "it is impossible today to speak of Europe in the present tense."[20] From the vantage point of Europeans--looking out rather than in--there are a number of interrelated transitions unfolding in three geopolitical concentric circles:

> The first is the EC itself, the most homogeneous circle, moving toward political union. The Europe of the Twelve will play a central role in guiding the transformation of the Continent. The second circle consists of the Community, EFTA countries, and the Central and East European countries.... The last circle embraces Europe in the political sense, the Europe that stretches from San Francisco to Vladivostok. This includes the US and Canada, on the one hand, and the [remnants of the] Soviet Union, including its Asian dimension, on the other.[21]

Intra-European relations today are immensely more complicated than they were a few years ago. For one thing, the European diplomatic agenda today is much more crowded: economic integration is continuing amid growing concerns about the singular and asymmetrical role of Germany in areas of regional finance, trade, and aid. "German questions" are linked to new questions about *Mitteleuropa*, the potential revival of "Ostpolitik" policies by which Germany turns eastward in its foreign policy priorities. These questions are accompanied by

121

Charles W. Kegley, Jr.

such equally familiar concerns as British resistance to widening
political integration, French preoccupation with continental
security interdependence, and the desires of less affluent
European states such as Portugal and Greece for development
assistance.

Many of the international political and economic solutions
of the last era have become today's problems for Europeans. The
EC, for example, united Europe in the Cold War era, but it
divides Europe today into a peninsula of prosperity that juts
from a mainland of economic decay. German partition assured an
outward- and Westward-looking Bundesrepublik, but German
unity produces momentary introspection and a diffusion of
resources to the east and west.

From 1949 to 1989, NATO simplified West European
security, but today it complicates pan-European security.
Weakening and ultimately crippling the Soviet Union was the
Western cold warriors' singular and simplistic task. Strengthening
Russia and the former Soviet satellites is the more complex
challenge today.   For Central and East Europeans, former
problems of how to live with single-party governments and
centrally planned economies have been exchanged for current
problems of adapting to political pluralism and unplanned
economies. The CMEA countries' former problem of how to
avoid economic relations with the West has been exchanged for
the current problem of how to increase economic contact with the
West. The might of the Soviet Union was the solution for
Warsaw Pact governments' security problems, and the Warsaw
Pact was at least part of the solution for the Soviet Union's
security problems. Today the Warsaw Pact is defunct and the
former members have become each others' potential security
threats.

122

Contrasting Policy Choices

Given this disorderly environment, and given US interest in abating European disorder, what combination of institutional frameworks can best advance that goal? Let us take a snapshot of the delineated options.

The United Nations

The UN has heightened its profile during this epoch; many hope it can begin to perform the security-maintenance functions proposed in its Charter. But the United Nations remains unprepared to keep the peace through the use of force except in the most extreme circumstances. And the UN's ability to maintain world order is still contingent upon Security Council consensus--a requirement exceedingly difficult to achieve in the absence of a common culture and sense of shared destiny, and even more difficult to sustain. In the post-Cold War era, consensus is likely to be fragile--perhaps more so than before. In addition, the UN is a universal, not a regional organization, responsible for the global community as a whole rather than its constituent regional parts. This dilutes common interests and reduces the prospects for mounting a prompt collective response to the onset of regionalized aggression. The US and European states cannot be expected to entrust their future security to UN peacekeeping and preventive diplomacy, even if such efforts are directed toward European stability. Reliance on the UN for collective security is likely to provoke distrust, not confidence. The absence of attention to the UN as a shield to protect Europeans from themselves is not surprising in this context. The more than $860 million in back dues owed by the US at the end of April 1992 for the UN's peacekeeping operations is an indication of the barriers that remain to an expanded UN collective security role under Article 43 in Europe.[22]

The European Community

The EC, now more than ever the center of gravity in European politics, is not a viable security arrangement either. "The identity of the Europe of the Twelve is gradually being dissolved into a pan-European association of states."[23] More importantly, the EC is functionally a trade, not a security, bloc, designed more to make business than to make peace. As primarily a customs union, the EC is likely to compete with the US economically and remain disunited on security issues, despite the Maastricht pledge to forge a common EC foreign policy and the tightened linkages between it and the WEU. In fact, these are likely to drive the United States further away from abiding involvement. As trade competition mounts, as appears likely, a coordinated EC foreign policy is likely to present a mixed blessing for the US. When US and European interests diverge--as inevitably they will, especially on trade policy--US willingness to invest in EC security can be expected to decline. The emergent mood is suggested by Senator Richard Lugar's warning in February 1992: "I don't think the Europeans understand how far they have to move on track. If they don't back down, it ... could undermine American participation." Indeed, a US withdrawal from Europe is possible given the EC's profound differences with the US on trade policies and the spillover this could have in defense policy, over which US influence will wane now that US military might is no longer needed to balance Soviet might.

The Cold War's demise devalues military power and elevates economic power, thus eroding the scope of convergent US and EC interests. If Europeans don't look to the US as an equal partner--indeed, if they perceive the US as an economic competitor--there is little possibility that the US can exercise leverage, and its voice in European security debates will weaken. The EC is, therefore, not a hospitable institution for the US to influence its West European allies' decisions about peacekeeping; it may even pose an obstacle for this purpose.

The North Atlantic Treaty Organization

Having successfully managed the Atlantic Alliance during the Cold War, NATO represents a tempting option for anchoring European security. Yet for the US, there are many costs to continuing this relationship in its present extended deterrence form, and in the contemporary world NATO may be more an anachronism than an anchor.

The usefulness of any alliance is destined to diminish when the common external threat that brought it together disintegrates. Today, the Soviet threat that once tied European states to one another has literally disappeared. Without that unifying force, it is not surprising that intra-alliance fissures have widened. NATO is likely to weaken, even dissolve, without an external threat to preserve its internal cohesion. A US policy predicated on an enduring NATO role is a wager against the historic propensity of alliances to crumble after the common enemy has been defeated.

According to Lord Ismay, the first Secretary General of NATO, the original purpose of the Atlantic Alliance was "to keep the Russians out, the Americans in, and the Germans down." If NATO has a role to play, it must transform this mission. NATO could be preserved if it were restructured, not to contain enemies, but to control allies. Yet for that, *all* the countries in Europe, including Russia, would be required to coordinate their defense policies, and NATO would have to jettison the sphere-of-influence conceptions on which it has been based since its advent. To end the division of Europe, the East European and Commonwealth republics must be brought into the alliance and assured of protection in the event of remilitarization and renewed authoritarianism and aggression there. "The Alliance's New Strategic Concept," embraced at the Rome summit, seeks to create just that kind of partnership in the new North Atlantic Cooperation Council, but giving the former Warsaw Pact members and the successor states of the Soviet Union a voice (but not a "say") in the new security agreement, as well as a forum for exploring a "defensive defense" strategy that accommodates the new and more promising military realities.

Yet for all the speculation about a broadened, reconfigured NATO, it is instructive that the members of NATO itself have looked elsewhere for answers. The Rome Declaration of November 1991 defined a new agenda and mission that turned to other complementary institutions (the NACC, the WEU, and the CSCE) as the preferred mechanisms for preserving Europe as a democratic zone of peace. By NATO's own admission, to stabilize the rush of events following the Soviet collapse and to deal with the threats emanating from nearby regions along Europe's southern extremities, a framework of other interlocked institutions is better equipped. It can even be advanced, as a hypothesis, that NATO perpetuated the Cold War rather than accelerated its end, and today remains ill-equipped to transform itself 180 degrees from the goal of protecting the West from the East to protecting security *in* Central and Eastern Europe as well as in contiguous "out of area" regions where ethnic and minority problems present a clear and present danger to peace and stability in the area. NATO's impotence in dealing with the

Greek-Turkish conflict over Cyprus does not inspire confidence that NATO is prepared to come to grips with these kinds of issues that are likely to pose the greatest threat in the immediate future.

Likewise, although NATO will likely remain a complementary cornerstone for *West* European security until a powerful substitute system is created, NATO is not a realistic magnet for US political participation in European affairs. As Gregory F. Treverton observed,

> The alliance has been one of the great postwar successes, so some nostalgia for it is understandable, all the more so for Americans who have dominated it. It remains the only serious security game in town. But it is fruitless in the long run for American policy to acknowledge, on the one hand, that the Soviet threat which NATO was constructed to contain is no more and yet insist, on the other, that NATO must remain the preeminent European security institution.[24]

It goes without saying, moreover, that pressures to "Europeanize" NATO would only antagonize and alienate the US, and remove incentives for it to remain engaged. Such a quest to save NATO would thus, ironically, destroy it.

NATO served its original purpose well, but now that the threat that provided its raison d'etre has vanished, NATO is no longer needed. "NATO will be at best a bit player."[25] It survives largely by the power of inertia, and remains a symbol of division, not unity. It should be buried, with suitable monuments to its achievements, in the archives where historians record such rare successes.

The CSCE

Europe needs an "anchor" in a rough nationalistic sea. A tightly integrated Europe would create a "zone of stability" within a broader, more turbulent economic and political environment. Integrated states can legitimize, articulate, and disseminate liberal values much more readily than atomistic states in a Hobbesian state of war.

The most comprehensive and visionary mechanism for the promotion of liberal values of democratization, privatization, free markets, and human rights, in addition to the renunciation of war and territorial expansion, are the norms that emerged out of the Helsinki process that commenced nearly two decades ago. Its widening diplomatic theater now encircles the globe, extending from the west coast of the United States to the east coast of Russia. Arguably, the CSCE served as a potent agent of system transformation, helping to create and institutionalize East-West detente, to end the Cold War, and to redraw the map of Europe. Moreover, its contribution to the revolutions in Central and Eastern Europe, and to trans-European cooperation generally, was made, it should not be forgotten, from a position of political weakness.

This CSCE Zone incorporates all the countries on whom intra-European peace depends. The CSCE is the most inclusive of Europe's tiered and interlocking security institutions, and the most viable umbrella through which their missions can be tied together and coordinated. Fifty-two countries are members, including all the NATO countries and former Warsaw Pact countries and the European neutrals. CSCE is symbolically important because it bridges former Cold War cleavages and unites old enemies as new friends. If there is a "common European home," this is it. No other regional institution so comprehensively encompasses the new geopolitical landscape and allows the countries within it to respond constructively to crises erupting in any part of the far-flung region.[26]

More importantly to our query, access and membership make the CSCE the most inviting forum to perpetuate the instilled US habit of engagement in Europe. As noted, NATO is still symbolically exclusionary; the EC and EFTA countries are separate economic unions that compete with the US. The CSCE is the only pan-European mechanism of which the US is already a part, that touches all the European states, and in which US participation as an equal member is enthusiastically greeted. The CSCE is, as the Rome Declaration acknowledged, "the only forum that brings together all countries of Europe and Canada and the US under a common code of human rights, fundamental freedoms, democracy, rule of law, security, and economic liberty." The US is not, nor will ever be, part of Europe's "common home." But it is, and can remain, ideologically at home in the CSCE apparatus, where commitments to the same values are shared, and where active US involvement is welcomed.

In his analysis of NATO's London Declaration on a Transformed North Atlantic Alliance, Ambassador Henning Wegener stressed that the post-Cold War "challenge is to create a continent--encompassing both the North American democracies and the [former] Soviet Union--that will increasingly derive security from peaceful cooperative interaction and interdependence of states."[27] A sign of the post-Cold War times is that few question that security must follow from making peace more valuable, instead of from making war appear more dreadful. The states and peoples in this zone are today integrating into a security community that promises to exploit the positive and proactive as well as the preventive aspects of

129

integration. The family's expanding competence represents a logical progression of its capabilities, and testifies to its past success while inspiring growing confidence in its future as the primary locus for management of security issues. The CSCE is the vehicle best suited for a transition from collective defense to collective security.

Yet, satisfying the political-military needs of more than four dozen countries is laden with pitfalls, as the political obstacles to launching the ambitious European Union illuminate. Like the far-flung United Nations, the CSCE must reconcile the divergent interests of its polyglot membership. By minimal definition, security in the CSCE Zone will require muscular institutions that

- encourage greater Russian-Western security cooperation;

- provide insurance against a revival of Russian expansionism, while guarding against the more pressing and pregnant problems posed by Russian weakness rather than strength;

- bind Germany to the pursuit of regional and multilateral security and embed it in European unification, and provide Germany with a non-German nuclear deterrent;

- foster the movement toward an integrated military command and away from reliance on strictly national defense;

- cope with the security vacuum that will follow the implosion of the Warsaw Pact, as well as "spillouts" that might accompany civil strife in Eastern Europe and the CIS;

- provide crisis management and conflict resolution mechanisms with enforcement capabilities, as well as long-term efforts toward arms control;

- provide for decisive "out-of-area" activities;

- allow for the neutral and nonaligned (N+N) countries to participate in the diplomatic dialogue surrounding a new European security framework;

- ensure a continued US military presence in Europe.[28]

In many respects, the preconditions necessary for this transformed, expanded role are now in place or rapidly gaining momentum. The November 1990 CSCE summit in Paris solemnized the ending of the Cold War division of Europe and the opening of a new era wherein former antagonists are pledged to nonaggression and formally committed to political cooperation and arms control. It provided a clear demonstration to NATO of how a post-Cold War security system might operate, which is perhaps why in the Rome Declaration NATO pledged to support and strengthen the CSCE. This is also the reason that sentiment has shifted from the view of the CSCE as an adjunct to NATO to the view of it as an independent and serviceable peacekeeping organization, to which NATO capabilities might productively be made available for peacekeeping operations.

Moreover, the Paris Summit made a CSCE *organization* out of what was formerly merely a CSCE *process*. After the NATO-Warsaw Pact negotiating relationship produced the historic reductions of conventional military forces in Europe (CFE), CSCE is now positioned to become the primary arms control negotiating forum to mandate even deeper cuts in offensive capabilities and for the maintenance of balanced military power on the continent. Despite foot-dragging by the US, which is behind the curve of unfolding developments, the CSCE has expanded its mission and jurisdiction for collectively made decisions to manage this expanded agenda. In its new organizational form, the CSCE can become the institutional nucleus for crisis management--a point reflected in the wide agreement reached at the March 1992 ministerial session that the CSCE should be given a peacekeeping capability and perhaps accept the proposal of German Foreign Minister Hans-Dietrich Genscher that the CSCE create its own peacekeeping forces.

The CSCE's capabilities as a security organization must greatly expand if the organization is to take on this function. At present, the CSCE remains constitutionally incapable of performing as a military organization. It is not an alliance, and does not yet have multilateral peacekeeping forces of its own; it can only call on NATO, the WEU, or the UN to deal with threats to the peace. For this reason, advocates are likely to recommend continued reliance on these institutions as an "insurance policy," for until the CSCE absorbs their role they alone remain prepared to act in response to a security threat. Moreover, concerted action depends on consensus, and in the CSCE this is difficult to obtain among more than four dozen governments, however high their level of ideological agreement. The arrangement whereby any member has theoretically been able to veto any joint CSCE reaction to an act of aggression paralyzes its collective security function. If the CSCE is to move from a cumbersome voluntary association confined to promoting the vision of pan-European unity to a security community equipped to deter aggression, it must be empowered to make credible the threat that aggression will be met by collective defense of the victim.

Even though the requirement of unanimity for any CSCE action is in the process of being relaxed, institutional enhancements such as the creation of a body with enforcement powers are unlikely, since the smaller European countries would not tolerate larger-power control. Given the problems the CSCE and other security regimes invariably face, how might a structure for peace be created that enables the US to play a constructive role?

Toward a Concert-Based Security Organization

Integration in the CSCE Zone, growing from deepening economic interdependence, must be followed by the emergence of a true collective security apparatus. Already the continuing arms control processes currently demilitarizing Europe are creating the conditions conducive to the construction of an intercontinental security system much more complex than the "nuclear umbrella" that lent an anxious stability to the Cold War era. "The ultimate goal must be to create a single security system in which every country feels protected from every other and not just from an opposing alliance."[29]

The inescapable parallel here is the Concert of Europe, the group of powers that policed the continent's disputes after the Napoleonic Wars. This, too, operated in the absence of bipolarity, and preserved peace for four decades in a multipolar system through joint decisions for collective security. A Concert is an idea whose time has once again come.[30]

The CSCE can become the leading institution through which such a new supranational Concert of pooled sovereignty might emerge and be managed, and national disintegration fed by resurgent hypernationalism might be controlled. The Helsinki

Final Act and the ongoing CSCE talks have established principles for Europe's political and economic reintegration that create the necessary preconditions for this next institutional step,[31] providing a two-tier formula can be found that gives the great powers incentives to share responsibilities and their costs for core security threats without reducing the lesser powers to second-class citizens. Finding this common ground is a substantial institutional challenge. But finding some principle is a prerequisite to overcoming the obstacle to full-membership unanimity that prevents the creation of a true collective security organization. The CSCE establishes all its principles on the basis of consensus, but if its security-enforcement powers are to increase with US support, a regime requiring less than unanimous consent ("consensus minus") will need to be constructed to enforce, in the event of clear and flagrant violations, those principles to which the 52 member states have formally agreed.

The CSCE is the logical and desirable security institution to replace NATO and the Warsaw Pact. It has numerous advantages because it

- incorporates the two leading military powers, the US and Russia, and presents an institutional catalyst to their cooperation and a barrier to their renewed rivalry;

- allows the US to remain involved as an equal partner, by encouraging its participation but deterring its potential heavy-handed, hegemonic intervention;

- accommodates representation of the breakaway CIS republics, provides a framework for their assimilation, and gives them a stake and voice in European security;

- provides a mechanism for dealing with the security concerns of the Central and East Europeans--precisely those countries most unstable in the wake of the Cold War;

- is the only forum that explicitly links political, social, and economic issues to the military aspects of security;

- fosters democratic governance--a powerful contribution to peace, because throughout modern history democracies have almost never gone to war with one another;[32]

- spreads the costs of collective security through burden sharing, which enables each member to diminish its defense expenditures;

- includes all the EC, EFTA, and former Warsaw Pact states;

- coordinates the policies of the leading powers in ways that reduce the ability of each to upset the balance of power;

- restrains the capacity of any actor, including the US, to pursue dysfunctional policies that, with the best of intentions, produce the worst of effects.[33]

A CSCE-based Concert opens the door to other options and linkages. For example, the integration of a CSCE security system into the United Nations collective security mechanism as advocated in Articles 51-54 of the UN Charter represents another possibility. Though fogged in symbolism and sloganism and presently highly politicized in the US, an embryonic global post-Cold War security system may be in an incipient stage of development. Its activation during the war against Iraq may be a harbinger of the future. The CSCE Zone is the nucleus of Europe and crosses into the UN security system by virtue of the fact that four of the five permanent members of the Security Council--the US, France, the UK, and Russia--are CSCE countries, and at least one East European and one Nordic country regularly appear among the Security Council's non-permanent members. In addition, there is currently discussion in Europe concerning the earmarking of German and possibly of WEU forces for service in UN peacekeeping operations very much in the way that Sweden, other Nordic countries, and the Netherlands routinely prepare forces for UN assignments.

Most importantly, restructuring the jurisdiction and the decision-making procedures of the CSCE to enable the great powers to act in concert would give the CSCE the muscle its emaciated military frame currently lacks. Only through institutional reform that unites the great powers as equal members of the European family but (like the UN Security Council) preserves their right to veto military action can paralyzing schisms be avoided--and enthusiastic US support be assured. In its absence, defense cooperation and full US participation are not reasonable to expect; what the Germans call *alleingang* (going it alone) is a highly probable US response.

Needless to say, great uncertainties surround the processes by which global security and European security could dovetail. There also lingers the gnawing US penchant for unilateralism that must be resisted, as well as its short-sighted urge to preempt ascendant great-power rivals from sharing leadership responsibilities.[34] Indeed, everything is now in transition. This will not end until a unified Europe emerges and begins to play a role in a genuinely multipolar world. At that point, distance from the US may become more important to Europe than attachment. If the US wants to secure a say in that world when it forms later, it must act now. By becoming an active participant, the US can help prevent an emergent multipolar system from culminating in another general war.[35] In the near term, the CSCE is the most attractive arrangement for enlarging the zone of stability in a multipolar system. For that purpose, the US must get serious about its European role, and help to activate the further expansion of the domain of CSCE competence.

Conclusion: Keeping the US in Europe

In his renowned farewell address, President George Washington dismissed the "primary interests" of Europe as having, at most, "a very remote relation" to US interests. He counseled against "interweaving our destiny with that of any part of Europe [which would] entangle our peace and prosperity in the toils of European ambition, rivalship, interest, humor, or caprice."[36]

Washington's warning properly detached a fledgling, nation-building US from the machinations of 19th-century European politics, which were dominated by autocratic monarchies. Today, however, European states generally uphold the liberal democratic principles outlined by the Founding Fathers. And the US, long beyond its nation-building preoccupations, stands to benefit from a concert of cooperation among the now ideologically compatible states of modern

Europe.

Throughout its history, US diplomacy has alternated ambivalently between periods of involvement in and withdrawal from European affairs. These approach-avoidance cycles have co-varied with the country's cyclical swings between internationalism and isolationism. Since the end of World War II, active entanglement has prevailed. The US was involved in Europe economically, politically, and militarily. This entailed uniting US and West European defenses while facilitating European economic reconstruction, a liberal trade regime, and continental integration. Now, however, there is danger that the cycle will reassert itself, and a new period of US wariness about and rejection of European affairs (like the retreat that occurred in 1919) will again take root. To some, putting America first means putting Europe a distant second and treating it as a rival.

The proper US response is neither another retreat into isolationism nor a hegemonic effort to manage the new European order. The proper response is for the US to act in concert with Europeans and to strengthen the security-maintenance role of the multilateral institutions.

In order to combat domestic isolationist and nationalist tendencies, *the US needs Europe to need the US*. The US requires not only support from European allies in specific issue areas, but also their generalized backing of a US vision of a new world order based on Western ideals. Most West and East European governments already prefer some continuing US presence in Europe, and this pressure can help US leaders combat those segments of US opinion that prefer decoupling Europe and having a marginalized US play a passive spectator role. Some middle ground between isolationism and unilateralism--the two polarized traditions of US diplomatic history--is essential.

138

Europeans can help the United States avoid the poles of undiscriminating indifference and a power politics equally undiscriminating.

To balance commitments with resources, some measure of retrenchment from a hegemonic leadership role for the US proportionate to its relative power is inevitable, and arguably warranted. The unrestrained scale of post-World War II US globalism[37] must be reduced, and US pursuit of a predominant role in managing European affairs must be jettisoned. The capacity--indeed, the moral qualification of the US to shape European conditions--is questionable. Moreover, the uniting Europe is a power equal to the US, positioned to declare its independence from the US nuclear umbrella and justifiably no longer willing to acquiesce to a Pax Americana hegemony, however benign. The day has passed when Europe requires the US to protect it from external attack and regulate its internal disputes.

However, although it is no longer realistic for the US to follow Paul Nitze's 1952 advice to seek preponderant power, unrestrained US retrenchment also must be rejected. Instead of these extremes, the US response to the new European system should draw on the vision inspired by Woodrow Wilson's idealism and Franklin Roosevelt's internationalism. A new Concert under the auspices of a strengthened CSCE that subsumes NATO and the EC provides the US with the means to practice selective engagement[38] in European affairs while avoiding full-scale withdrawal. This role is consistent with traditional US values, emerging national interests, and the exigencies of a multipolar world. It would enable US leaders to redress urgent domestic problems while preserving the vital US role in European diplomacy. And it is cost-effective, as "a central coalition would be a much cheaper international regulatory device than either an inefficient and dilatory balance of power or an expensive deterrence."[39]

Traditional US distrust of "permanent alliances" must give way to Euro-American collaboration and shared decision-making powers. Only through concerted action can states on both sides of the Atlantic preserve stability while putting their own houses in order. Current circumstances have made it both prudent and pragmatic to empower the CSCE and thereby give Wilson's program for collective security the chance to succeed it never was given.

Notes

This paper has benefitted from the comments and criticisms of P. Terrence Hopmann, Donald J. Puchala, Steven Hook, and Jeffrey Morton.

1. Charles Krauthammer, "The Unipolar Moment," *Foreign Affairs* 70, no. 1 (1990), pp. 23-33.

2. See Eugene R. Wittkopf, *Faces of Internationalism* (Durham, NC: Duke University Press, 1990).

3. Hans J. Morgenthau, *In Defense of the National Interest* (New York: Knopf, 1951), p. 242.

4. See Joseph S. Nye, Jr., *Bound to Lead: The Changing Nature of American Power* (New York: Basic Books, 1990).

5. Edward Luttwak, "From Geopolitics to Geo-Economics," *The National Interest* 20 (Summer 1990), pp. 17-23.

6. Theodore H. Moran, "International Economics and US Security," in *The Future of American Foreign Policy*, ed. Charles W. Kegley, Jr. and Eugene R. Wittkopf (New York: St. Martin's Press, 1992), p. 317.

7. See Benjamin Barber, "Jihad vs. McWorld," *The Atlantic* 269 (March 1992), pp. 53-63.

8. For example, see Lester Thurow, *Head to Head: Coming Economic Battles Among Japan, Europe, and America* (New York: Morrow, 1992).

9. Karen Elliott House, "As Power Is Dispersed Among Nations, Need for Leadership Grows," *The Wall Street Journal*, Feb. 21, 1989, p. A10.

10. Joseph S. Nye, Jr., "The Changing Nature of World Power," in *The Global Agenda*, 3rd ed., ed. Charles W. Kegley, Jr. and Eugene R. Wittkopf (New York: McGraw-Hill, 1992), p. 318.

11. Walter Lippmann, *US Foreign Policy: Shield of the Republic* (Boston: Little, Brown, 1943), p. 9.

12. Samuel P. Huntington, "Coping with the Lippmann Gap," *Foreign Affairs* 66, no. 3 (1988), pp. 453-77.

13. James Chace, "A New Grand Strategy," *Foreign Policy* 70 (Spring 1988), p. 3.

14. Paul Kennedy, *The Rise and Fall of the Great Powers* (New York: Random House, 1987), pp. 514-15.

15. David Calleo, "American National Interests and the New Europe: The Millennium Has Not Yet Arrived," in *The Future of American Foreign Policy*, ed. Kegley and Wittkopf, p. 190.

16. See Ted Galen Carpenter, "The New World Disorder," *Foreign Policy* 84 (Fall 1991), pp. 24-39.

17. See Charles W. Kegley, "The New Global Order: The Power of Principle in a Pluralistic World," *Ethics and International Affairs* 6 (1992), pp. 21-40.

18. Fred Charles Iklé, "Comrades in Arms: The Case for a Russian-American Defense Community," *The National Interest* 26 (Winter 1992), pp. 22-32. This typology, of course, does not exhaust the possibilities. A complete picture would need to treat the potential for working with the Western European Union, the CFE process, and the European Economic Area (EEA), alongside the other layers of institutional linkages that exist among active and dormant structures.

19. Thomas Kielinger, "Waking Up in the New Europe--With a Headache," *International Affairs* 66 (April 1990), pp. 249-63. The characterization of the new European landscape that follows is indebted to Donald J. Puchala.

20. Pierre Hassner, "Europe Beyond Partition and Unity: Disintegration or Reconstruction?" *International Affairs* 66, no. 3 (July 1990), p. 461.

21. Gianni De Michelis, "Reaching Out to the East," *Foreign Policy* 79 (Summer 1990), pp. 53-54.

22. "UN, Weighing Bosnia Role, Cites $2 Billion in Arrears," *International Herald Tribune*, April 30, 1992, p. 3.

23. Anthony Hartley, "The Once and Future Europe," *The National Interest* 26 (Winter 1992), p. 53. The EC's enlargement to include the neutral and nonaligned states, and its new trade agreements with Bulgaria, Czechoslovakia, Hungary, Poland, and Romania, will accelerate this trend.

24. Gregory F. Treverton, "The New Europe," *Foreign Affairs* 71, no. 1 (1992), p. 110.

25. Jenonne Walker, "Keeping America in Europe," *Foreign Policy* 83 (Summer 1991), p. 129.

26. For a penetrating discussion, see Alpo M. Rusi, *After the Cold War: Europe's New Political Architecture* (New York: St. Martin's Press, 1991). For an assessment of alternative scenarios and the barriers to a CSCE-based security system in Europe, see Stefan Lehne, *The CSCE in the 1990s: Common European House or Potemkin Village?* (Vienna: Austrian Institute for International Affairs, 1992).

27. Henning Wegener,"The Transformed Alliance," *NATO Review* (August 1990), p. 7.

28. This list of security needs expands those identified by Hans Binnendijk in "What Kind of New Order for Europe?" *The World Today* (February 1991), pp. 19-21.

29. De Michelis, "Reaching Out to the East," p. 59.

30. Advocates of this option include John Mueller, "A New Concert of Europe," *Foreign Policy* 77 (Winter 1990), pp. 3-16; Richard H. Ullman, *Securing Europe* (Princeton: Princeton University Press, 1991); Hans Günter Brouch, "From Collective Self-Defense to a Collective Security System in Europe," *Disarmament* 14, no. 1 (1991), pp. 1-20; Malcolm Chalmers, "Beyond the Alliance System: The Case for a European Security Organization," *World Policy Journal* 7 (Spring 1990), pp. 215-50; James Goodby, "A New European Concert: Settling Disputes in CSCE," *Arms Control Today* 21 (January/February 1991), pp. 3-6; Richard Rosecrance, "A New Concert of Powers," *Foreign Affairs* 71, no. 2 (Spring 1992), pp. 64-82; and K.J. Holsti, "A 'Zone of Civility' in European Diplomatic Relations? The CSCE and Conflict Resolution" (Paper presented at the annual meeting of the Interntional Studies Association, Atlanta, March 31-April 4, 1992).

31. For a forceful argument on the capacity of the CSCE to play this role, see Charles H. Kupchan and Clifford A. Kupchan, "Concerts, Collective Security, and the Future Europe," *International Security* 16 (Summer 1991), pp. 114-61.

32. See Peter Manicas, *Democracy and War* (Cambridge: Cambridge University Press, 1989).

33. "If the United States pursues fickle or short-sighted policies," warns Steven Van Evera, "the American presence in Europe could cause more problems than it solves." "Primed for Peace: Europe after the Cold War," *International Security* 15 (Winter 1989), p. 56.

34. The latter response, which rejects collective internationalism, is advocated by the Defense Department's mission statement. See Patrick E. Tyler, "A One-Superpower World: Pentagon's Document Outlines Ways to Thwart Challenges to Primacy of America," *The New York Times International*, March 8, 1992, pp. 1, 4.

35. For a discussion of the means for preserving peace under conditions of multipolarity, see Charles W. Kegley, Jr. and Gregory A. Raymond, "Must We Fear a Post-Cold War Multipolar System?" *Journal of Conflict Resolution* 36 (September 1992), forthcoming.

36. From Armin Rapaport, ed., *Sources in American Diplomacy* (New York: Macmillan, 1966), p. 29.

37. See Charles W. Kegley, Jr. and Eugene R. Wittkopf, *American Foreign Policy*, 4th ed. (New York: St. Martin's Press, 1991).

38. For an elaboration of this position, see Zbigniew Brzezinski, "Selective Global Commitment," *Foreign Affairs* 70, no. 4 (Fall 1991), pp. 1-20.

39. Rosecrance, "A New Concert of Powers," p. 82.

Part III

145-229

Regional
Approaches
to European
Security

6

The Role of the Commonwealth of Independent States in the New European Security System

Oleg N. Bykov

The political landscape of Europe has changed dramatically. Seen for over four decades as a threat to European security, "the Evil Empire" has collapsed. The tide of democracy has swept over Eastern Europe. With the Berlin Wall removed, Germany unified, the Warsaw Pact dissolved, and the former Soviet forces withdrawing, the ideological division of the continent--the source of the military confrontation of the Cold War--has thus been overcome.

Europe's transition to the post-confrontation era was substantially enhanced by the policy of "new thinking" initiated by leaders of the former Soviet Union. NATO has put forward a new strategic concept oriented towards the establishment of a just and lasting peaceful order in Europe. The countries of the European Community have been promoting the principles of political union, including the development of a distinct European security identity. The CSCE process has moved towards establishing institutional arrangements and a contractual framework for consultation and cooperation in Europe. The Treaty on Conventional Armed Forces in Europe (CFE) has significantly enhanced stability through deep arm reductions, unprecedented military transparency, and greater mutual confidence. A new European security architecture has begun to take shape through the interaction of the various institutions, which complement each other. The people of North America and the whole of Europe are now in a position to join in a community of shared values based on democracy, human rights, the rule of law, and a market economy.

While these fundamental changes have significantly reduced the threat of East-West conflict, problems of security in Europe still remain. They stem from a wide range of instabilities and a great deal of uncertainty about the future.

The most obvious case among the present instabilities is that of Yugoslavia, where an extremely volatile situation has highly destabilizing ramifications far beyond its borders. There is also the potential for instability in other countries of Eastern Europe, all of which face severe economic, political, and social problems. Given the accumulated dissatisfaction and unrealized expectations among the populace in these countries, the democratic model may yet be rejected in favor of authoritarian or totalitarian regimes based on aggressively nationalist policies. Ethnic conflicts could erupt and escalate, leading to greater tensions in interstate relations in Eastern Europe.

However, overshadowing all other instabilities are the dangers stemming from the breakup of the Soviet Union. The continued disintegration of the old union structures and the proliferation of contradictions between and within the former Soviet republics are fraught with all sorts of threats, including the possibility of full-scale civil war. Conflicts over the control of military capabilities could lead to extremely dangerous collisions that will be difficult to contain within the territory of the former USSR. In such a situation, the accidental or unauthorized use of nuclear weapons remains a serious possibility. It is impossible to rule out the ominous prospect of massive and extensive radioactive contamination resulting from destruction of many nuclear power stations--a catastrophe that would dwarf the effects of the Chernobyl disaster. Of course, these are the worst-case scenarios. But even barring such calamities, the very fact of persistent instability in Russia and other former Soviet republics inevitably affects the security of the rest of Europe.

Commitments and Constraints

Their current predicaments notwithstanding, the Soviet Union's successors, the Russian leadership in particular, remain deeply committed to the strengthening of European security. Indeed, it is vital to their objectives of surmounting the tremendous domestic difficulties and making the process of democratic reform irreversible. There is an emerging commonality of national interests of the post-Soviet states and the democratic countries of Europe and North America. For the first time since the Bolshevik Revolution, the external issues of national interests in both East and West have become increasingly compatible, devoid of serious ideological or security conflicts. Given the cooperative stance of the Western democracies, the only real source of threat to the progressive transformations of the former Soviet republics is to be found in their internal problems.

If economic hardship, political disarray, ethnic unrest, and civil strife are permitted to become unmanageable, the developments might well lead to a situation that could be exploited by those whose vested interests require restoration of a totalitarian order. For them, no domestic sacrifice would be too great to bear in the name of underpinning military power. The entire West, this time together with many former Soviet allies and friends, would then have to brace for another Cold War. This would in all likelihood leave the prospective neo-totalitarian leadership with virtually no chance for success or even long-term survival in the face of a stepped-up arms race and resumed confrontation.

A blending of democracy and security has long been taken for granted in the West; post-Soviet realities make its adoption universally imperative. One premise of post-Soviet policies has been focused on the recognition of this essential prerequisite for European affairs. Yet this generalization, though adequate in principle, is perhaps too sweeping. When applied to the actual situation, the common denominator of democracy and security clashes with a host of limitations and inhibitions. Foremost among these limitations is the fact that the normal process of foreign and security policy formation has been largely disrupted since the dissolution of the USSR. The emergence of the Commonwealth of Independent States holds the promise of some political stability, but the danger remains that the Commonwealth will prove to be little more than a forum for discussion among its member states. Although CIS leaders recognize the need to cooperate, they continue to have serious differences over the sharing of power and resources. Under these circumstances, there may well need to be separate policies toward Europe by the Russian Federation and other former Soviet republics. While conceptually similar now, such policies will almost certainly differ in many practical ways in the future. The CIS will hardly be able to influence the behavior of the individual sovereign nations when they emerge on the European scene. Nor is it likely that the Commonwealth, or Russia, for that matter, will be successful in fostering cohesiveness among the new participants on the European political scene by linking involvement with the need for enhancing domestic democratic change and making such change irrevocable.

The degree of allegiance to democracy varies considerably from one new state to another. In some of them, conservative leaders in whatever disguise--pseudo-democratic or nationalist-- are concerned less with safeguarding freedoms and reforms than with retaining their positions of power and independence. While eager to play conspicuous roles in European affairs for their own political and economic purposes, they are reluctant to permit the introduction of Western democratic values into their own fiefdoms.

To make matters more complex and troublesome, the recently recovered sovereignty has put the former Soviet republics in an entirely new geopolitical context. Each is in search of a new foreign policy and security identity. Some tend to gravitate westward, while others seem to be east- or south- bound, with Russia itself apparently torn between Europe and Asia. The actual picture is certainly more blurred. Yet there are few clearcut choices and many straws in the wind across the vast expanse of the former Soviet Union. These point to various, often criss-crossing, directions to the ongoing reorientation of security priorities.

Russia is in the throes of redefining its national security priorities, with a discernible trend towards an "all azimuths partnership." An organic linkage must be developed between the European and Asian aspects of the country's national objectives. This need is further accentuated by Russia's membership in the CIS, an entity with diversified geopolitical characteristics. The Eurasian dimension of Russian security policy is also essential for coping with a new set of bilateral relations with the newly sovereign countries on both sides of the Ural continental divide. The same geopolitical duality is reflected in Russia's emerging

151

capacity as an intercontinental connection between the Atlantic and the Pacific worlds. At the same time, Russia is definitely not deemphasizing its strategic interaction with the United States.

In any assessment of Russia's present geopolitical posture, one important circumstance should be taken into account. Russian territory, in purely physical terms, has been effectively cut off from Western Europe, its major partner in any European security arrangement. This separation has been brought about in two stages; first, with the formation of a wide belt of fully sovereign states following the democratic revolution in Central and Eastern Europe and the unification of the German Democratic Republic with the Federal Republic of Germany; and later, with the secession of the three Baltic republics--Lithuania, Latvia, and Estonia--and subsequently with the dissolution of the Soviet Union, thus placing Ukraine, Belarus, and Moldova as additional barriers between Russia and Western Europe. Today, Russia has direct access to Western Europe only by air or by way of the Baltic Sea via the ports of St. Petersburg and Kaliningrad (itself an enclave surrounded by Lithuania and Poland), with the option of more distant routes from the Black or the White and Barents Seas. While far from totally disrupting the established system of East-West security interaction, the relative detachment of Russia from Western Europe (and vice versa) causes considerable logistical complications. Facing these overwhelming odds, a possible role for the CIS as a "bridge builder" between Russia and Western Europe seems dubious.

Nonetheless, the predominant national security interests of Russia, by far the biggest among the ex-Soviet republics and the pivot of the Commonwealth, remain firmly Europe-oriented. This is not only because of Russia's early commitments and deep involvement, but also because of the government's determination to enter the global community of advanced free market democracies, of which Western Europe is a central part. Russia's non-European or rather non-Atlantic security concerns, however distracting, will remain for the foreseeable future subordinate to the overriding interest in keeping peace and stability in Europe. (One hypothetical deviation from this consistent course might be related to China, but for the time being, there is no detectable menace looming from that direction.)

While reappraising and reordering some of its national security priorities, Russia is conducting its global and regional political and military activities with the objective of minimizing any collateral damage to the stability of its posture in Europe. More importantly, whatever is being done by Russia elsewhere (e.g., improvement in relations with the US and China) has a mostly countervailing impact on the country's efforts to consolidate the system of cooperative security in Europe. This is specifically relevant to the Russian-American strategic interaction. Rather than diminishing the value of Russia's input into European security, however, the country's partnership with the US, the strategic mainstay of the whole Western world, augments immeasurably the effectiveness of Russia's contribution to overall stability within Europe, by ensuring that different views and interests continue to be part of the evolving security debate.

Ukraine clearly has the potential to play an important role in European affairs. With a population of over 50 million and rich industrial and agricultural resources, Ukraine's claim to be a middle European power appears to be warranted. Kiev's reorientation from East to West is already taking place as the country's leaders search for political recognition and economic assistance. Europe's interest in welcoming Ukraine into its fold is beyond doubt.

At the same time, complicating Ukraine's entry into Europe is the rift between Kiev and Moscow. The two biggest powers in the CIS have become bogged down in quarrels over a wide range of burning issues. A great deal of rivalry, especially with regard to security and economic matters, often hampers their respective approaches to practical problems of European security. To counterbalance Russian power, Ukraine seeks closer regional cooperation with such neighbors as Belarus, Poland, Hungary, and Romania. Despite major obstacles, Ukrainian policy is rapidly adjusting to new realities. With or without Russia, Ukraine seems bound to become part of Europe.

Belarus is following Ukraine's lead, although with a lower profile and a willingness to avoid serious conflicts with Russia. With more limited resources, Belarus cannot afford a substantial contribution to common security arrangements, but Minsk's political attitude is definitely pro-Europe.

Lithuania, Latvia, and Estonia, first to quit the crumbling Soviet empire and resolutely holding on to their independence, have already established an irresistible momentum that is propelling them into Europe. Their disengagement from economic and military connections with Russia can slow down this movement, but its final result will certainly be full-fledged integration of the three Baltic states into the European structures, with an emphasis on closer cooperation with the Nordic countries.

Moldova is something of a special case. Its affiliation can only be European, but incessant, violent ethnic clashes and internal instability, exacerbated by heated controversy over unification with Romania, have so far constrained Moldova's ability to actively participate in European politics.

Since the breakup of the Soviet Union, a new world has

opened up for a number of nations formerly not known for close association with Europe, namely the republics of the Caucasus, Kazakhstan, and Central Asia. Europe and the US have offered them an opportunity for cooperation, prompted by the compelling factors of interdependence, which have broadened the very concept of "Europe," first westward and now eastward. In the same spirit of geopolitical novelty, the newly independent states have for the most part responded positively. Yet confronted with the need to reveal their true identity and genuine preferences, leaders of most of these former republics remain ambivalent.

What is unfolding can hardly be perceived as unexpected. The conglomerate of these vast and varied regions is in flux. The newly born sovereign states are confronted with hard choices involving not merely geopolitics and economics but, more importantly, religion. It has been difficult for the states of these regions to resist the magnetism generated by powerful Muslim neighbors, primarily Iran and Turkey (and to a lesser extent Pakistan, Afghanistan, and the Mideast Arab countries; of course, China is also nearby and seeking to expand its own spheres of influence). Iran-style Islam and the Turkish secular model, competing for influence in the region, may produce results that vary from one country to another. However, it is almost certain that Islamic fundamentalism has a good chance of spreading throughout the Muslim republics of the CIS.

The West hopes to encourage these states to look towards Europe for guidance and strategic orientation, and away from their Islamic neighbors to the south. The proximity of these states to the Middle East, which is of the utmost importance to the West, primarily because of oil and potential threats to its flow, has made the area strategically significant for the US and Europe.

Western countries have become concerned that radical political change and ethnic conflicts in the former Soviet republics may spill over to the Middle East, thus exacerbating the critical impact on US and European interests. The result is a flurry of US and other Western diplomatic activity in these states.

Sitting on the dividing line between East and West has been an excruciating balancing act for most of the newly independent states. With fateful decisions to make, it is not implausible to expect the boundary between the Christian and Muslim republics to eventually become the most important partition within the Commonwealth, as well as between Europe and Asia.

Such a cleavage has already become stark reality in the Caucasus and Central Asia. Armenia has been locked in a protracted bloody conflict with Azerbaijan over ownership of Nagorno-Karabakh, a mostly Armenian-populated enclave in the middle of Azerbaijan. The war between the two Caucasian states has all but incapacitated them in terms of any external activity beyond their pleas for international mediation. If not for this tragedy, Armenia, with its ancient Christian heritage, propensity to Western values, and extensive international ties, could long have been an active participant in European affairs. Some effort would have been required to overcome the longstanding animosity between Armenia and Turkey, but otherwise the republic was the most inclined in the region to join the West. As for the internally unstable Azerbaijan, its European inclination is far less pronounced. While displaying some interest in maintaining peace in Europe, Azerbaijan is much more predisposed to develop contacts with its Islamic neighbors--the secular Turkey and/or the fundamentalist Iran.

Georgia has been so far, deplorably, an odd man out.

Predominantly pro-democracy, this Caucasian state has been deeply submerged in civil strife and economic degradation. Violation of human rights under a brief authoritarian rule has interfered with Georgia's entry into various international organizations, including the UN and the CSCE. It is highly probable that, given internal normalization, Georgia will be actively engaged in cooperative efforts towards enhancing European security.

Kazakhstan, the largest among the CIS Asian republics, with substantial economic resources and significant military capabilities, is clearly entitled to share Russia's burden of European security involvement. What apparently restrains Kazakhstan (apart from obvious reasons of bargaining) is its dual geopolitical position between East and West. Bordering on China and Muslim countries on the southern periphery of former Soviet lands, Kazakhstan has deferred decisions on security commitments with regard to Europe. At the same time, the Kazakh leadership has been seeking direct approaches to European economic and political institutions, as well as to various Asian countries, such as India or Turkey. Islamic fundamentalism has so far held little appeal for Kazakhstan's Muslims despite a revival of religion, although all this could change in the event of economic collapse.

Situated deep inside the continental land mass, Central Asia is far from Europe. It is nevertheless relevant to European security. As the devolution of the former Soviet Union continues, the import of this remote region's future path(s) has begun to loom larger. Choices the newly independent states will make in their governments, economies, and international ties can influence East-West relationships far beyond their boundaries.

Three of the region's four republics--Uzbekistan,

Tajikistan, and Turkmenistan--were the last bastions of the old, if recently somewhat camouflaged, regimes. Kyrgyzstan is the only quasi-democracy in Central Asia. All four republics are impoverished and in need of outside help.

For the West, the challenge is to foster and expand its influence in the predominantly Muslim states through diplomatic recognition or economic aid to keep them away from their neighbors to the south, particularly Iran, without further entrenching undemocratic rule. On the other hand, pan-Islamism is gathering momentum in most of the republics. While the Turkish secular brand has some appeal in more sophisticated quarters, the Iran-style fundamentalism is becoming increasingly popular with ordinary people and many old and new leaders. As a result, the prospect of Central Asia's constructive contribution to European security appears rather dim.

The creation of an adequate balance of commitments and constraints across the entire board of national and European security interests of Russia and other CIS or non-CIS states requires that a number of additional considerations be taken into account. They stem from the uniqueness of the conditions that confront these states since the breakup of the union. The scale and pace of radical change have been unprecedented, without parallel in modern history. Against this tempestuous background, evaluation and prognostication are extremely difficult. Incessant instability, structural fragmentation, multifarious conflicts, civil unrest, and political posturing impair credibility and predictability. External projection of security interests is confounded by the fact that too much attention has to be directed towards intractable internal problems.

Nonetheless, there are sufficient grounds to conclude that the essential national security objectives of Russia and most other ex-Soviet republics, including Ukraine, Belarus, and Kazakhstan, will continue to be distinctly and consistently Europe-oriented. Short of a complete collapse of democratic reform and a return to totalitarian rule, these newly independent states will be contributing substantially to the common cause of enhancing cooperative security for a Europe whole and free.

Defusing Explosive Structures

The issue that has the most far-reaching consequences for the security concerns of Europe and for that matter, the whole world, is the management of military capabilities. Of common concern is the disposition of Soviet military power, particularly nuclear weapons. The context of confrontation and competition is gone, but the lethal means of mass destruction remain. Both Moscow and Washington are ready to begin dismantling most of their long-range nuclear weaponry, with which each superpower threatened the very existence of the other.

However, the chief concern is not about designing new stable balances or modified patterns of mutual deterrence. Instead, it is about a possible loss of control over nuclear capabilities that could lead to accidental or unauthorized use of these deadly weapons. These are known to be well protected, but given their numbers, estimated at 27,000-32,000, there is never a full guarantee, particularly when command and control begin to deteriorate. This is where the residual Soviet military structures are most vulnerable and explosive. Joint efforts are urgently needed to defuse this time bomb.

There are also other insistent security issues stemming from the demise of the USSR. The former Soviet armed forces, still the largest and most heavily armed in the world, now has no clear mission or well-defined chain of command, and its traditional means of life support are drying up. The army is becoming frustrated by its sudden fragmentation, loss of social prestige, and precipitously declining living standards. Several ex-Soviet republics are attempting to take over the military forces and equipment on their territory, in spite of resistance from Moscow. Some units are switching allegiance to local authorities on their own. In some areas, weapons are being seized by warring paramilitary groups, thus increasing the risks of an all-out civil war, which could involve outside powers or spill over into Western countries.

Putting first things first, some urgent measures have already been taken to keep the former Soviet nuclear weapons under secure, reliable, and responsible control. As Russia and the other new states sort out relations with each other, the CIS framework has proved to be instrumental in beginning an intricate set of negotiations with regard to the nuclear legacy of the defunct USSR.

Most importantly, the Commonwealth states have agreed to take a number of steps to place the former Soviet nuclear arsenal under unified control. The four CIS states on whose territory nuclear forces are actually deployed--Russia, Ukraine, Belarus, and Kazakhstan--have all indicated their readiness to observe and implement START obligations. Ukraine and Belarus have expressed their intention to become nuclear-free states, and all nuclear weapons will be removed from Ukraine by the end of 1994. It appears that Kazakhstan may also eventually become a nuclear-free state. If so, all strategic nuclear systems will in the end be deployed on Russian territory. The ultimate future of these weapons will take some time to resolve, however, though Commonwealth leaders have unanimously agreed to retain unified control over nuclear capabilities. While final launch authority is vested in the president of Russia, the Minsk agreement specifies that he or she act only with the consent of the leaders of Ukraine, Belarus, and Kazakhstan and in consultation with the remaining Commonwealth leaders.

These commitments are vitally important for the new states in the territory of the former Soviet Union, for the whole of Europe, and for the rest of the world. So far the nuclear command and control mechanisms have proved to be more reliable than many would have anticipated. However, a deterioration of relations among these states could undermine the Commonwealth's ability to keep nuclear weapons under firm control. Moreover, the very prospect of the Commonwealth would rest in the balance. If the CIS dissolved, Russia and other states in actual possession of nuclear weapons would face enormous difficulties sorting out responsibilities. Such difficulties could be further exacerbated if the future internal integrity of some of these states might be in doubt. It is therefore of utmost importance both for the successors to the former Soviet nuclear arsenal and for the West to persist in jointly developing the necessary safeguards against the possibility of a nuclear catastrophe.

Fears have heightened around the world that the Soviet Union's breakup will spur nuclear proliferation, particularly to such countries as Iran, Libya, or Iraq, and thus enable terrorists to acquire weapons of mass destruction. Deep concern has been expressed that nuclear arms--as well as conventional weapons--may find their way to international black markets from the former USSR, where hard currency is in short supply. With the cutbacks in former Soviet weapons programs and the rapid deterioration of the economy, there is a strong temptation for

161

unemployed nuclear scientists to work abroad, especially in the so-called nuclear threshold countries in the less developed world.

The acute problem of "loose nukes" and "loose brains" has to be addressed urgently. Initial steps have already been taken. The US and Russia, in consultation with Ukraine, Belarus, and Kazakhstan, have sought to tighten export controls on nuclear arms, materials, and technology, with other Commonwealth states to follow suit. The US has offered Russian nuclear scientists contracts in the US or funds to finance their peaceful research work in Russia. There is a need to develop similar cooperation between Russia and Western Europe.

Overall, the CIS has so far proved to be an effective instrument for keeping nuclear weapons under unified command and control. Yet uncertainties have persisted since the Minsk agreement. While Ukraine and Belarus seem to be committed to eventual non-nuclear status, Kazakhstan has been reluctant to make its final position clear. As distinct from strategic systems effectively under CIS control, short-range nuclear weapons have been widely dispersed in Russia, Ukraine, Belarus, and Kazakhstan. The security systems on tactical weapons are less foolproof than those on strategic weapons, and some of the oldest may not have double locking devices and are insufficiently secure against theft or terrorism. By mid-1992, all battlefield and sea-based nuclear weapons are to be concentrated in Russia.

Another area of common concern is that of possible widespread environmental damage resulting from destruction of the huge stocks of chemical and biological weapons on the territory of the former USSR. As Moscow's destruction capabilities are limited, the US is determining how best to assist, technically and financially. Again, there is room for Western Europe's active participation in preventing disaster.

Attention also still needs to be paid to the fate of the former Soviet general purpose forces. Although it is unlikely that a large-scale conventional challenge to European security will reemerge from the Eurasian heartland for many years to come, some new leadership in Moscow could, hypothetically, try to recover the USSR's lost empire in Eastern Europe. In this event, however, the reduction of the former Soviet conventional capabilities over the past several years would make the chances for success exceedingly remote without prolonged and massive force generation and redeployment; but even residual forces, if clear reduction is not properly managed, could be a destabilizing factor.

Recent events are having a devastating impact on the capabilities of the former Soviet military. Combat readiness and force levels are falling; there are problems with conscription; units withdrawn from Eastern Europe and Germany are having serious logistical and housing difficulties back home; a large amount of military spending is being diverted to personnel costs from operations and procurement expenditures to prevent a total breakdown of living standards for the troops and their dependents. Troop loyalties are becoming divided and uncertain. Implementation of arms control agreements will further reduce any threatening military potential. So will redirection of resources from military to civilian purposes.

Had such a deterioration of Soviet military power happened during the East-West confrontation, this surely would have pleased the Atlantic community and the entire free world. However, the end of the Cold War and the development of nonadversarial and cooperative relationships have placed this process in the broader context of common European security interests. From this new point of view, the predicament through

163

which Russia and the other newly independent states are muddling has to be approached in a different way. On the one hand, the risk of major conflict in Europe has been greatly reduced. On the other, there is a greater risk of various conflicts of a lesser magnitude, particularly within the former USSR or Eastern Europe, which could quickly spread westward and require a rapid response. Moreover, such a risk is likely to grow if the former Soviet army, virtually the only functioning institution of the old union, disintegrates into a series of disjointed and often hostile contingents. But even barring these highly destabilizing developments, there is a natural Western interest in how the former Soviet armed forces are divided among the CIS and the non-CIS states and then reconfigured and redeployed.

While in the throes of force reconstruction, Russia and other militarily significant members of the Commonwealth rightly expect that, in the interests of European security and stability, the West will take their enormous difficulties into consideration.

Regardless of differences in their circumstances or in their national military capabilities relative to each other, the independent states have been engaged in a process of strategic reorientation with regard to the US and Europe. They have been moving away from the concept of forward offensive deployment towards a reduced forward presence in tune with the requirements of purely defensive sufficiency. The changes stemming from the new strategic environment necessitate significant modifications to be made in the missions of the military forces and in their posture at a substantially reduced level.

Simultaneously, Russia has to sort out its military-political relations with its former Warsaw Pact allies and its new counterparts within the CIS. These new relationships often do not conform with Russia's strategic reconstitution vis-a-vis Europe. Ukraine, Moldova, Azerbaijan, Belarus, and Kazakhstan have moved to form armed forces of their own, thereby disrupting whatever cohesiveness could be expected of a unified CIS force reconstruction. A potentially explosive dispute has erupted between Russia and Ukraine over control of military capabilities, including the Black Sea Fleet. Azerbaijan, virtually at war already with Armenia, has taken over some CIS armaments and equipment on its territory. Moldova has been doing the same to restore internal stability by force. Moves by Ukraine to assert full-fledged military sovereignty have raised questions about the impact on the overall force balances across Europe. As the former union's second most populous republic, Ukraine has been home to roughly 1.5 million troops and 6,000 tanks. In its newly formed national army, Ukraine already has over 400,000 troops, more than most other countries in Europe.

The Russian leadership has pushed hard to hold as much of the former Soviet armed forces together as possible under a unified command. With a Russian in charge of the CIS forces, this would postpone the changes Russia would have to make in its military posture. It is still hoped that the Commonwealth command would evolve into an alliance similar to NATO, which would ensure the security of Russia and other CIS members. Yet the geopolitical situation of Commonwealth states being different, odds are that most if not all of them would opt for their own armies.

Under such circumstances, Russia is hard pressed to draft a military doctrine and create an army of its own. Russian civilian and military leaders envision their country's new armed forces in a strictly defensive posture, devoid of any intention to project its influence to distant regions and free of any claim to superpower parity with the US. They suggest Russia's total armed forces should be scaled down to less than one-third of the 3.7 million troops maintained by the former Soviet Union.

These developments, of course, have a direct bearing on European security. Apart from the vexing problems of force structures and deployments, much depends on the implementation of the CFE treaty, the backbone of European arms control.

The former Soviet republics with territory in the treaty's area of application (Armenia, Azerbaijan, Belarus, Estonia, Georgia, Latvia, Lithuania, Moldova, Russia, and Ukraine) have agreed to join the CFE regime from the Atlantic to the Urals without requiring any modification of its provisions. The main challenge was to divide the treaty-limited equipment (TLE) that the Soviet Union had been permitted to keep so as to ensure that the independent states keep their combined forces within the formerly Soviet share of the CFE treaty's various ceilings. The success of the negotiations was connected to the issue of what kind of military establishments the new states plan for themselves.

However, the most difficult obstacle for the independent states was undoubtedly the geographic disposition of TLE deployments. The boundaries for the treaty's zones are defined in terms of the old Soviet military districts. This implies that the new states must be lumped together. As it happens, the "Flanks" zone is especially complicated: it includes four military districts in the territory of Armenia, Azerbaijan, Georgia, Moldova, and portions of Russia and Ukraine. (Bulgaria and Romania, former Warsaw Pact allies, are also included in the "Flanks" zone.) The treaty's tank, artillery, armored combat vehicle, armored infantry fighting vehicle, combat aircraft, and other entitlement for this zone are very low because they reflected the realities of the bloc-to-bloc confrontation. The Soviet military accepted these limits on the assumption that they would always have the option of moving forces from the center of the country. Now six independent states are compelled to fit themselves into the framework of a treaty designed under the rubric of East-West standoff and agree on a permanent balance of reduced forces (while two of them, Armenia and Azerbaijan, have been at war).

Russia and Ukraine may face additional difficulties with some of the treaty's other zonal limits. The CFE accord sets ceilings for three concentric rings, as a means of pushing forces away from the Cold War's old central front. The forces in the inner rings are included within the ceilings of the outer rings. If the whole quota of an inner ring is used, fewer forces will be allowed in the outer ones. But the second ring is comprised mostly of Ukrainian territory and the outermost ring is entirely Russian territory. Consequently, the levels permitted within Russia will depend directly on the quota to be assumed by Ukraine. So far, the Russian government has not indicated whether it will be sensitive about how many forces remain on Russian territory.

Although the independent states have not requested any revisions in the CFE arrangements and have promised to restructure and redeploy their forces within the treaty's confines, it is doubtful that they have yet fully comprehended what is actually involved in such commitments. Even without enormous political-military differences, the costs and complexities of destroying equipment will present serious difficulties. Extending the deadline for carrying out the reductions may be necessary. At

167

any rate, the West's active cooperation is imperative to help guide the complex process of ratification and implementation of the CFE treaty (as agreed, with some updating but without renegotiation) within the new requirements of European security.

An Emerging Security Architecture

Since the end of the Soviet Union, Russia and the other independent states, though deeply submerged in internal turmoil, have nevertheless been moving to intensify their participation in the dynamic political affairs of a post-Cold War Europe. Moreover, they have been in the midst of a thorough conceptual reappraisal of their approaches to the various European security institutions and structures. Their attention also has been drawn to ways in which these institutions and structures can effectively interact in creating a new system of cooperative security vitally needed for them and their partners in Europe. Indeed, the former republics' immediate concern, out of urgent necessity, has been focused on what should be done collectively to avoid a social and political explosion, which could confront them with a new array of challenges to their own security and inevitably to the common security of Europe and the world community.

Despite overwhelming domestic difficulties, democratic leaders of Russia and other new states have consolidated their positions to an extent that enables them to contemplate changes in the European security system unthinkable even one year ago. They have become convinced that the challenges they are facing on the home front and in Europe cannot be comprehensively addressed by one institution alone, but only in a framework of interlocking institutions tying together all European and North American nations. Consequently, the CIS states' attitudes have been reoriented from a predominant fixation on the CSCE, as the key element of European security, towards a wider range of dynamics in Europe's politics.

While engaging the people in even more vigorous participation in the so-called Helsinki process, Russian and other democratic leaders now envision a new European security architecture in which the CSCE interacts with NATO, the European Community, the Western European Union, the Council of Europe, and other institutions formerly associated with "the opposite side." Regional frameworks and bilateral relationships are also seen as important. This broad interaction across the board of European institutions is considered to be of greatest significance in preventing instability and divisions that could result from various causes, such as economic disparities, social unrest, or violent nationalism.

One novelty in these revised approaches to the problems of European security is the fact that they clearly signify a drastic departure from a great power's usual desire to chart Europe's future. Gone from these approaches are "grand designs" or all-embracing programs. Rather, pragmatism and realism are the new features of Russia's policy and that of other independent states with regard to Europe.

Another specific feature is the lack of cohesiveness and uniformity in dealing with the different European institutions. The Commonwealth mechanism, barely capable of coping with control over nuclear weaponry, can do very little by way of coordinating the independent states' activities along these lines. Although the most influential (and the most experienced) state in European affairs, Russia is not in a position to play a unifying role. In fact, a great deal of competition or even rivalry is involved in the currently expanding (and often chaotic) ties of the new sovereign states with a wide range of European institutions.

Such a phenomenon is not entirely negative; its silver lining is that it stimulates involvement in European politics based on democratic values, which in itself is helpful for those independent states whose political experience over decades has been determined by clearly undemocratic standards. It should also be admitted that in their race for Western recognition the new states are tempted to indulge in some sort of competitive posturing related to their domestic politics or the unsettled relationships between them. A typical case is that of Russia and Ukraine, both trying to "mend fences" in Europe to strengthen their respective stands in their strained bilateral relations. Yet the thrust of pro-Europe efforts by the newly independent nations is definitely positive. Its net result can be of significant assistance to the establishment of a multidimensional system of European security.

There is renewed interest among practically all ex-Soviet republics in the process led by the CSCE, especially in light of the decisions taken at its Paris summit in 1990, which have opened up a variety of overarching institutional arrangements in the fields of political and military security. A convincing consensus of opinion in the former USSR in favor of further active involvement in the CSCE has been reflected in the almost unanimous application for membership by the new states.

It is of the utmost importance, both for the independent states and for Europe, that with the admission of Asian as well as European countries into the CSCE one more division has been overcome--that of geography, which in the case of Eurasian indivisibility has always been artificial. Now with the new Asian states in, it is to be expected that theirs will be a fresh, constructive input into European politics. Conversely, and perhaps more importantly, the impact of European democratic values and procedures on these states will certainly be highly beneficial, particularly in such matters as human rights. This, naturally, is one issue on which most Central Asian republics remain rather reticent--generally due to their less than perfect human rights records and persistent undemocratic practices. Nor is this attitude confined to the Asian states. Democracy still does not enjoy a sufficiently stable status in some of the European republics either, including Russia itself.

Specific interests of the independent states in the CSCE vary widely in emphasis but have much in common when it comes to substance. Russia, Ukraine, and Belarus seem to be especially keen on participation in the CSCE summitry and the ministerial meetings proposed by the Paris summit. Most of the states favor the creation of a CSCE parliamentary assembly (an "Assembly of Europe"), possibly based on the Parliamentary Assembly of the Council of Europe. Russia and many other states are interested in the work of the Conflict Prevention Center (CPC) in Vienna as well as the framework of the new confidence- and security-building measures, mechanisms used for consultation and cooperation regarding unusual military activities and to create a communications network for transmission of messages relating to agreed measures. The Paris summit's establishment of an Office for Free Elections in Warsaw has caused mixed reaction, however, particularly in the Central Asian republics.

Looking beyond this list of the well-known proposals, some diplomats and experts in Russia suggest the creation of an All-European Security Council, which would combine the security-related functions of the entire range of the present European and Atlantic institutions, including the CSCE, NATO, and the European Community. They also think in terms of establishing a set of permanent "security forums" under CSCE auspices to address such issues as arms control to follow through on the agenda of the CFE IA and CSBM talks; "information dialogue" on new possible transparency measures to open up budget and force planning data to international (and, in the case of the post-USSR republics, also to domestic) scrutiny; nonproliferation and regulations on export control; and regional arms control and military deployments, sponsoring talks between and among neighbors (a burning issue for some Commonwealth and non-Commonwealth countries, particularly Latvia, Lithuania, and Estonia, as well as for the biggest military powers of the CIS -Russia and Ukraine). Other cooperative measures are urged, such as more regular liaison between military officers and "operational" arms control regimes that would govern the readiness level of forces.

However, it would be asking too much, and too soon, to expect the newly formed sovereign states (most of them with very little knowledge about the outside world and its international institutions) to direct their undivided attention towards the CSCE's longer-range problems. Considering the current crisis-level conditions in most republics, it is only natural for them to concentrate on internal issues of utter urgency and seek outside assistance in settling them as the necessary prerequisite for further activities. Hence their preoccupation with the possibility of engaging the CSCE and other European institutions in peacekeeping missions inside the troubled areas of their own relationships, such as Europe's fiercest civil war in Nagorno-Karabakh.

Involvement in this specific case is seen by many in the newly independent states as a promising pattern of things to come from Europe in the form of political mediation and, if need be, military peacekeeping. Although a great deal of national and local patriotic resentment necessarily accompanies such external intrusions, both Armenia and Azerbaijan, hopelessly submerged in a protracted shooting war, have welcomed what may develop as an effective exercise in joint peacemaking, with the CSCE, NATO, and the European Community pooling their political (and potentially military) resources to put an end to this bloody conflict, which neither the Commonwealth nor Russia and Kazakhstan have been able to resolve.

NATO, formerly the main antagonist to the now defunct Soviet empire, has been increasingly perceived by Russia and the other independent states as their natural partner and eventually even an ally in a post-confrontation Europe. They have noted with satisfaction the Alliance's profound transformation as tremendous changes swept the global and European security environment. They have welcomed NATO's readiness to extend the hand of friendship and establish regular diplomatic liaisons, as well as its enhanced commitment to the CSCE. High-level visits, exchanges of views on security and other related issues, intensified military contacts, and exchanges of expertise in various fields have demonstrated the value of such dialogue and contributed greatly to building a cooperative relationship between NATO and the ex-Soviet republics. This is a dynamic process: the growth of democracy throughout Eastern Europe and the former USSR, as well as the desire of these countries for closer ties, now calls for relationships to be broadened, intensified, and raised to a qualitatively new level.

Russia has been the first to break the ice, perhaps somewhat awkwardly, by indicating its willingness to join NATO. The Alliance has been noncommittal from the outset, suggesting that it may not be possible for Eurasian Russia's armed forces to be integrated into NATO's military structures, which are strictly defined by the North Atlantic Treaty's geopolitical confines. Of course, mutual adjustment by former enemies to the radically changed situation will require patience and circumspection. As subsequent events have taken an evolutionary course, the former Soviet republics and the Alliance have developed some flexible models for a growing partnership without prejudice to respective institutional constraints. A new security body has been set up, the North Atlantic Cooperation Council, which has brought together the 16 NATO nations, five East European countries, three Baltic states, and 11 members of the CIS.

With the institutional relationship of consultation and cooperation established, Russia and other independent nations, together with NATO and other European institutions and, of course, the United Nations, are ready to define further the modalities and content of this process. In particular, there are suggestions relative to the establishment of regular contacts with the Military Committee of the Alliance. Consultations and cooperation should focus on security and related issues such as defense planning, democratic concepts of civilian-military relations, civil-military coordination of air traffic management, and the redirection of military production to civilian purposes. It is also urged that the military help overcome the divisions of the past, not least through intensified military contacts and greater military transparency.

The newly independent states are clearly interested in NATO's activities towards cooperating with all countries in Europe on the basis of the principles set out in the Charter of Paris for a New Europe. Together they should seek to develop broader and more productive patterns of bilateral and multilateral cooperation in all relevant fields of European security, with the primary aim of preventing crises or, should they arise, ensuring effective management at an early stage. Of particular importance should be NATO's contribution to the strengthening of the means available for the Conflict Prevention Center in Vienna to fulfill the specific tasks entrusted to it by the Paris Charter and assigned to it by the CSCE Council.

Again, as in similar cases with other European institutions, the most urgent need is for the Atlantic Alliance to be invited as peacemaker by warring states in the former Soviet Union. NATO is believed by many to be particularly effective in such a role, given its military credibility.

There is a considerable degree of flexibility involved in the emerging military-political relationships across Europe. Obviously uncomfortable within the CIS framework, Ukraine, for example, is seeking a military alliance with Hungary, which in turn is believed to be working with Poland and Czechoslovakia towards a Central European defense "triangle."

The European Community, a powerful economic magnet for Eastern Europe and the former Soviet republics, now is seen by them also as another pillar of European security. The states welcome the prospect of the European political union, which will reinforce the development of a European security identity, in particular through the strengthening of the Western European Union. They are no longer alarmed by the growing cooperation among the Atlantic Alliance and the emerging military component of the European integration process, because such developments contribute to overall stability in Europe. This serves the national interests of the newly independent states.

Realistically, it will be a long time before these states

fulfill conditions for EC membership (although Kazakhstan has already announced its intention to join the Community). With Nordic and East European countries queuing up to enter a Community that is already unwieldy with its current 12 members, it would be extremely difficult for all ex-Soviet republics, not excluding the Baltics, to prove preferential eligibility.

At the same time, there is ample room for economic and political cooperation with the EC short of full membership. Russia, Ukraine, Belarus, and the Baltic states consider themselves to be within an "inner circle" of those physically nearer Brussels and with sufficient levels of economic and political development. Latvia, Lithuania, and Estonia may be offered association accords with the EC similar to those it has signed with Poland, Czechoslovakia, and Hungary. The three Baltic states also hope to strengthen their ties with the EC through their membership in the newly created Council of Baltic Sea States. Countries in "outer rings," such as Azerbaijan, Uzbekistan, and Kazakhstan, intend to gain indirect access to the EC through cooperation with Turkey.

As far as specifics of European security are concerned, the new independent states primarily consider the EC a unique, politically influential force capable of effective peace efforts. Appropriate links and consultation procedures between the Twelve and the WEU and the Atlantic Alliance will undoubtedly be developed to enable them to be collectively prepared for crisis management and conflict prevention in a new Europe, which now includes a vast unstable area within the boundaries of the former Soviet Union.

The stakes are enormous. If Russia, Ukraine, and other Commonwealth states make the transition to a new political and economic system, the next century is likely to be marked by peace and prosperity. If they fail, Europe and the entire world will have to face unpredictable threats to security. Unfortunately, all the elements are currently building up to an outcome that would eliminate the very assumptions underpinning the common desire for a Europe whole and free. A disastrous economic situation may not be reparable in time to avoid total social and political collapse. Continuing differences within the CIS are being exacerbated by the absence of a tradition of either democracy or free enterprises, weak governing institutions, divisions within the military, ethnic conflicts, strikes, and stoppages. Psychologically, the atmosphere is being polluted with persistent totalitarian ideology, popular resentments, xenophobia, and nostalgia for the lost empire.

The possibility, indeed the probability, of failure of the democratic experiment cannot be wished away. There is real danger that a destructive dictatorship will seize power to restore the old regime and again intimidate Europe and the free world. This might provoke a civil war or reverse the process of democratization in Eastern Europe. It could even precipitate a nuclear conflagration with unpredictable consequences for all of humanity.

Nonetheless, despite the potential calamities, the current trend of events provides grounds for cautious optimism. If democracy matures in Russia and other key states of the Commonwealth, there is every possibility that these countries will be forces for peace and stability in Europe and beyond. This is where the emerging cooperation between the new independent states, Europe, and North America may make a difference. Each region can join in a community based on shared values of freedom, democracy, human rights, market economics, and the rule of law. It is likely that uncertainties will be faced for over a decade or longer. But these are inevitable--the price of victory over the Cold War. The change from the past and the promise of the future make this a price worth paying.

7
New Democracies in East Central Europe: Expectations for the EC and the CSCE

Andrej Cima

Introduction

The Conference on Security and Cooperation in Europe, as well as other European and transatlantic institutions, operates today in a profoundly changed environment. The changes are still under way and some have resulted in fierce armed conflicts. It is therefore too early to develop coherent ideas and suggestions as to how international organizations and institutions should act in order to meet the new challenges. One may, however, define basic areas where common action is required. It should be pointed out that the CSCE, the EC, and other institutions are not waiting passively for new strategies to be developed, and in many respects they have already started refocusing their activities. What they are doing should be carefully studied so that optimal policies can be identified and implemented.

With the end of the Cold War, both parts of Europe rejoiced that the external threat to their security had disappeared. But the continent's central and eastern parts soon discovered that internal threats had replaced the external ones. The concepts of security and national interest had to be substantially reconsidered and revised. In the late 1980s, when deep political changes were about to occur in East Central Europe (ECE), most of the countries of the region were members of the WTO and the CSCE. Membership in the former organization was in a way imposed by historical circumstances, and analyzing the pros and cons of participation in the WTO is senseless. The CSCE, as an institution heralding new norms of relations between the states of Europe, was of much livelier interest for both the political leadership and the general public.

This attitude has been reversed in the past. Politicians who supported the signature of the Helsinki Final Act were content that the postwar borders in Europe were recognized, and through that recognition, at least in their opinion, so was the political division of Europe. Some were unhappy with the "concessions" to the West in the field of human rights, but finally they accepted that, as the price for maintaining the political status quo in Europe, these concessions were not so important. The general public was, on the contrary, happy about the commitments of their governments in the area of human rights but was afraid that the "first basket" of the Helsinki Final Act provisions would petrify the Soviet sphere of influence in East Central Europe.

At the same time, a powerful, vibrant integration was gaining force in the vicinity. The EC, which in the past was often described in the official East European press as an arena of conflict and competition, was clearly better off than the Moscow-based Council for Mutual Economic Assistance (CMEA), which its economically more developed participants resented as a forum for one-way assistance they were supposed to provide to the less advanced members. The proclaimed goal of gradually evening the levels of all CMEA members was a frightening prospect for officials in Berlin, Prague, and Budapest.

When the EC agreed in 1986 to open internal borders and

establish one market by 1992, even official sources in Eastern Europe and the Soviet Union could not deny that West European integration was making significant progress. However, while some CMEA states bordered the EC, CMEA and the EC seemed so politically distant and inaccessible that no economists in East Central Europe were seriously studying the possibilities and consequences of eventually joining the EC.

There was also the North Atlantic Treaty Organization. In the course of more than three decades, it was portrayed as an aggressive organization, and the psychological barrier was too deep even for shrewd politicians to think of the East Central European countries seeking security within NATO ranks. This barrier was obviously working on both sides; it was thus no wonder that the first Hungarian "coquetries" about joining NATO stirred bewilderment in Brussels as well as among beleaguered WTO generals.

When by the autumn of 1989 Hungary decisively joined Poland on its way towards political pluralism, and the flow of citizens from the German Democratic Republic streamed through Hungary and Czechoslovakia to the FRG, the scene was set for the radical political changes that ensued with unexpected rapidity. A completely new situation was created in intra-European relations, and the political environment in which the CSCE, the EC, and other European and transatlantic institutions operated was profoundly changed.

The successes of the first months were spectacular. Virtually within weeks or months, the ECE countries managed to organize fully democratic elections based on a multiparty system. This was a period of decisive internal change, and amid the euphoria the construction of "new democracies" was launched. However, it takes time to create a working market economy and longer still for the benefits to be widely felt. The early stages of the road to democracy were hampered by a number of domestic problems, but also by difficulties caused by external developments. Soon it became obvious that the transition required adequate international support.

The CSCE, especially in view of its human dimension, was immediately "accepted" by the new political leaders, but there were well-founded doubts about whether it could be an appropriate framework for new security arrangements.

There was no time for a thorough analysis in the dynamically changing situation. The negotiations on the withdrawal of Soviet troops stationed in Eastern Europe and on the gradual dismantling of the WTO were launched, and it was only during this process that the first serious considerations were given to the question of how the security of the new democracies could best be ensured in the changing Europe.

The CSCE and Changes in Europe

The new generation of politicians and security experts in the ECE countries tried to approach the security needs of their countries with open minds, free of any prejudice. When it became obvious that the WTO was seen not as a security framework but rather as a menace to the sovereignty even of its participants, the possibility of joining NATO was, as mentioned above, explored unsuccessfully. Ideas to establish regional or subregional security organizations or buffer zones were considered. Security was also seen as related to regional economic cooperation and integration, e.g., within the Pentagonale (later Hexagonale).

Not having any reliable security framework at hand, the ECE countries had to concentrate on bilateral relations, on building security networks through new treaties with neighbors and through closer cooperation with individual NATO member states.

On the multilateral level it soon became obvious that there was no better framework than the CSCE, albeit in its form at that time it was far from being in a position to offer its participants any tangible security guarantees. The Helsinki process moved forward slowly under a regular schedule, in "waves" topped by follow-up meetings every two or three years, each of which usually went on for a year or two, so it was difficult to come to any agreements on new recommendations. This working scheme needed to be changed in order to give the CSCE the ability to react more quickly to new requirements.

The ECE countries sought an accelerated schedule and started to demand the deeper institutionalization of the CSCE, which, in view of many, acted like a "circus," moving its follow-up meetings from one town to another without having a single permanent organ. This was the background that led to the decision to convene an extraordinary CSCE summit in Paris in November 1990.

During the preparations for the Paris summit, a number of new, sometimes bold proposals were advanced. Some of them inadvertently had a double effect, like the Czechoslovak proposal to establish a European Security Commission, which had been advanced at the meeting of the WTO foreign ministers in March 1990 in Prague. This proposal could be seen as aimed at both weakening the security or military dimension of the WTO and establishing a new security body with full CSCE participation regardless of military bloc affiliations.

Though it was not accepted, this proposal was very useful, since reactions to it were extremely instructive. After decades of prepared, sterile debates at WTO high-level meetings, it prompted Soviet Foreign Minister Eduard Shevardnadze and other foreign ministers to pick up their pencils and start drafting on the spot. Poland had earlier advanced a similar proposal at the prime minister level, but the Soviets were obviously still not prepared to accept a non-bloc approach to security. The proposal, however, turned out to be very appealing to all the other WTO member states, and it accelerated the debate that ultimately led to the dismantling of the WTO.

The intention to seek security not through military blocs but rather through cooperation on a democratic, all-European basis was communicated also to NATO officials. Their answers, which unanimously ended in insisting that "NATO must exist," revealed to the supporters of the proposal even more than they had asked for. It was not proposed that NATO be dismantled in the near future, but NATO officials and high-level supporters responded as if that were the case. Thus, the architects of the new collective, or rather cooperative, security arrangements were told from the beginning that the bloc approach to security may be considered finished, but one military alliance was not yet ready to dissolve.

The lesson was learned quickly. The calls for the replacement of the military blocs by a collective security system were replaced by suggestions that NATO should modify and adjust to present needs. Still later, some political representatives of the ECE countries went to Brussels and inquired about the possibility of their countries being admitted to NATO.

It should be noted that at this early stage, when the new democracies were impatient to join any organization in Western Europe, be it NATO or the EC, most of the organizations' member states explained to East European officials on all possible levels that they simply could not be admitted because, especially in the case of the EC, they were not yet ready, that they would be "sucked in" and exploited by the huge EC market.

Finally, the East Central European countries had no choice other than to seek a multilateral security framework within the CSCE, because it is the only organization that embraces all European countries and that also has an Atlantic dimension. Efforts by a number of countries from East and West focused on preparing numerous steps aimed at strengthening the institutionalization of the CSCE process. The Paris summit, though criticized as another bombastic gathering that would bring little practical benefit, was important because it established a number of permanent institutions that the CSCE had previously lacked. Regular yearly meetings by the Council of Foreign Ministers were institutionalized, as were the meetings of the Committee of Senior Officials in Prague and the Conflict Prevention Center in Vienna. The Office for Free Elections, recently renamed the Office for Democratic Institutions and Human Rights, was established in Warsaw. The permanent Secretariat of the CSCE was installed in Prague; envisaged as a relatively small administrative unit, it has done a marvelous job preparing the meetings of individual bodies within the CSCE and ensuring communications and sharing of information among CSCE participants between official meetings.

Another important change introduced after the Paris summit was the chairmanship of the CSCE, which goes to the country that organized the meeting of the Council of Ministers. After the council meeting in Berlin in June 1991, it was German Foreign Minister Hans-Dietrich Genscher who acted as the chairman-in-office of the CSCE until the end of January 1992, when the chairmanship was assumed by CSFR Foreign Minister

Jiří Dienstbier. This rotating function cannot be seen as comparable, to the post of UN Secretary General, for example, or to directors of other international organizations. It is unclear to what extent the chairman-in-office can represent the CSCE in strictly legal terms. But it is quite obvious that the creation of this post strengthened the CSCE capacity for action and promoted continuity in its functioning.

If one compares the skeptics' low expectations for the Paris summit meeting with the present state of affairs, the results are more than surprising. The new CSCE institutions were barely established when they had to be put into action. The escalating Yugoslav conflict provided the first opportunity.

Austria initiated the convening of the Consultative Committee of the Conflict Prevention Center under the provision of the 1990 Vienna Document on unusual military activity. This was immediately followed by a succession of meetings of the Committee of Senior Officials in Prague under the agreed "emergency mechanism." Apparently, none of these meetings tangibly influenced the developments in Yugoslavia. Neither CSCE nor EC efforts could prevent what was already under way --the disintegration of a CSCE participating state for a variety of political, historical, ethnic, and economic reasons. It was often pointed out that the CSCE could try to deal with disputes between sovereign states, but it could not prevent or control a crisis situation like that in Yugoslavia.

However, the CSCE was for the first time involved. Yugoslav representatives repeatedly travelled to Prague, where they reiterated the positions of officials in Belgrade and answered questions. Foreign Minister Genscher acted not only in the name of the EC but also on behalf of the CSCE. In all these diplomatic maneuvers on Yugoslavia, it appeared that the CSCE had one obvious advantage compared to other institutions--Yugoslavia itself, as well as other ECE countries, including the USSR, were directly represented. That universality of the CSCE can be seen as its indisputable advantage compared to NATO or the EC.

The widest possible representation is an important asset of the CSCE if one believes security in Europe is indivisible. Moreover, the new democracies were increasingly encountering economic difficulties, and their officials warned that the former political and military "iron curtain" should not be replaced by an economic division of Europe into "haves and have nots." Thus, security had to be perceived and treated through a wider basket, where economic, social, and ethnic problems would not be seen as secondary.

Since the EC, NATO, and the WEU are all limited in membership, it was only natural that gradually those institutions became more and more interested in the activities of the CSCE. This interest was generally welcomed, though occasionally their presence at CSCE-sponsored conferences became a controversial issue. For instance, when the second CSCE seminar on military doctrine was organized in Vienna in the fall of 1991, the US insisted that NATO be represented at the seminar by its staff in Brussels. France and some other NATO member states objected, arguing that NATO was sufficiently represented through its 16 member states in Vienna.

NATO was not represented separately at that meeting, but from then on the participation of "other institutions" at CSCE gatherings has become an issue. To a large extent, that is apparently caused by procedural or protocol reasons, but in some cases the US-supported presence of NATO has become a real political problem. For instance, when a seminar on military conversion was organized in Bratislava in February 1992 under the auspices of the CSCE, the final decision on the seminar was blocked for about two months because of disputes about the relevance of NATO expertise, cited in support of NATO's participation.

It· may be paradoxical to see multilateral institutions competing in not very friendly ways, when defense conversion, for example--a problem whose solution depends on ECE countries receiving exceptionally well coordinated aid--is being discussed. Greater coordination of aid seems to be one of the essential preconditions for rendering aid efficiently.

While the CSCE "hawks" were still surprised by the unexpected interest displayed by other organizations in their activities, the events that followed the aborted coup in Moscow pushed the Helsinki process even further to the forefront. New independent states were appearing on the territory of the former Soviet Union, and it was considered useful to keep them within the CSCE framework.

It was still not clear whether Ukraine and other possible future participants would be admitted before the Prague meeting of the CSCE Council of Ministers at the end of January 1992. In the meantime, conflicts developed in Georgia and flared again in Nagorno-Karabakh and in Moldova, and uneasy neighborly relations prevailed between the former Soviet republics, especially between Ukraine and Russia. There was more than one reason to believe that, in addition to Yugoslavia, a variety of conflicts could soon be at hand elsewhere in the original Helsinki process area.

Taking into account the consequences of the crisis in Yugoslavia, and perhaps motivated by a number of other political considerations, the CSCE was persuaded to act quickly; on January 30, 1992, all former Soviet republics, in addition to the three Baltic states but still without Georgia, were admitted as CSCE participating states. The process happened so quickly that some of the new participants had difficulty preparing their request for admission properly, and indeed, some did not make it in time. It is an important fact that while in principle the CSCE territory remained the same, the problems of various regions, especially in Asia, will be much more present at the CSCE through the new local governments than they were through the former central government in Moscow. The long-term consequences of that decision remain to be seen.

With the ten new countries, to which Georgia, Slovenia, and Croatia were added in March 1992, the CSCE became a somewhat extraordinary regional organization covering three continents with far from homogeneous participants, from the developed Western countries through new postcommunist democracies to the literally developing states with deep economic and social problems. Before it is clear how the CSCE can influence developments in its new participating states, it appears that the developments in these states have already influenced the CSCE's procedural functions.

The first fact-finding mission to Albania was followed by similar missions to other new participants. A number of countries responded positively, offering planes and other services because the CSCE could not cover the expenses for the seven or eight missions.

But in some cases the original fact-finding venture was clearly insufficient, and it was necessary to send two additional missions, aimed at mediation, to Nagorno-Karabakh. The mission by Foreign Minister Dienstbier in late March and early April 1992 resulted in the decision to dispatch advance teams and monitors to the area of conflict. Still earlier, the ministers had decided in

Helsinki to convene a conference on Nagorno-Karabakh.

It may be concluded that the CSCE is about to embark on new practices that may eventually lead to a kind of enhanced monitoring or peacekeeping operation, either in cooperation with the UN or on its own. This policy is still far from being accepted by all the participants. The monitor missions as well as the conference on Nagorno-Karabakh will be financed predominantly by their participants. But it may be reasonably expected that these types of activities, on a wider or narrower scale, will gradually become part and parcel of routine CSCE practice.

Many of the East Central European countries were somewhat taken aback by such a rapid development of events. If they had had more time for consideration, some would probably have voiced their concerns about adopting all the former Soviet republics at the same time, since this may limit the CSCE's potential for action, especially in conflict prevention and crisis management. It may be argued that the republics with armed conflicts on their territory can hardly guarantee the fulfillment of all the CSCE commitments, particularly in the field of human rights.

Besides, any modest benefits that people in East Central Europe may have expected from cooperation within the CSCE will now have to be shared with new members whose needs are obviously more urgent. But there was no time to consider all this in depth, since many CSCE participants were very much interested in ensuring that democratic development prevailed in the former Soviet republics. The interest in getting the new states "on board" was evident, and during the Prague meeting there was no open opposition to that. All accepted that it was less risky to invite these countries to the CSCE and to exert all necessary effort to incorporate them into the system described in the Paris

Charter for a New Europe than to let them remain exposed to local conflicts or possible hostile religious or ethnic influence.

A somewhat similar process occurred when the former WTO member states were invited to cooperate closely with NATO member states through the new North Atlantic Cooperation Council (NACC), established at the NATO ministerial meeting in Rome in late autumn of 1991. The new independent republics were later invited to participate in what was informally described as the "second NATO." The establishment of the NACC was perhaps necessary to strengthen the pressure on the former Soviet republics to respect the spirit and letter of the disarmament treaties and regimes agreed in Vienna, which seemed directly threatened after the collapse of the USSR. It would have been more diplomatic to consult the nonaligned and neutral countries and prepare them for the creation of an institution described by some as the symbol of preservation of the bloc approach to security issues. Perhaps there was no time to do so; keeping disarmament treaties alive was more important than diplomatic subtleties. Overall, only a couple of representatives of those "left outside" displayed their disdain. The prevailing reaction was a stoic reply that an eventual invitation to participate in the NACC would be contrary to the neutral status some countries still cherished.

The Helsinki Follow-Up Meeting is now engaged in a debate that should determine the future activities of the CSCE in the areas of conflict prevention and crisis management. Perhaps there is no need to profoundly change the institutional framework established by the Paris Charter. What is required is a better coordination and division of labor in the activities of individual CSCE institutions. If the negotiators in Helsinki cannot prepare well-balanced proposals for the July 1992 summit, it can

191

hardly be expected that the CSCE will be in a position to coordinate or supplement its actions in this field with other relevant organizations. And it may be taken for granted that East Central Europe, which seems to be transforming itself into a theater of conflicts and rivalries, has no doubts about the need for the key European and transatlantic organizations to act in a more coordinated way.

East Central Europe and the Security Dimension of the CSCE

After 1989, negotiations on conventional disarmament in Europe moved from the "closed club" of the endless and completely unsuccessful MBFR (Mutual and Balanced Force Reduction) talks with limited participation to a full-scale NATO and WTO negotiation under CSCE auspices, thus joining the all-European forum on confidence- and security-building measures (CSBMs).

During the Vienna Review Meeting, many officials from East Central Europe already preferred the convening of a single disarmament forum with full CSCE participation. As a compromise, it was agreed that NATO and the WTO member states would first agree on the reduction of their conventional armed forces while further CSBMs would be agreed by all CSCE participants. A new all-European disarmament and security forum would be convened afterwards.

The established plan worked remarkably well. In spite of the progressive disintegration of the USSR, or perhaps thanks to it, the Treaty on Conventional Armed Forces in Europe (CFE) was agreed to with unprecedented speed, and was signed in 1990 at the Paris summit. The final stages of its negotiation provided a serious test for the WTO group of states, who had to distribute among themselves the so-called national levels of holdings in five key categories of conventional weapons (tanks, artillery, APCs, aircraft, and helicopters), while knowing that the WTO would soon be dismantled and that they might then perceive one another as uneasy neighbors if not potential adversaries. Meetings of the WTO special commission for disarmament were repeatedly convened in Bratislava and Prague, since Czechoslovakia was acting, in accordance with the principle of rotation, as the last WTO coordinator. In the meantime, NATO member states managed to distribute their quota quietly at special group meetings in Brussels.

The prolonged negotiations were extremely tense, and the final compromise achieved in Budapest left unclear the issue of the number of weapons that individual countries had to place in permanent storage. The East Central European countries refused the relevant commitment, since, in their view, permanent storage sites were originally envisaged for US and Soviet weaponry. All this can now be seen as a rehearsal for the similar exercise among the former Soviet republics. This agreement was finally signed at the CIS summit in Tashkent on May 15, 1992.

The way the CFE treaty was negotiated (at the final stage almost imposed on the majority of participants) and the "flexibility" of its implementation are unique examples of multilateral diplomacy. Many negotiators from East Central Europe were unhappy about the exercise and saw it as the continuation of the bipolarity in international relations.

Nevertheless, in the final account it was accepted that the CFE treaty was in the interest of a new Europe, and the treaty's entry into force, with all the possible drawbacks, was better than trying to renegotiate it or negotiate a new treaty. For the same reason the efforts by the newly established NACC to ensure the entry into force of the CFE treaty, even in the profoundly changed political environment, were basically accepted in spite of the fact that many thought the NACC was unduly replacing or supplementing the Vienna negotiating forum under CSCE auspices. Some officials from the former WTO countries also expressed dissatisfaction with the NACC because they were not treated as equal partners. Since that view is being expressed more and more often, it may be questioned whether the NACC will be in a position to play, in perspective, the role of a body that streamlines efforts towards arms control and disarmament, as originally intended.

The CFE treaty's entry into force is still not quite certain. However, if one can ignore the diplomatic and protocol missteps, it is obvious that there are no alternatives to this treaty. The limits on the weaponry imposed by the treaty still allow for bloody conflicts to be waged. The CFE treaty provides for a considerable decrease compared to the present levels of armed forces in Europe, and renders larger military operations unlikely. This is a considerable asset in today's unstable situation in some parts of Europe, and one has to believe that the responsible politicians in East Central Europe, those in power today as well as those who may be in control tomorrow, will not break the disarmament process, which, after years of protracted and sterile debates, has been so dynamically launched in Europe.

Extensive debate carried on so far on the mandate for the new, post-Helsinki all-European disarmament and security forum also confirmed that a vast majority of countries are sincerely interested in the continuation of all the positive security arrangements achieved over the past two years.

In the course of 1991 a protracted debate was under way in Vienna, and has continued in Helsinki, on the modalities of conflict prevention and crisis management. Often more attention was paid to which CSCE body was going to be responsible for something than to the efficiency and feasibility of proposed solutions. While this often repetitive debate was going on, the EC dispatched monitors to Yugoslavia, and the UN put together a peacekeeping force that is already deployed at locations where until recently fierce fighting was going on.

The case of Yugoslavia can hardly be seen realistically as a failure of the CSCE or any other organization. But the reactions to the Yugoslav crisis very visibly demonstrated again a point that was known anyway--that the CSCE ascribed to itself in the Paris Charter a number of functions in conflict prevention and crisis management that it was not sufficiently equipped to carry out. The relevant political conclusions will need to be made soon. While the UN is involved in peacekeeping in Yugoslavia, the CSCE is in the process of dispatching monitor teams to Nagorno-Karabakh. Needless to say, the conflict in the Caucasus may have a direct bearing on a number of UN member states who are not participants in the CSCE.

Certainly, problems need to be solved as they arise and according to their urgency. Both the UN involvement in Yugoslavia and an eventual CSCE presence in the Caucasus were reactions to crisis situations. However, in the future a question may be justifiably raised as to whether regional institutions would not be more appropriate for dealing with regional conflicts while the universal international organizations should be called in when there is the risk that a conflict may spill over into other regions. It may well happen that with the CSCE's meager resources spread thin through involvement in Nagorno-Karabakh, the UN would remain the only organization capable of action should the Moldova situation deteriorate, for example.

East Central Europe and the EC: Association or Membership?

Though East Central European officials on all levels had been constantly reminded that they were not prepared for admission to the EC, the more they listened to the warning the more fascinated they seemed to be by the prospect of getting as close as possible. It may be safely concluded that the motives were twofold--political as much as economic.

It is not surprising that after decades of one-sided orientation to the East, the sudden possibility of seriously exploring eventual membership in the EC was irresistible. There was no time for a serious and detailed study of the economic consequences of such a step. The EC was perceived as a symbol of West European integration, and the countries from "another Europe" quite understandably wanted to become part of such an integration. It was and still is regarded as the best guarantee against finding themselves again within an "unfortunate" part of Europe in case any future attempts to divide it were to succeed.

The negative and reserved position by some EC member states somewhat cooled the initial optimism, but never really undermined the determination of the East Central European countries to join the West European integration. They were encouraged by rapidly improving cooperation with individual West European countries and their admission to the Council of Europe. The interest in the EC was sustained and even further increased as the economic difficulties of the countries in transition to market economy were aggravated.

The insistence paid off. As a first step the EC concluded association agreements at the end of 1991 with Poland, Hungary, and Czechoslovakia, which should assist them in adapting their economies to the standards of the EC. These so-called European Agreements recognize the fact that the relevant countries' ultimate objective is to join the Community and that this association will help them achieve this objective. Article 1 refers to the need to provide an appropriate framework for these countries' gradual integration into the Community. Article 2 stipulates that economic rapprochement will lead to greater political convergence, and it also calls for the rapprochement of the parties' positions on security issues. The association agreements, the possibility of which has also been explored with Bulgaria and Romania, will serve as the centerpiece of the EC's relations with East Central Europe in the 1990s.

All this may greatly increase the popularity of West European integration among experts and the general public in East Central Europe. However, much more ambitious cooperation is required than simply easing mutual trade. And such cooperation cannot be seen as a kind of moral obligation of the more developed to aid the less fortunate. Americans know how to define problems in a pragmatic way. In mid-February Deputy Secretary of State Lawrence Eagleburger emphasized that the US is assisting East Central Europe as the region joins the democratic world. But the US does so primarily to support the well-being of its own people. The US cannot itself force the ECE countries to put their own houses in order. If the ECE countries cannot attract foreign investors, those investors will be directed elsewhere.

There is no reason to believe that the EC's approach would be less pragmatic than that described by Eagleburger. Maastricht, occasionally described as a boost for Europe, is willingly interpreted in East Central Europe as reflecting the recognition of the fact that economic stabilization and deep structural reform in the ECE countries is also in the interest of Europe as a whole.

The year 2000 is frequently mentioned as a possible date for the acceptance of some ECE countries into the EC. The president of the EC Commission, Jacques Delors, recently disagreed with French President François Mitterrand, who expressed the view that Poland, Hungary, and Czechoslovakia would have to wait decades before acceptance. Mr. Delors believes the "troika" could enter the EC at the beginning of the next century. Immediate entry would ruin them in spite of all gifts, subsidies, or exceptions they could be accorded.

The race for membership in the EC has undoubtedly been stimulated by global economic and political considerations. In the view of a number of political analysts, the space between Germany and Russia will either evolve into unstable territory, with small states engaged in quarrels over minorities and borders, or else, as a better alternative, a sort of regional Central European integration may develop either around the "troika" or on a wider scale, e.g., as the continuation of the Pentagonale/Hexagonale scheme.

The local strategists obviously hope for the more positive destiny. Too weak an integration would leave the states vulnerable to strong economic and/or political influence from the West, from the East, or from both. Since one cannot build capitalism without the necessary capital, investments into a smaller area of integration would undoubtedly tend to lead to the creation of spheres of economic, and thus also political, influence. Not that modern economic colonization would be something unthinkable or unheard of in the region. But the prospect of wider European integration, in which the EC remains the only efficient vehicle, is and will remain a much more attractive alternative not only for the "troika" in East Central Europe but also for countries like Bulgaria, Romania, Ukraine, the new states emerging from Yugoslavia, and with time also Russia, not to speak of the Baltic states.

But there are few reasons to believe that further accessions to the EC will unfold within a smooth, regular process. As Delors noted in early April 1992, the EC Commission is preparing a report for the Lisbon EC summit in June. The reports will contain a warning that further expansion of the EC will represent a "political, intellectual and institutional shock" for the EC membership. It will deal with the objective contradiction between the expansion of the EC and the further deepening of cooperation within its framework.

The general attraction of the EC is caused mainly by the successful pace at which it realizes its own ambitious schedule. The agreements achieved at the December 1991 Maastricht summit seem to be taken seriously, a fact that was confirmed by another meeting in Maastricht, this time of ministers for foreign affairs and finance, who signed the Treaty on European Union. On April 7, 1992, the European Parliament approved it and recommended its early ratification by the parliaments of the 12 EC countries. The treaty may thus enter into force in early 1993, opening the way to a further deepening of integration within the EC in the economic, monetary, and political areas. This is quite different from the situation in East Central Europe, where, at present, opposite tendencies prevail, with disintegration, conflicts over minorities, and declining economic performance at the top of the agenda.

All in all, the EC is now confronted with a dilemma--either it accepts only very limited expansion and continues to focus on further deepening of cooperation between its members, or it responds to the challenge of spreading the integration processes eastward. Undoubtedly, in some respects it may be easier to remain "in the smaller family"; on the other hand, the sooner the EC meets the challenge of incorporating postcommunist societies, the sooner it may opt for creating a huge, consolidated, continent-wide market capable of competing with any other economic center in the world.

As to present developments, it may be argued that the ECE countries should be more directly involved or associated with the mechanism of political consultations, which has been strengthened following the Maastricht summit. On the basis of article 2 of the association agreement, mutual dialogue on security issues, until now absent, should develop. In this connection the interest of East Central Europe in the WEU is increasing. The Maastricht agreement assigned the WEU the task of elaborating a common defense policy for the EC, in accordance with NATO member states' commitments. In view of the fact that the ECE countries' interest in accession to NATO has recently been considerably revived, the WEU (with its new security tasks, and for the first time formally tied to the EC) is further gaining in attractiveness, and observer status for the ECE countries will persistently be sought. Asymmetry in the rapprochement with the WEU will be favored by some ECE countries. And it should be clear that this interest in the WEU could only be strengthened by the concern that, through enhanced political and economic integration with the WEU as its security mechanism, the EC may ultimately be tempted by a concept of a "small Europe" rather than expansion.

A number of experienced politicians seem to have to come to a similar conclusion. Former German Foreign Minister Genscher had invited the WEU foreign ministers as well as the foreign ministers of the nine Central and East European countries to Mainz. The intention is to establish a consultative council for cooperation with the East Central European countries in the security field.

The EC can influence the situation in individual ECE countries more than it necessarily realizes or admits. For instance, it is well known that the representatives of some republics, forming at present part of federative states, interpret the tendency towards wider European integration as requiring the achievement of national sovereignty with eventual independence so that they can enter Europe as members entitled to full rights. It would be beneficial if EC officials succeeded in finding ways of explaining to the representatives of the regional or republican authorities in some ECE countries that the dismantling or atomization of internationally recognized states is not seen as improving anyone's chances of getting into the EC.

The EC can play a highly positive role in East Central Europe's efforts to achieve macroeconomic stabilization. The Community's readiness to hold a follow-up conference on assistance to the CIS later this spring is encouraging. Programs like PHARE, which has dispensed two billion ECUs during the three years of its existence, have great economic as well as political impact.

The year-old European Bank for Reconstruction and Development is another excellent example of how the ECE countries may be assisted in building the infrastructure for their democratic future. Besides direct economic assistance through loans and common projects, the EBRD sponsors educational programs for present and future political and economic officials. The EBRD also provides consultants to governments, universities, and other similar institutions who offer advice on privatization, solving ecological and energy problems, nuclear security, the development of freedom of the press, etc.

The involvement of the EBRD, together with the World Bank, in the process of the reform of the Russian banking system and agricultural sector is an example of assistance in specific areas that may, in the long run, prove decisive for maintaining the transition to a market economy. The reform processes in some East Central European countries may, in the foreseeable future, find themselves at a critical point at which timely and qualified assistance will be invaluable. Neither the EC, nor the EBRD, nor any other West European institution alone can solve the economic and social problems of the ECE countries and thus save democracy there. Philanthropic gestures are neither required nor feasible. What can be of tremendous importance, however, are the coordinated actions of West European institutions towards East Central Europe with the aim of making the rules that govern economic and political life in the region compatible with those in Western Europe. Thus, the means of economic and political support could be channelled effectively should democracy in the region be threatened.

This possibility seems remote as euphoria over the political changes still persists, though in considerably more modest forms. But for the time being there is no guarantee whatsoever that political leaders, either democratically elected or otherwise nominated, may not seek to find a solution to acute economic, political, or ethnic conflicts through nonconstitutional means. Yugoslavia is only too alarming an example of what is still possible in Europe.

Each of the West European or other regional institutions can influence developments in East Central Europe in its own way. While the CSCE can offer a wider political framework for cooperation, mainly in the security and humanitarian fields, the EC has the potential to gradually involve individual ECE countries in economic and political integration. The security aspects, which cannot be raised effectively in the CSCE, can in the near future be dealt with through NATO and its consultative mechanisms. This may prove useful, especially with regard to those countries that cannot consider joining the EC in the foreseeable future but whose security has a direct bearing on the general security situation in Europe.

And what would be the price of ensuring the readiness of Western Europe and the two transatlantic allies to undertake concerted actions aimed at assisting East Central Europe? That is hard to estimate, but the dividend would be enormous--Europe may eventually evolve into a region with no conflicts, with no significant flows of refugees, and with no need for monitors or peacekeepers to be dispatched into neighboring countries. Besides, members of the huge 320 million-strong EC market, already the largest in the world, may feel more comfortable in the vicinity of another large, high-absorption market, albeit in the beginning a somewhat nonhomogeneous and disorganized one, rather than representing an island of prosperity in a troubled continent.

Conclusion

Organizations like the CSCE, the EC, and other institutions play or may soon play important roles in both the domestic and foreign policy efforts of the countries of East

Central Europe. These countries have many common problems that stem mainly from the fact that they are trying to rebuild their societies on democratic values. At the same time, though, it would be a mistake to think that these countries form a homogeneous group.

While some have already established a solid basis for viable democratic institutions, others have not yet succeeded in setting up governments and parliaments through democratic procedures. It would be an illusion, or a gross miscalculation, to think that the postcommunist states will continue to form a group or a common category of states for a longer period.

Europe will have a better chance of becoming a continent of peace and cooperation, as it clearly wanted to become in 1975 when adopting the CSCE Final Act, if the activities of the international organizations do not overlap but rather complement each other. A flexible mechanism would be needed, perhaps regularly reviewing the main problems of coordination on the margins of the yearly meetings of the CSCE Council of Ministers. Operative contacts between the "troikas," acting within the CSCE and the EC with the chief executives of the other organizations, could be useful. The UN General Assembly sessions represent another suitable forum for the exchange of views on how the activity of the universal and regional organizations are contributing to promoting international peace and stability and what may be done in order to streamline their activities wherever appropriate.

Paradoxically enough, the present conflicts are forcing the CSCE participating states to take all the talks about security much more seriously than would have been the case under normal conditions. At the Helsinki Follow-Up Meeting, the mandate for a new all-European disarmament and security forum is being designed with a new, security-related permanent standing committee, which the CSCE lacked hitherto. The operative capability of the CSCE may also be further increased if proposals to establish smaller executive organs with more powers are accepted, e.g., the troika, consisting of the present, former, and future Chairmen-in-Office. Ad hoc steering committees may in future be established, consisting of five to ten countries, including the troika, depending on the questions to be discussed. Such steering committees could serve as central, decision-making CSCE bodies on urgent operative issues. The establishment of the functions of personal representatives of the Chairman-in-Office could also increase the operative capabilities of the CSCE.

On May 1, 1992, the Council of Ministers took a historic decision to establish a monitor mission in connection with the situation in and around Nagorno-Karabakh. However, until recently it was not capable of putting this decision into effect or to decide on when to convene its first ever peace conference of a limited participation on the same problem. So for the time being, rapporteur and other missions are being dispatched to the regions of conflict, crisis situations are being discussed at length at various CSCE forums, and a new procedure called "consensus minus one"--excluding a country violating the CSCE principles from decision-making--was painfully and not very convincingly applied in the case of Yugoslavia after protracted, exhaustive debate.

It would not be realistic to expect that the CSCE will be in a position to quickly develop security mechanisms that could be applied to conflicts within its participating states or between them. While the dispatch of monitoring missions could be feasible rather soon, the prospects for CSCE peacekeeping capability are still remote.

However, the need for such activities is imperative. The CSCE should not be shy; it should ask, preferably at its July 1992 summit in Helsinki, for direct cooperation in peacekeeping with other international organizations or institutions.

The former Yugoslav territory can be looked to as an example insofar as monitoring and peacekeeping activities there are shared by the UN, the EC, and four non-EC states. The United Nations, with rich experience in peacekeeping, would be a logical partner for common action in this field. Its financial constraints are, unfortunately, well known. Apparently, the Western European Union, now seen as a European pillar of security, and NATO can bring in required human and material resources. The missing experience could be provided by the UN and the mandate and political guidance by the CSCE.

Specific modalities will need to be discussed among experts. However, this discussion, which is informally already under way, needs a strong political impulse. If the heads of state or government could express their direct commitment in this regard, common action in conflict prevention and crisis management would be greatly facilitated.

206

8

The Future of the CSCE: The Needs of East Central Europe

Andrzej Karkoszka

This chapter deals with the future challenges posed by the security environment of the East Central European states, Poland, Czechoslovakia, and Hungary, and the ability of the CSCE to meet these specific needs. It is thus only the functional abilities of the CSCE, not its structural or purely procedural strengths or weaknesses, that is the subject here. The term "security environment of the ECE" encompasses the European security order within the ECE area (including the internal situation in the ECE states), in its vicinity, and whenever directly applicable to the security and well-being of the ECE states. Naturally, when discussed in the context of the CSCE, "security" connotes all aspects of "being free from threats," both physical and nonphysical--first of all military threats, but also economic, ecological, and other threats.

Internal Developments

The future security environment of the ECE states will be shaped most decisively by their future economic strength and social development. This complex issue remains basically outside the purview of this discussion. Internal developments have to be mentioned, however, because of their influence on the relative and actual position of a given state within the international community, and on the national self-perception of relative security and well-being, and thus on the willingness to enter into far-reaching interactions with other nations. Their impact on the ability of the newly democratic states in the region to carry out the most appropriate foreign and security policy cannot be overestimated.

The most characteristic features of the ECE states at present are the deterioration in living standards, the rapid pace of change in virtually all aspects of life, and the uncertainty as to the final outcome of the changes within states and in the surrounding international system. (It is interesting to note that the difference in this respect between the ECE states and areas further to the east is not one of substance but degree--the same conditions exist everywhere, but they permeate day-to-day life and are far more painful in the post-Soviet republics.)

In the case of Poland, the economic crisis or stagnation has already lasted more than a decade, and the transformations of the last two years have added still more strains to everyday life. In all three ECE states, the introduction of a market economy, though indispensable in the long run, has caused serious disruptions to their traditional international trade patterns, domestic production, and market structures. Inflation is a common problem, the cost of living is often unbearable for ordinary citizens, unemployment is constantly growing, social mobility is restrained by the lack of housing and retraining opportunities, and the crime rate has surpassed all heretofore known standards. Privatization is being achieved more slowly than desired and expected; foreign investment has been restrained throughout the ECE region, particularly in Poland, and has failed to live up to expectations. The degradation of the natural environment, the worst on the continent, has begun to be perceived more strongly than ever before. National politics are dominated by inter-party frictions and disrupted by the weaknesses of the newly established administrations, fraud scandals, and the new social divisions between the recently established affluent and impoverished groups. Added to this are the tension and fear caused by the painful "screening" processes being directed against the representatives and supporters of the former communist regimes. The fundamental achievements of these societies--a democratic system, assurances of individual rights and freedoms, new economic prospects for private enterprises, and generally expanded contacts with prosperous Western countries--are cherished, but at least for the time being, such largely intangible positive developments cannot balance the negative aspects of day-to-day life.

In short, it seems that the traumatic experiences of the last decade have brought about, at least in Poland, a new appreciation of the importance of material and social factors in a state's and nation's standing in the international community. For the first time it is being understood that a nation's economic, technological, ecological, and cultural progress is more important than old threats, power politics, enemy images, or stereotypes concerning neighboring nations, national pride, and symbols. This "enlightenment" germinating in the ECE societies may seem trivial to West Europeans, but for some nations, especially Poland, built as it is around romantic and lofty but volatile and often parochial symbols, it is quite a change.

Dependence on the Outside World

The future political and social stability of the ECE countries depends on the ability of their respective governments to first of all provide hope for an improvement in living standards, and then to deliver on that hope. The difficulty stems from the fact that the delivery cannot be executed without a protracted period of aggravation. Thus, the most difficult problem in these countries is how to achieve the assurance of decent living standards and technological progress without, however, jeopardizing short-term social stability. Ensuring that this disruption is limited in time and intensity is greatly dependent on the preservation of propitious external conditions. What the ECE states need most are foreign investments and unhindered access to foreign markets, not the financial hand-outs or well-meant but ineffective and costly advice. All forms of international cooperation, expansion of trade and technological exchanges, and harmonization of legal, bureaucratic, and organizational standards between the backward East and the advanced West are seen by governments and populations in the region as the best guarantee of internal political stability. In order to materialize this guarantee, the ECE states have no other option but to enmesh themselves in the network of existing European organizations and institutions, especially those that may help to bridge the aforementioned gap in social and economic development.

One Goal--Many Routes

The supposition that internal social and economic developments will have a decisive effect on the stability and future standing of the ECE states within the international community leads to the logical conclusion that the integration of these states with the European Community is of primary importance. No other global or regional organization is as significant, for reasons of geography, history, policy and culture. This importance and closeness does not, however, diminish the attractiveness and usefulness of other organizations and institutions, particularly NATO, the WEU, the Council of Europe, and the CSCE. Each of them has specific virtues and abilities (and weaknesses, of course). The ECE states are willing to participate fully in their work, seeing no contradiction but rather a mutual reinforcement between them. After all, they are all based on the same fundamental values and norms, and all of them, the EC included, are in a dynamic process of transformation and realignment, leading, it is to be hoped, to a single European system, although that system's shape, scope, and structure remain as yet obscure.

The evolution of existing European organizations has led to a substantial overlap in membership and functions. The European Community is in the process of a gradual expansion of its membership that will soon include members of EFTA and possibly in the not too distant future the ECE states, and its members are undertaking to develop a European Political Union, accepting the WEU as its defense subsidiary. The Council of Europe will soon cross the threshold of 30 members. NATO is striving to expand its political role and has engaged, although not on an equal footing, all its former antagonists, including the Asiatic and Transcaucasian republics of the former USSR, in its North Atlantic Cooperation Council (NACC). Finally, the CSCE is striving to transform itself into an institutionalized organization, able to cooperate with all the existing European and extra-European institutions. Only the hard practice of interstate relations will determine the final outcome of all these processes and solve the question of the functional interrelation between the various organizations. As was stated above, participation in all these processes is vital for the future security and prosperity of the ECE states.

211

Significance of the CSCE

It is important to underline the fact that at present it is solely the CSCE that embraces all the European states, aligned and nonaligned alike, and gives them the same rights and an equal status. Small and medium-sized states, like those of the ECE, are rarely able to exert political pressure in order to advance their own particular national interests. The CSCE procedures, with all their inherent weaknesses, permit these states to be subjects, not objects, in the international endeavors to establish new norms for states' behavior and in the pursuit of joint actions. It is also the only European organization that encompasses, in more or less stringent fashion, all categories of states' concerns. Because it is all-inclusive, politically rather than legally binding in its functioning, and ephemeral despite its continuity as a process, the CSCE could not and still cannot respond to most of the concrete needs and requirements of member states. It has, however, an enormous growth potential on its own and, moreover, it may become much more important by fortifying its particular ability to mandate a concrete action to those more specialized organizations that acquiesce to such a role. Thus, for the ECE states, the importance of the CSCE's existence and further development is beyond any doubt, all the more so as the future may carry a host of challenges to the security and well-being of the ECE states that they are unlikely to be able to confront and overcome alone and that can be addressed only in a cooperative international framework, of which the CSCE may become the most expeditious element.

Future Challenges

Preservation of Stability--Prevention of Instability

The most benign challenge facing the CSCE and the one for which it is best equipped is the preservation of stability where it exists but where it is considered, for various reasons, to be fragile but not seriously jeopardized. This description may apply to the present situation in the ECE states and to some of the latent contradictions that have existed for years inside and between various West European states. However, the CSCE may actually be deprived of an opportunity to work directly on such a case of potential instability, because that would probably be tackled primarily by one of the other existing European organizations. There are no grounds to doubt that the norms of behavior established by these organizations and by the CSCE, which are followed rather strictly by West Europeans and are strongly aspired to by the ECE states, as well as the consultative mechanism already in place, will enable a successful containment of, if not a solution to, potential disputes and contradictions between these states.

What has already been achieved on a large part of the European continent, with the beneficial involvement of the CSCE, is an effective security system, in which the probability of interstate or civil war is very small and where a local military conflict would probably be contained by joint diplomatic action. It can safely be assumed that the ECE states belong to this area despite all their internal economic and social instabilities and problems. However, the vast areas of the CSCE geographic space, including the Balkans and the majority of the post-Soviet states, suffer from an inherent instability and, most probably, will witness military hostilities of varying intensity. The ability to

213

preserve stability and to prevent instability in these areas seems to be the most important present aspiration of the CSCE and the biggest hope of the ECE states.

The task of building up the CSCE conflict prevention mechanism enjoys wide political and diplomatic support, including support from the ECE states. This is understandable, as their exposure to potential dangers is relatively greater. The belt of potentially bloody conflicts emanating from the ethnic, religious, border, and political contradictions between different local groups, small autonomous regions and republics, up to and including the newly established states covers an area a number of times larger than the territory of Western and Central Europe taken together. Some of these conflicts taking place in the vicinity of the ECE states will have a direct and negative bearing on their security. As a result, the ECE states feel very concretely the meaning of the notion that peace and stability are indivisible in Europe.

Theoretically speaking, in order to fulfill the aforementioned CSCE aspirations to establish an effective preventive mechanism against various categories of instabilities and conflicts, an institution established for such purposes should have access, on its own or through its members, to a continuous inflow of data, with all relevant information on ethnic, religious, military and political developments. The data should be stored, analyzed, and presented to the appropriate international bodies in time to permit them to formulate a proper reaction. The procedures of the organization, on the diplomatic as well as on the bureaucratic level, should permit timely and adequate action. The material and financial resources at the disposal of the organization or provided on an ad hoc basis by its members should be available promptly for the execution of whatever action was decided on by member states. Finally, the legal grounds for the actions, some of them perhaps involving an imposition of international norms over the sovereign rights of a state, should be entirely clear in advance.

The above cursory rendition of theoretical conditions required by any international organization to become effective in complex, controversial, and often distant affairs indicates clearly all the shortcomings of the existing CSCE mechanisms. But in reality, all intelligence about irregularities and deviations from CSCE norms and rules, which may lead to instabilities or conflicts, originates in and is presented by the individual states. The sole exception where the CSCE has its own source of information is the Conflict Prevention Center. However, the mandate of the CPC seems too restricted to enable a prompt preventive action. In a case where the deterioration of a given situation does not fit the criteria of a "military emergency," or where it does not concern an abrogation of human rights but has, for example, economic or ecological ramifications, or where it does not involve state entities but social groups within a state, then neither the "Berlin mechanism" (an emergency meeting called by 12 plus one states) nor the "Moscow mechanism" (pertaining to human rights), nor the "Valetta mechanism" (peaceful settlement of disputes) may be invoked. The CSCE would not, most probably, react to such contingencies. In fact, the CSCE, apart from its general legal, political, and military normative functions, does not as yet address the future mechanisms of conflict prevention.

However, the CSCE's existing and proposed (as far as they are already known) mechanisms for prevention of instabilities and conflicts should not be examined, much less designed, against the background of purely theoretical demands.

215

The mechanisms are concerned primarily with interstate, not intrastate, relations; thus the information on potential contradictions is readily available. The mechanisms are in an early stage of development, and the process is of a delicate nature, as it often touches upon an area of states' sovereign rights. The evolution of the CSCE procedures for calling meetings, the institutionalization of chairman's prerogatives, the differentiations in voting mechanisms according to the type of decisions to be taken, and other gradual procedural evolutions may eventually bring enough flexibility to the CSCE's modus operandi to permit it to act in a preventive rather than reactive mode.

Conflict Resolution, Peacekeeping, and Peace Enforcing

The experience gained by the CSCE (as well as by the UN, the EC, and NATO) from their involvement in the Yugoslav civil war and the armed conflicts in Nagorno-Karabakh and Moldova is, at best, not very encouraging. On the one hand, the existing procedures for emergency consultations (on Yugoslavia, both in the CPC and the Committee of Senior Officials) and fact-finding missions (to Nagorno-Karabakh and Moldova) were applied successfully. This proves the point that these rudimentary forms of conflict prevention function well in the framework of the CSCE, permitting a more effective diplomatic and political pressure to be exerted on the belligerents by this and other international organizations involved.

On the other hand, the practical influence of the CSCE efforts on the course of events in Yugoslavia and, so far, also on the conflicts in Nagorno-Karabakh and Moldova has been nil. Even the collusion of pressures exerted by the CSCE, the UN, the EC, and NATO, amplified by the international economic sanctions in the case of Yugoslavia, could not stop the hostilities. The lesson is clear and already well known: once an ethnic or religious conflict turns into armed violence, it takes enormous material losses and human casualties, as well as time, before it can be stopped. This is even more true when the conflict is an internal one and thus the freedom of direct action on the part of the international community is restricted.

The international mechanisms available and practiced on different occasions to settle interstate disputes, be it mediation, arbitration, judicial services or others, presume the consent of all parties involved. Even an open and large-scale military conflict may be defused in this way. The CSCE is visibly on the way to incorporate such good offices into its statutory procedures. However, in the realm of ethnic or religious struggles, as well as the nationalistic drive to regain territory lost in the past, there is nearly no chance for a cooperative attitude on the part of the antagonists, whatever the pressure by the international community. And it seems that these kinds of conflicts will be the most typical in the years to come.

Among the often proposed new instruments designed to strengthen the CSCE peacekeeping functions is the concept of CSCE-operated (mandated) but nationally located and budgeted military forces, which would probably have to be NATO-supported in terms of transport, logistics, and C^3I systems. The concept quickly gained support in a number of states, including the NATO and ECE states, and it now seems likely to be implemented when the right opportunity arises. The positive outcome of several UN peacekeeping operations serves as the main argument in favor of adopting this type of more muscular capability to back up the CSCE's mediation efforts.

The value of a neutral force disengaging armed

opponents is indisputable. Again, however, the aforementioned requirement for the mutual consent of the feuding parties is a difficult precondition. Moreover, on the negative side of this type of peacekeeping is usually the duration of the operation, which is sometimes very long, and thus the incessant drain on the finances of those who pay for the intervention force. Given the fact that the list of potential conflicts that might flare up in the eastern and southern parts of the continent is quite extensive, the establishment and support of such peacekeeping forces may become a serious, even unbearable, burden to the participating states and organizations.

Once the military instruments of the CSCE are created, a question will have to be answered about the advisability of military coercion or punitive actions against a transgressor state or, reaching still further, against a militant group within a state. Such an eventuality opens a number of very painful and complex issues as to the legal procedures that would have to be adopted in the CSCE context to permit such action. It seems that such an arrangement would perhaps be possible only at a very advanced stage of the process of political integration of the European states. If it is adopted before that stage of integration is reached, it may create insurmountable frictions within the ranks of the CSCE member states.

As in the case of conflict prevention, the CSCE potential for conflict resolution, peacekeeping, and peace enforcement seems to be very restricted, most probably to the cases in which virtually all parties involved support the CSCE's role. The procedural hurdles and the financial costs involved would certainly impose strict limits on the number and scale of such operations. It may be imagined that at times the number of calls for action may surpass the ability of the CSCE to respond or, even worse, the prospect of peace enforcement operation directed against a state may prompt it to abrogate its links with the CSCE. The presently restricted and uncertain CSCE capacity to foresee and control emerging instabilities, a capability crucial to conflict prevention, as well as its rather doubtful efficiency in conflict resolution or peace enforcement, should be carefully considered by the ECE states, which are among those countries potentially most exposed to the various destabilizing influences from the east and south of Europe and beyond. Without depreciating in any way the normative and all-embracing values of the CSCE, its importance as a future security "guarantor" for these states may be perceived as limited.

Restraining Military Capabilities

The future challenges posed by military developments in Europe to the security of the ECE states do not look as serious as they were in the past. Nevertheless, these states continue to attach great importance to the problems of European military security, because after the dissolution of the Warsaw Treaty Organization, each state has had to tend to its own security and defense, while the military powers to the East and West are many times larger. Although they are voicing some of their concerns at the NACC and are striving to foster various forms of military cooperation with the West European states and the US, they believe that a further diminution in influence of military power in European relations, through the CSCE-based disarmament, arms control, and confidence-building measures, may be the best way to look after their security.

These states are vitally interested in the implementation of the CFE 1 and Vienna 1990 CSBM agreements. The accords are not only a proof of the diminished importance of military power

219

in European politics, nor are they merely a term of reference for all the European states in their military planning. For the ECE states, they are also the best possible multilateral constraint imposed on the military capabilities of their much more powerful neighbors.

Concerns over the implementation of the agreements seem to be well founded. The agreements are very complex and the execution of their stipulations may be quite demanding to any military and state bureaucracy, and an even greater burden to the administrations of the post-Soviet states, which are newly organized and working under various strains. The final quantitative distribution of the Soviet-assigned treaty-limited items (TLIs) has only recently been decided by the former Soviet republics. Their respective territories are constantly crisscrossed by various military units, weapons' transports, and soldiers, all attempting to join their native forces. Several national armies, border guards units, and national militias are in the process of being created. Several high-quality former Soviet divisions are being partially and gradually withdrawn from Germany and Poland. It seems that this process is being carried out in an orderly fashion; nevertheless it cannot but add to the overall chaos within the former USSR. How the various ceilings and restrictions will be accounted for and verified remains to be seen.

The ECE states are confident that at present there are no direct military threats to their security. No one challenges their borders. Each of the three states has signed treaties of good neighborliness, friendship, and cooperation with all states in the vicinity. Good will and a spirit of cooperation seem to prevail in the region. However, as has been mentioned above, the neighbor states are powerful, and some at least are engaged in a steady improvement of their forces. And as long as armed forces remain deployed in such quantities and quality as is the case today around the ECE states, they have to remain concerned.

The feeling of relative insecurity resulting from the ongoing potential threat assessment is, admittedly, partly of their own making. The present economic difficulties of the ECE states have had a serious effect on their military and security policies. After regaining their sovereignty from Soviet domination, which had been exerted particularly through the Warsaw Treaty Organization, the ECE states have each undertaken ambitious programs aimed at transforming their military capabilities, including, among other measures, the reduction, redeployment, restructuring, modernization, and professionalization of their armed forces. Military industries in the region were to be partially converted to civilian purposes. The end result of the processes was to be a military capability that was truly defensive, small in size but modern and capable of guarding against small-scale intrusions and giving as painful as possible a resistance to a large-scale aggression. After more than two years, however, the programs remain to a large extent unfulfilled. The budgetary squeeze has imposed severe reductions in personnel and equipment in all ECE states, much below the ceilings prescribed by the CFE 1 treaty but without any restructuring taking place to improve the efficiency and effectiveness of the remaining forces. Also precluded are the normal training routines at all levels and in every category of forces, and the lack of resources has all but halted any acquisition of new weapons and equipment. Officer corps function under increasing pressures, caused by professional insecurity and the deterioration in their living standards. All in all, if these trends are prolonged--and prospects for an improvement of the situation are dim--the relative capabilities of these armies will deteriorate to an unacceptable level. It is thus

221

in the vital interest of the ECE states to strive, through the CSCE negotiations, which remain the sole forum of such endeavors in Europe, for further general reductions in European armed forces.

An important aspect of the future military security of the ECE states is the mobilization capabilities of other European states. The matter has an obvious sensitivity in the framework of the CSCE, as it touches on the basic aspect of the military preparedness of several states, particularly the neutral ones. However, it should be addressed by the CSCE, as the ability to mobilize large military forces on short notice, the existence of a large pool of trained reservists and extensive stocks of military materials, and the pattern of deployment of these stocks, are all indications of a state's real military preparedness, its actual peacetime operational forces notwithstanding. The progress achieved so far in rationalizing European military capabilities, remarkable as it is, will not be satisfactory if the mobilization potentials of states are not rearranged accordingly. The particular interest of the ECE states in this regard is directly linked to the enormous mobilization potentials of the surrounding states.

Another aspect of future military developments that raises concern in the ECE states and that they hope can be considered and acted upon within the framework of the CSCE is the question of the qualitative sophistication of weapons and armed forces. The existing transparency in this regard, as introduced by the CFE 1 treaty, is seen as a good precedent. However, the exchange of information on the planned introduction of new weapon systems does not give early enough warning about the emerging capabilities of other states and does not constitute any form of restraining measure on the rapid progress of military technology. Again, it is the relative inability of the ECE states to cope with technological progress in weaponry and all kinds of the auxiliary military systems that shapes their initial position. However, their attitude is not altogether based on selfish concerns: internationally accepted restrictions on the freedom of individual states to continue fielding ever new weapons systems, some of them with particularly dangerous features, or increased international cooperation in controlling military R&D outlays would benefit nearly everyone. It seems that in the future only a very few states will be able to cope with the increasing costs and technical complexity of new weapons and military systems. Modern electronic warfare, air defense and air combat systems, communication and control systems, and highly mobile and destructive weapons systems will soon become the domain of a few leading military powers, giving them in turn several political, military, and economic advantages over the vast majority of other states. A periodic review of technological advances in weaponry and their consequences for the international stability ("stability impact statements"), an exchange of plans on the future acquisitions of modern weapons, and joint efforts in finding mutually acceptable restrictions on the military applications of super-modern technology might be taken as the possible means.

The CSCE should also turn more attention to the regional and subregional security and military arrangements that could directly improve the sense of security of the respective areas and by the same token promote stability in a more general context. Geographically restricted measures, bilateral or multilateral, have the best chance of responding to local security concerns and go much further than general arrangements applicable to the whole continent. Any regional or subregional solution would naturally be handled by the governments concerned, and thus would not be negotiated within the scope of the CSCE proceedings. Once agreed upon, however, they should be functionally incorporated into the wider settings of the CSCE pattern of security-related agreements: other states could be informed about the process of implementation of a regional undertaking, and they should be able to express their assessment of its consequences. In this way a network of regional commitments would be part and parcel of the whole European security concert.

The military-industrial base of the CSCE states is the primary source of today's world armaments. Its output is at present and will in the foreseeable future be excessive, in view of the diminishing demand for weapons and military equipment in most parts of the world. This is particularly true in Europe, where this demand has dwindled most rapidly. The ECE states had also developed large military industries, oriented toward the large arms market of the WTO and some of their clients in the developing nations. Now, after the disappearance of the Soviet and all other outside markets as well as because of the reductions in their own forces and a complete halt to the acquisition of new weapons due to budgetary constraints, these indigenous military industries have become a heavy economic liability to the states concerned. Only some of the production facilities have a chance to survive and be useful as suppliers of military hardware. The great majority of them, however, must convert to civilian production or vanish altogether. The trouble is that neither solution is practical. Conversion requires ample financial resources measured in several hundreds of millions of dollars. And on the other hand, the factories support hundreds of thousands of workers, entire towns and regions; thus, closing them down is socially impossible. On top of that, the problem of conversion is both technically, economically, and organizationally very demanding and sometimes controversial because of its linkage with a state's security concerns. The Western countries are in a much better position with regard to conversion of military industry. They have appropriate resources and can afford spatial reallocation and reeducation of labor. They also have substantial experience in these matters.

The interest in addressing military conversion in the framework of the CSCE should not be seen as an effort to raise money for this particular need. A specialized forum, convened within the CSCE, could concentrate on an exchange of information and experiences, a debate as to the methods used, a joint analysis of social and economic consequences, and technical assistance required and possessed by various states. Such a forum could be also seen as a confidence-building measure, since a general knowledge about such conversion processes could be useful in military-industrial planning.

One of the interesting ideas circulating in various states, and officially espoused by the ECE states, is the concept of a defensive military posture. Notwithstanding the details of various proposals connected with this concept and the debate on various definitions, the fact remains that aspects of the size, structure, deployment, technological content, and other material and doctrinal features of military capabilities leads them to be identified as offensively or defensively oriented. Overall stability on the continent could be strengthened, though not assured, by the spread and eventual universal acceptance of defensive rather than offensive postures, with forces and capabilities to match. It seems that the CSCE's new Security Forum, where discussions devoted to military doctrines and related matters will in all likelihood take place, would be particularly well equipped to undertake the task of identifying such criteria and supervising their implementation.

225

Coping With Nonmilitary Threats

The notion of nonmilitary threats to a state's security encompasses many things. States and societies can be threatened by natural disasters, famine, economic exploitation, political or cultural domination, and, most importantly, degradation or even destruction of the natural environment. However, not all degradations or disasters are of such a magnitude or duration to represent a threat to a state's security by decimating or degenerating large segments of the population, destroying a large part of its nutritional basis, and the like.

It is not an exaggeration to say that the degradation of the natural environment in the entire ECE region has already assumed proportions that endanger their security. Over four decades, the states of the region have acquired a very dense network of heavy industries, based predominantly on the use of coal for energy, the major source of the very high concentration of destructive "acid rain" and several other poisonous substances. The forests in these countries are already half destroyed. Their soil is contaminated with heavy metals. Foodstuff is increasingly deteriorating in quality. There are few relatively clean lakes and rivers remaining: fertilizers and saline water from the coal mines have killed the rest of them. Most villages, as well as small, medium, and even large towns, along with the majority of small and large enterprises, live and operate without any sewage treatment. As a result of this catastrophic situation, the incidence of various diseases in this region is much higher than in other European states, which devote substantially higher resources to environmental and medical protection of their populations. Thus, the populations of the ECE countries are finding that the quality and average length of their lives are being seriously limited.

Several neighboring states in Western Europe, though

adding their own dose of pollutants to the region, are nevertheless suffering from cross-border emissions. Pollutants do not recognize state frontiers, and the ECE states do not possess the financial and technological resources commensurate with the problems they face in this area.

Another basically nonmilitary problem of even graver potential consequences for the long-term well-being of Europe is the existence of a number of old-fashioned Soviet-built nuclear reactors. The problem is well known; it is mentioned here only as a reminder of the wide spectrum of challenges to be confronted by the CSCE in the immediate future.

One could ask why the CSCE should undertake an action in such a technical and highly specialized field. Bilateral and multilateral cooperation in the ecological domain has long been established, to mention only the Baltic cooperation or the Oder bilateral and trilateral efforts. There exists strong public pressure on governments to address the issue. However, the problem should be tackled on a continental scale (not to mention a global one). It has become obvious that the degradation of the natural environment constitutes at present an immediate and rapidly growing menace to the security of Europe, and particularly to its central region. Thus the answer to the above question is that there is a need to organize official and public opinion, to put together various technical expertise represented by different specialized organizations, to harmonize efforts on a regional and continental scale, to set common standards and norms that will have not only technical but also legal and political meaning, and to create a mechanism enabling a strong and unified international reaction in cases when international assistance is needed or when norms have been transgressed.

Conclusions

The ECE region's vital interests concerning the CSCE stem from their geopolitical and economic position: they are going through a profound economic and political reform, and their neighbors include very economically successful and militarily powerful West European states as well as inherently unstable, economically backward and militarily still very potent states. Thus they are first of all interested in their own economic progress, which is seen, together with the their democratic social system, as the best guarantee of their stability and security. This progress is dependent on their ability to join the more advanced industrial and democratic states in their integrative processes. Participation in the CSCE and its further development facilitate the ECE efforts.

In the opinion of the ECE states, the crucial tasks confronting the CSCE are, first, the preservation of stability in the eastern and southern regions of the continent and, second, the advancement of measures directed at a further reduction of the role played by military factors in European affairs. While the CSCE seems well prepared to handle the second of these tasks, it remains to be seen how the CSCE's limited resources are to be expanded and organized to meet the first. Although ethnic contradictions are generally considered the greatest threat to the future stability of the continent, the ECE states stress also the importance of progress in the economic and social spheres and in the democratic institutions in their own as well as in the post-Soviet states, as a vital prerequisite of the future long-term stability in Europe.

The ECE states continue to regard the CSCE as the sole forum in which they are able to participate as equals with their

Western neighbors. Their approach to the CSCE is designed to demonstrate their continuing interest in this institution as well as their reliability and responsibility as actors in the international arena. They view their successful participation in the CSCE as one of the complements to their membership in other European organizations such as the European Community. As such, their stake in the success of the CSCE, in all its facets, is large, and they have been and will continue to be among its most tireless proponents.

229

Part IV
231-301

An Evolving
Agenda for
the CSCE

9

The Future of Institutionalization: The CSCE Example

Heinz Gärtner

In the two decades since it was launched in Helsinki in 1973, the CSCE process has developed a set of principles, rules, and codes to reduce East-West tension and confrontation. Its continuity has been sustained through periodic follow-up meetings (Belgrade, Madrid, Vienna, Helsinki) and numerous expert meetings. The political changes in the East since 1989 have raised expectations that the CSCE would become an all-European security system with regular and permanent institutions. With the 1990 Charter of Paris for a New Europe, the CSCE process has become institutionalized and regularized, and mechanisms have been created and further developed.

Institutions and Mechanisms

The CSCE institutions are designed to assist the regular and other meetings on a day-to-day basis. The participating states have agreed not only to the regularization of consultations and institutionalization, but also to several so-called mechanisms or procedures for acting either more quickly or without having first to achieve the consensus of all participating states to do so. The mechanisms are designed to respond to emergency situations or to situations not conducive to regular decision-making processes;[1] they can provide for bilateral meetings or the establishment of a group to act as a fact-finding or mediating party.

The regular CSCE meetings consist of:

- The CSCE Summit of Heads of State or Government, which convenes on the occasion of follow-up meetings and meets at least once every two years.

- The Council of Ministers for Foreign Affairs, which provides a forum for regular and high-level political consultation and meets at least every year.

- The Committee of Senior Officials (CSO), which prepares Council meetings and implements Council decisions, and meets at least every three months. Thirteen member states can request emergency meetings; subsidiary meetings take place between the regular sessions.

Other CSCE meetings include:

- Inter-sessional/subsidiary meetings, such as experts meetings, seminars, symposia, etc.
- Negotiations on CSBMs, Vienna.
- Negotiations on Conventional Forces (CFE), Vienna.

The CSCE institutions comprise:

- The CSCE Secretariat, Prague.
- The Conflict Prevention Center (CPC), Vienna, which includes a Consultative Committee.
- The Office of Democratic Institutions and Human Rights (ODIHR), Warsaw (formerly the Office for Free Elections).
- Probably a Standing/Permanent Committee (housed in the Security Forum).

Other bodies of the CSCE include:

- The Parliamentary Assembly,
- The Economic Forum,
- Probably a Forum for Security (FSE), Vienna (negotiations on measures of arms control, e.g., harmonization, security enhancement and cooperation, nonproliferation, stabilizing measures, confidence-building, risk reduction, and conflict prevention).

The CSCE mechanisms are as follows:

- Human dimension mechanism (housed at the ODIHR), which provides for information exchange, mediation, and fact-finding missions as agreed in the Vienna, Copenhagen, and Moscow documents and by the Prague Council meeting and subject to efforts of one, six, and ten states respectively.

- Dispute settlement mechanism (housed at the CPC), which provides for the formation of a third-party group to facilitate peaceful settlement of disputes, as agreed in the 1991 Valletta document and according to the mutual consent of two states.

- Unusual military activities (housed at the CPC), which provides for information exchange and bilateral and multilateral meetings, as agreed in the 1990 and 1992 Vienna CSBM documents and subject to efforts of one state only.

- Emergency meeting mechanism (of the Committee of Senior Officials), as agreed in the 1991 Berlin Council meeting and subject to efforts of 12 or more states.

- Council/CSO rapporteur missions (subject to full consensus).

Theoretical Assumptions

The assessment of whether the CSCE institutions and mechanisms provide efficient instruments for conflict prevention or resolution and collective security depends very much on underlying theoretical assumptions that very often are not made explicit.

Basically there are two theoretical approaches. The neoliberal approach[2] places great faith in the capabilities of the CSCE institutions and mechanisms to promote cooperation between states and to prevent and resolve conflicts among them. The CSCE institutions and mechanisms are seen to be of great importance for peace building. They would act independently of the interests of states, yet would affect the policies, expectations, and behavior of those states. According to this theory, compliance with institutions comes first; hence, the CSCE institutions and mechanisms are the independent variable. States would realize that the costs of noncooperation are higher than the costs of compliance; they would realize that cooperation and compliance provide gains to all participants. Therefore, the rule of law and institutional procedures are crucial to peace building. In sum, CSCE institutions and mechanisms, procedures, and rules would effectively and decisively reinforce and strengthen a state's willingness to cooperate to promote stability and peace.

The neorealist approach[3] emphasizes that states fail to cooperate if vital interests are at stake. CSCE institutions and mechanisms would reflect state interests and would influence the behavior of states only marginally. According to this theory, the self-interest of states is the independent variable. States are always afraid that other states will gain more from cooperation than they do. The main concern of states is their security. They cannot rely on the good intentions of other states; what counts are states' capabilities, not their intentions. CSCE institutions and mechanisms would never be able to constrain states with bad intentions and strong capabilities. According to this theory, CSCE institutions do not really matter. States cooperate if they think cooperation is to their advantage. If they really wanted to cooperate, they would do so even without institutions. CSCE institutions and mechanisms would work only when they were not vital.

High Expectations

The Paris Charter and the documents of the 1992 Prague meeting of the CSCE Council of Foreign Ministers created a network of regular consultations and cooperation at various levels. The assessment that the enunciation of norms is sufficient for the prevention of violence and for peace building was prevalent before the Yugoslav crisis. It was caused mainly by the enthusiasm spread by politicians and diplomats after the Charter of Paris was adopted. The Paris Charter constituted a culmination of the normative efforts of the CSCE.[4] The Charter and the newly established institutions and mechanisms are based on the assumption that states are willing to comply with the rules, procedures, and norms laid out by the CSCE. An institutional network itself would be the basis if not the guarantee for conflict prevention, management, and resolution. The number of norms would limit the use of force and protect human rights and the rights of national minorities. Politicians, diplomats, and scholars held high expectations about the conflict resolution and prevention capability of the new institutions.

The mechanisms have been triggered in the wake of the Yugoslav crisis. It turned out that they worked as planned, but they could not prevent further escalation of the violence or resolve the conflict.[5] They did not fail, but they did not lead to the intended success. The result was widespread disappointment about the CSCE institutions and mechanisms.[6]

Future Tasks

In January 1992 in Prague, the CSCE Foreign Ministers called for the "further development of the CSCE institutions and mechanisms and structures" and stressed "the need to strengthen the effectiveness of CSCE institutions and mechanisms by matching their functions more closely to the achievement of these objectives."

Besides stronger institutions and stronger democracy, more effective mechanisms to contain the use of force were called for. Before and during the Helsinki Follow-Up Meeting, several proposals to improve the capacity of CSCE institutions and the mechanisms for emergency situations were called for:[7]

- the reaction time should be shortened. The time allowed under the present arrangements between a request for implementation and the reply could be dispensed with.

- in the framework of the CSBM regime, the Conflict Prevention Center should be able to call on the Consultative Committee or the Committee of Senior Officials to act quickly when unusual military activities are detected. At present, the requested state must reply within 48 hours; if the requesting state is not satisfied, it may call a bilateral meeting and/or a meeting with all the participating states at the CPC to discuss its concerns. The Consultative Committee may subsequently decide, by consensus, to send a rapporteur mission to the area of concern.

- effective crisis management can work properly only with a flexible decision-making procedure. Under certain conditions, decisions should be made by majority voting and not by consensus. The rule of consensus for the decision-making process was seen as a major obstacle to the adoption of effective measures. New decision-making processes such as "consensus-minus-one" to react to major violations of CSCE commitments were discussed and adopted at the Prague meeting.[8] In the area of dispute settlement between two or three parties, a "consensus minus two or three" procedure is being considered. Hans-Dietrich Genscher, then Germany's foreign minister, proposed the appointment of an ad hoc "steering committee" for each emerging conflict.

- fact-finding missions should be used as a method for containing emerging crisis situations.

- early warning systems should be installed to prevent conflicts from becoming violent.

- France proposed a "security treaty" that would be more binding than the Helsinki Final Act and the Paris Charter. If an agreement on this cannot be achieved right away, adoption of a "code of conduct" could be a first step.

- mediation and arbitration in crisis situations could assist parties to solve disputes through negotiation. The Valletta mechanism on the peaceful settlement of disputes already developed such procedures; they are so cumbersome and time consuming, however, that they are not applicable in emergency situations. France and Germany also proposed the establishment of a "Court of Conciliation" as a permanent tribunal that would strengthen the legal standing of the CSCE mechanisms and principles.[9]

The shift from the setting of norms, rules, and procedures to operative measures proved that an institutional network is not sufficient for peace building. If the rule of law or an international norm is violated, action must be taken against the lawbreaker so as to preserve the rule of law. This is a recognition that states must at least sometimes be forced to comply with rules and norms, and that these are not always compatible with states' interests. One step further would be to establish some sort of peacekeeping forces. An even more forceful measure is the creation of a system of collective security.

Peacekeeping

There is growing support for the idea that the CSCE should be able to carry out peacekeeping operations. CSCE peacekeeping forces could conduct several operations, acting according to United Nations principles of conduct: they could observe a crisis situation, monitor a cease-fire, separate conflicting military forces.

The CPC and peacekeeping forces could also develop some sort of "escalation control" capacity, thereby reducing the chances of the outbreak of large-scale violence and also increasing the participating states' ability to react if the situation threatens to escalate. The countries would then earmark some of their armed forces for "CSCE escalation control" duties. The participating countries can offer their expertise and services to the escalation-control (ESCON) forces[10] where conflict resolution might be possible. Escalation control could benefit from the concept of Open Skies and the observation of activities made possible thereby.

Peacekeeping or ESCON forces could also be sent to sensitive regions, either before a conflict, or when a dispute is unsolved, or after a truce or settlement. They could be deployed on one side at the request or with the consent of only one party, even if the other party objects.[11]

The open question is which forces should carry out the operations. In April 1992, the Netherlands proposed that NATO (which has since taken up the idea) should carry out peacekeeping operations on behalf of a CSCE mandate on a case-by-case basis, because "NATO is the only organization which has the infrastructure, politico-military resources, logistics and operational capability to implement a CSCE mandate for peace-keeping on short notice and a cost effective way." The Dutch proposal says that the CSCE could also call on the Western European Union. But the WEU lacks infrastructure, command and control systems, and intelligence resources.[12] In June 1992 in Oslo, the NATO foreign ministers decided that NATO would support the CSCE in certain peacekeeping missions. The communiqué leaves open the possibility that groups of states could or could not participate as they chose. Neutral countries, however, which have some experience from UN peacekeeping operations, cannot utilize the NATO infrastructure for peacekeeping activities.

241

Collective Security

The boldest method for upholding the rule of law would be a system of collective security.[13] The idea is that delinquent states would be treated the same way that criminals are dealt with under domestic law.[14] A discussion of whether the CSCE could turn into a collective security system has been going on for quite some time.[15] This would imply the commitment by all participating states to take effective and coercive measures, including the use of military force against any state that violates the peace.

Collective security rests on the notion of all against one.[16] States would be committed to join a coalition to confront any aggression whenever and wherever it occurs. The concept assumes a very high degree of congruent interests among members, whether they are weak or powerful. A system of collective security implies that all members would be willing to come to the assistance of one of its members if it were attacked or threatened.

The concept of collective security is based on the assumption that neither CSCE institution building nor "peacekeeping" is enough to keep the peace. It relies on the means of peace enforcement to maintain the rule of law and international norms. It is idealistic insofar as it assumes that all states share common security interests, that every state perceives every challenge in the same way, and that every state is prepared to run the same risks to preserve peace.

In reality, however, for most of the states different interests are at stake; they define aggression differently, and react in different ways. Neorealists would say that states do not commit themselves to punish a crime unless it is in their interest.

States also occupy different positions within the international hierarchy of power. Small states and large states may well have differing views on what constitutes aggression and when to engage in collective action. Not even Slovenia was willing to support Croatia militarily in 1991, although both had the same opponent and the same interests, and both are relatively weak states. Many conflicts are internally caused and are not border violations. Ethnic nationalities very rarely have clearly defined borders.

A collective security system also implies some risk for small states. If there was an automatic and binding commitment to collective action, small states would be dragged into wars of big powers. Big powers, however, would not always consider civil wars or military conflicts between small states to be aggression, and hence would not feel bound to act militarily and get involved.[17]

Collective security would work only if a major power was willing to take responsibility for it and the other nations were willing to fall in line. A war against a major power would probably not be carried out.[18]

An ideal collective security system does not exist and probably never will exist, even though it is a frequently considered goal for a European security system.

No CSCE institution or mechanism would be able to force a nation-state to use its forces against its will. The Yugoslav case already demonstrated that there is no agreement among CSCE states in the case of military involvement. The CSCE has neither the centralized structure nor a functioning military dimension that would enable and authorize coercive action against aggressors or "international criminals" that threaten the peace. None of the existing CSCE institutions and mechanisms questions

243

a nation's sovereignty over the decision on peace and war.[19] Thus, they do not point in the direction of a European collective security system.

The Charter of Paris "fully recognizes the freedom of States to choose their own security arrangements." The document of the CSCE meeting in Valletta (1991) on the peaceful settlement of conflicts "recognizes... that a settlement procedure ... is not incompatible with the sovereign equality of states." And if a "party to the dispute considers that because the dispute raises issues concerning its territorial integrity, or national defense, title to sovereignty.... the Mechanism should not be established or continued."

The Conflict Prevention Center will give support to the implementation of CSBMs: these are consultations regarding unusual military activities and the annual exchange of military information. Both the CSCE Council and the Consultative Committee work according to the CSCE procedures based on consensus.

The emergency mechanism agreed upon in 1991 in Berlin can convene without consensus. Thirteen members are necessary to call a meeting of senior officials for consultations, as happened in the case of Yugoslavia. Any decision requires consensus. Neither the CPC nor the emergency mechanism has an instrument to enforce sanctions.

The system of collective security thus raises the question of decision-making procedures. It has been repeatedly indicated that collective security could not function effectively as long as decisions are made by consensus.[20] Under present arrangements, a state violating its CSCE obligations has to expect strong criticism in CSCE bodies but need not fear any sanctions, least of all military ones, since any relevant decisions would require that state's consent.[21]

If the CSCE, however, agreed on majority voting, then two results would be likely, neither of which is compatible with the idea of collective security.[22] In the case of the risk of major military involvement, the decision to go to war, possibly against a great power, would not find a majority. In spite of majority voting, collective security would not be accomplished.

States would also be inclined to take advantage of the system without contributing an adequate share and getting involved themselves. They could take a free-rider position and rely on the collective security organization, which is supposed to provide the collective good, that is, to stop aggression.[23]

The second possible result is that if such a majority to stop aggression by military force exists, states would form a traditional ad hoc alliance (as in the Korean and Persian Gulf cases) under a strong leader that does not have much to do with a collective security system.[24]

Nationalization and Bilateralization of Security

Neither the CSCE, nor the EC, nor NATO is able or ready to provide security guarantees for the East European states. Each of these countries is developing its own national military strategies and doctrines, instead, and has put its armed forces under an exclusively national supreme command. National defense is so far the only real option against all sorts of threats for the former WTO countries.

Additionally, they are concluding bilateral treaties with security clauses among themselves and with West European states, according to the model of the German-Soviet treaty of 1990. There is a tendency towards "bilateralization" and "nationalization" of security. This trend runs counter to or replaces the efforts to create multinational forces and structures within a common or collective security system.[25]

Constraints on National Military Activities

According to the Vienna Document 1992 of the Negotiations on Confidence- and Security-Building Measures, no state will carry out more than six military activities involving 13,000-40,000 troops and 300-900 battle tanks within a year; and no state will carry out simultaneously more than three military activities involving more than 13,000 troops or 300 battle tanks.

Military activities (such as maneuvers) conducted by national armies near the border of neighboring states, even at lower levels of forces, may in time come to be considered the greatest threat to security and stability between states. The approximate limits for national military activities could be those of the Stockholm agreement on prior notification or observation, involving more than 13,000 or 17,000 troops. This threshold seems reasonable. A threshold for constraints on national military activities set between 13,000 and 17,000 troops appears to be well within the range of possibilities. Such restrictions on national armed forces would significantly decrease the intervention capability of individual states. They also could be applied to ethnic nationalities. The limits of constraints on national forces should not depend on population or territorial size.[26]

Regional constraints are also possible. Regional security arrangements, however, have not been successful so far. The "Central European Initiative" (before 1992 "Pentagonale" or "Hexagonale" group) has never dealt with security and defense issues. The "Visegrad" initiative (regional cooperation between

Poland, Czechoslovakia, and Hungary in 1991) failed to establish a regional security and defense cooperation.

CSCE and Democracy

The Charter of Paris for a New Europe stresses that the participating states

> undertake to build, consolidate and strengthen democracy as the only system of government of our nations.... Democracy is the best safeguard of freedom of expression, tolerance of all groups of society, and equality of opportunity for each person.
> Democracy, with its representative and pluralist character, entails accountability to the electorate, the obligation of public authorities to comply with the law and justice administered impartially. No one will be above the law.[27]

The Charter implies that democracy promotes compliance with international law and peace building. Norms of mutual respect, tolerance, and equality would prevail in the relationship between democracies. According to this line of thought, domestic democracy is vital for effective international peace; it is not institution building but democracy building that will promote peace and security. For the first approach (institution building), CSCE institutions and mechanisms, for the second (democracy building), domestic democracy are sufficient conditions to uphold international norms and the rule of law. However, if either one or both of them were sufficient for peace, security, and stability, no coercive measures would be necessary to uphold CSCE norms and the rule of law and to punish a defector.

CSCE and the Nation-State

The "peace through democracy" hypothesis[28] recognizes that the nation-state is the basis for peace building. It does not try to build peace by dissolving the nation-state but by equipping it with democracy. It recognizes that there is no developed democracy outside the nation-state.[29]

The functionalist strategy of institutionalization, on the other hand, suggests that European institutions represent a higher level of political authority in international relations and hence tries to bring different state functions gradually under a common authority. The nation-state would become less and less of a significant phenomenon and eventually would disappear and be replaced by the common authority.[30]

In Europe, new nation-states have emerged while old ones are fading away. What we are witnessing is a repetition of historic processes. If political units are dissolving, new ones emerge. It is a zero-sum game. Integration processes take place simultaneously with dissolution processes.[31]

The CSCE, along with the European Community and the United Nations, have recognized the existence of new nation-states. The creation of the new German nation-state in 1990 was immediately confirmed by the CSCE. The former Soviet republics and with some delay the new states on Yugoslav territory have been admitted to the CSCE process and the UN in early 1992. Those memberships can be taken as recognition of new nation-states.

The EC Foreign Ministers issued a "Declaration on the Guidelines on Recognition of New States in Eastern Europe and the Soviet Union" in December 1991, which stated that the recognition of these new states requires:

- respect for the provisions of the Charter of the UN and the commitments subscribed to in the Final Act of Helsinki and in the Charter of Paris, especially with regard to the rule of law, democracy and human rights;

- guarantees for the rights of the ethnic and national groups and minorities in accordance with the commitments subscribed to in the framework of the CSCE.[32]

In this declaration, the CSCE documents and the UN Charter provide the legal basis for the political recognition of new nation-states.

It is by no means certain whether and when institutional integration processes will become irreversible and prevail over national sovereignty. The weakness of the functionalist strategy is that it does not distinguish between different areas of integration and does not indicate the limits of integration. Where is the limit when states give up their sovereignty in security matters and their monopoly to decide on peace and war?

Integration is less likely to succeed if issues of national security are at stake. And integrated systems are most likely to fall apart if and when different security interests emerge. Examples are the Austrian-Hungarian Empire, but more recently also Yugoslavia and the Soviet Union.

CSCE and Germany

According to the neorealist theory mentioned earlier, the CSCE institutions and mechanisms would reflect states' interests and power. This theory stresses that foreign policies are in the first place determined by the place of states in the international system.

In Central Europe, Germany plays the dominant role in terms of economy, trade, politics, and culture. Germany itself is too big to be controlled by any European country. Of all European states, Germany has the biggest share of foreign trade with the East European countries and the highest share of investment in these countries. In 1991 Germany accounted for over one-third of trade between the West and Eastern Europe and for between one-fifth and one-fourth of investment in the East.[33] In the CSFR, the share of total foreign investment held by Germans has risen to 80%.

On the Yugoslav question, all Central European states, including Italy and Austria, took the same position as Germany, which recognized Croatia and Slovenia very quickly. All the other EC states followed, despite major misgivings on the part of some.

There is no major foreign policy issue--right or wrong-- within the CSCE where Central European states would take a position that is fundamentally different from that of Germany. Smaller Central European states join the stronger side if they believe that this is to their advantage.[34] They are attracted by economic and political strength. However, Germany is considered by many, and considers itself, to be a benign and benevolent power, which means that it does not activate all available power resources most of the time.[35] Furthermore, at this time in its history Germany is gaining power not through expansion but through attraction. It appears that Germany is becoming a great power almost against its will.

Summary and Conclusions

CSCE institutions and mechanisms consist of rules, norms, and principles. They are based on the expectation that governments comply with them and their rules of procedures,[36] and that consequently the institutions affect the behavior and politics of the participating states. The theoretical debate raises the question of whether institution building is sufficient for peace building. The neoliberal school tends to affirm this approach.

For the neorealist approach, on the other hand, institution building has little influence on states' politics because they act according to their interests and not according to international norms, rules, and principles.

CSCE institutions may reinforce cooperation among member states. But no matter how much the CSCE process influences the foreign policy of the participating states, the process itself and its new institutions alone are not sufficient to uphold CSCE norms and principles. The Yugoslav crisis raised the question of what the CSCE should do in the case of violation of its norms and principles. Means of coercion appear to be necessary to take action against defecting states. There is a wide range of possibilities being considered, including more effective decision-making procedures, economic sanctions, peacekeeping forces, and peace enforcement.

It seems inevitable that in the future the CSCE process will increasingly be characterized by the tension between coercion and accommodation.[37] Permanent solutions such as a collective security system do not seem achievable. The concept of collective security is itself idealistic and assumes that states do not act according to their own but in the common interest, and that security would be indivisible. It is highly unlikely, however,

251

that states would commit themselves to a system that would force them to get involved in military operations that were not in their direct interest. This concept also flies in the face of a strong trend towards nationalization and bilateralization of security, and not only in Eastern Europe. Under such conditions, more traditional approaches towards building confidence and security between states, such as greater constraints on exercises conducted by national armies, should be given more active consideration.

One answer to the question of whether and how much CSCE institutions contribute to peace building in Europe is that they can provide a forum for communication and negotiation. They can foster cooperation but they cannot force states to comply if they do not want to--you can lead a horse to water but you can't make him drink.[38]

Neither the CSCE nor any other pan-European security system is a panacea that can resolve all Europe's security problems. Creating a pan-European security system that would provide enduring and effective security under current conditions would overburden the CSCE institutions and mechanisms. Further changes in the attitude and conditions of individual states are needed before any such approach even begins to look worthwhile.

Domestic democracy--one basic principle of the Paris Charter--can be an additional element for peace. Those, however, who want to enable the CSCE to enforce measures do not consider it a sufficient condition for the maintenance of peace and security.

Even though some functionalists expect European institutions to replace national authorities in terms of democracy, there is so far no alternative to the democratic nation-state. The practice of admitting new members to the CSCE and the UN and the recognition of new states underline the continuing importance of the nation-state.

Notes

1. See the overview of the CSCE institutions in Commission on Security and Cooperation in Europe, *The Conference on Security and Cooperation in Europe: An Overview of the CSCE Process. Recent Meetings and Institutional Development* (Washington, DC, 1992).

2. For the neoliberal theory, see, among others, Robert O. Keohane, *International Institutions and State Power: Essays in International Relations* (Boulder: Westview, 1989); and Robert O. Keohane, "Correspondence: Back to the Future, Part II. International Relations Theory and Post-Cold War Europe," *International Security* 15, no. 2 (Fall 1990), pp. 192-94. For the application of the theory on military alliances, see Charles W. Kegley and Gregory A. Raymond, *When Trust Breaks Down: Alliance Norms and World Politics* (Columbia, SC: University of South Carolina Press, 1990); and Glenn H. Snyder, "Alliance Theory: A Neorealist First Cut," *Journal of International Affairs* 44, no. 1 (Spring/Summer 1990), pp. 103-23. See also Gunther Hellmann and Reinhard Wolf, "Neorealism, Neoliberal Institutionalism and the Future of NATO" (Paper presented at the 33rd annual convention of the International Studies Association (ISA), Atlanta, Georgia, March 31-April 4, 1992).

3. For the neorealist approach, see, among others, Kenneth N. Waltz, *Theory of International Politics* (Reading: Addison-Wesley, 1979); and John J. Mearsheimer, "Back to the Future: Instability in Europe After the Cold War," *International Security* 15, no. 1 (Summer 1990), pp. 5-56.

4. Stefan Lehne, *The CSCE in the 1990s: Common European House or Potemkin Village?* (Vienna: Austrian Institute for International Affairs, 1991), p. 90.

5. Austria and Italy have used the mechanism on unusual military activities to request information from Yugoslavia, and Hungary has held a bilateral meeting with Yugoslavia. The Committee of Senior Officials held several emergency meetings, offered "good offices" missions, and supported the observer missions of the EC.

6. Analysts began to study why the mechanisms that have raised such high expectations did not work properly according to conflict prevention and resolution theory. On the Valletta mechanism, see K.J. Holsti, "A 'Zone of Civility' in European Diplomatic Relations? The CSCE and Conflict Resolution" (Paper presented at the 33rd ISA annual convention, Atlanta, March 31-April 4, 1992).

7. See also Commission on Security and Cooperation in Europe, *The Conference on Security and Cooperation in Europe;* and Lehne, *The CSCE in the 1990s,* pp. 65-69.

8. Actions are limited to political measures outside the affected territory. It was first applied in May 1992 to suspend the Yugoslav delegation from decisions on Bosnia-Herzegovina.

9. For more about this French-German proposal see *Basic Reports,* no. 21, April 10, 1992.

10. Heinz Gärtner, "Constraints, 'Stabilizing Measures' and CSBMs," in *The Guns Fall Silent: The End of the Cold War and the Future of Conventional Disarmament,* ed. Ian M. Cuthbertson and Peter Volten, IEWSS Occasional Paper no. 16 (New York, 1990), pp. 127-40.

11. Brian Urquhart suggested that the UN peacekeeping forces should conduct those operations under Chapter 6 or 7: "Learning From the Gulf," *The New York Review of Books,* March 7, 1991, pp. 34-37. See also Stanley Hoffman, "Delusions of the World Order," *The New York Review of Books,* April 9, 1992, pp. 39-40.

12. The European Union may, according to the treaty signed at Maastricht in 1992, also "request ... the WEU to elaborate and implement decisions and actions of the Union which have defense implications." NATO decided that it could do the same, if it does not want to act itself. Everything remains open: the WEU can become the EC's defense instrument, but also the second pillar of NATO; it can also serve as a European bridge to NATO.

13. For details see Heinz Gärtner, *Wird Europa sicherer? Zwischen kollektiver und nationaler Sicherheit* (Vienna: Wilhelm Braumüller, 1992).

14. Hoffmann, "Delusions of World Order," p. 38.

15. Lehne, *The CSCE in the 1990s,* pp. 69-73.

254

16. See Charles A. Kupchan and Clifford A. Kupchan, "Concerts, Collective Security, and the Future of Europe," *International Security* 16, no. 1 (Summer 1991), p. 116-25.

17. The US and other NATO states did not want to become engaged in the Yugoslav conflict.

18. See Hoffmann, "Delusions of World Order," p. 38.

19. The Treaty of Maastricht also stresses that the policy of the Union "shall not prejudice the specific character of the security and defense policy of certain Member States." Even the North Atlantic Treaty leaves open what sort of action the parties would take individually or in concert with others against an armed attack. Article 5 states only that the parties will assist the attacked Party or Parties "by taking ... such action as it deems necessary, including the use of armed force, to restore and maintain the security."

20. A different viewpoint is taken in Janie Letherman, "Conflict Transformation, Learning and Institutionalization of the CSCE Achievements and Future Challenges" (Paper presented at the 33rd ISA annual convention, Atlanta, March 31-April 4, 1992). She argues that the consensus decision rule in the CSCE is exceedingly important as a learning process in terms of communication, the exchange of information, and building knowledge among all sides.

21. Lehne, *The CSCE in the 1990s,* p. 71.

22. Josef Joffe, "Collective Security and the Future of Europe," *Survival,* Spring 1922, p. 45.

23. See Kupchan and Kupchan, "Concerts, Collective Security," pp. 138-39.

24. Joffe, "Collective Security and the Future of Europe," p. 45.

25. With respect to the former republics in Yugoslavia and the Soviet Union, the trend towards "nationalism" has been visible since 1989 when the republics, which were striving for sovereign statehood, started to create their own militias. The independent defense strategies and the national armies of the former Soviet republics will probably lead to the end of the Commonwealth of Independent States as well.

26. Gärtner, "Constraints, 'Stabilizing Measures.'" For a summary and interpretation of the negotiations on CSBMs, see Ingo Peters, "Sicherheitspolitische Vertrauensbildung in neuen Europa. Herausforderungen und Entwicklungen in der VSBM-Politik," in *Sicherheitspolitische Stabilität im neuen Europa,* ed. Erhard Forndran and Hartmut Pohlmann (Baden-Baden: Nomos, forthcoming).

27. See the text of the Charter of Paris for a New Europe in Lehne, *The CSCE in the 1990s,* p. 113.

28. A good summary of the arguments of this hypothesis is given in Thomas Nielebock, "Once Again: Peace Through Democracy--But Which Kind of Peace and How to Explain It?" (Paper presented at the 33rd ISA annual convention, Atlanta, March 31-April 4, 1992).

29. The notion that the nation-state is responsible for international violence and war is widely represented among German scholars (among others, Michael Zürn, "Der Imperativ internationaler Verregelung: Über Nationalstaat und die internationalen Beziehungen," and Klaus Jürgen Gantzel, "Zu historischen Tendenzen und praxeologischen Orientierungen militärisch gestützter Sicherheitspolitik" (Papers presented at the Evangelical Academy conference on "Jenseits der Bipolarität: Aufbruch in eine 'Neue Weltordnung,'" Loccum, April 24-26, 1992). The German criticism of the nation-state may be influenced by the negative experiences with the German nation-state from Bismarck to Hitler. The argument may lose ground in Germany now that it has its identity back as a new nation-state after unification.

30. See Esko Antola, "Institutionalization of the CSCE in the Post-Hegemonic European Security System" (Paper presented at the 32nd ISA annual convention, Vancouver, March 20-23, 1991), p. 7.

31. The unification of Italy in the 1860s was possible only because the Austro-Hungarian Empire was in decline. The collapse of the Ottoman Empire gave birth to most of the nations in Eastern Europe.

32. See also Colin Warbrick, "Recognition of States: Recent European Practice" (Paper presented at the 33rd ISA annual convention, Atlanta, March 31-April 4, 1992).

33. Data from the UN Economic Commission for Europe.

34. Olav F. Knudsen, "Small States' Reactions to Sudden Power Shifts" (Paper presented at the 32nd ISA annual convention, Vancouver, March 20-23, 1991).

35. James March, "The Power of Power," in *Varieties of Political Theory*, ed. David Easton (Englewood Cliffs, NJ: Prentice Hall, 1966), pp. 58-61.

36. Kjell Goldman, "Peace-Building and War-Avoidance: Is There a Connection?" (Paper presented at the 33rd ISA annual convention, Atlanta, March 31-April 4, 1992), p. 5.

37. Ibid. Goldman calls this tension the "Internationalists' Dilemma"--"It is impossible to be both a consistent coercive internationalist and a consistent accommodative internationalist at the same time, and it is difficult to see how the problem could be solved other than ad hoc."

38. Heinz Gärtner, "Kollektive und nationale Sicherheit," in *Die Welt im Umbruch. Friedensbericht 1991. Friedensforscher zur Lage*, ed. Reiner Steinweg (Stadtschlaining: Institut für Friedensforschung, 1991), pp. 214-24.

10
The Challenges of Helsinki II
Michael R. Lucas

Introduction

The revolutions of 1989 and the end of the East-West conflict have left in their wake a still disunited Europe faced with the challenge of constructing a new framework of peace and stability. A pan-European security architecture of European and Euro-Atlantic institutions is rapidly evolving to address security, economic, human rights, interethnic, and ecological problems and conflicts.[1] The Conference on Security and Cooperation in Europe, with its 52 members encompassing the entire Northern hemisphere, has become the overarching geographical-political framework of this network of institutions. The CSCE has taken on the post-Cold War challenge of linking this highly heterogeneous group of nation-states in an evolving structure of interfaced institutions of cooperation.

A Theoretical Framework for
a Post-Cold War Security Architecture

The CSCE's Broadened Concept of Security

It is possible to distinguish between the following types of security:

1. *Antagonistic* or *military security*, which can take the form of military defense and confrontation, arms racing, the striving for military balance or superiority linked to notions of balance-of-

power, and conceptions of international order and general military-political tension of the type that existed during the postwar era, and the military standoff of NATO and the Warsaw Treaty Organization (WTO).

2. *Common security* can be defined as the striving of military-political protagonists to acknowledge and take account in their security policies of the security needs and perceptions of their opponents and enter into arms control, confidence-building, and disarmament treaties for this purpose. Throughout the late 1980s, the deepening cooperation between East and West in resolving regional conflicts and laying the basis for arms control, confidence-building, and disarmament treaties exemplifies this type of security.

3. *Collective security* denotes a relationship in which states in an international environment of diminishing confrontation or nonconfrontation enter into partnership to address what are perceived as common political or military threats to peace and stability. The United Nations alliance against Iraq following the Saddam Hussein regime's invasion of Kuwait as well as UN peacekeeping operations in Yugoslavia are examples of military action that can be understood as exemplifying this type of security.

4. *Comprehensive security* denotes a relationship in which evolving common and collective security partnerships are complemented and deepened with a broad set of economic, ecological, human rights-related, and other forms of informal and institutionalized cooperation among former or potential antagonists.

Comprehensive security is a qualitatively more complex and challenging form of security for a number of reasons, including its multidimensional character and the diversity of problems it seeks to address. Relationships of cooperation are sought in which unilateral policies, disagreements, and conflicts become subject to dialogue, cooperation, and forms of regulated conflict management. Comprehensive security can also be linked to the underlying general consensus that all actors are seeking to overcome potentially destabilizing asymmetries of economic or political power through mutually beneficial cooperation and, where appropriate, integration into institutionalized, regime-type structures of cooperation. In contrast to other forms of cooperative military security, comprehensive security also embraces forms of social and political interaction on the substate, that is, the transnational level, including social and political intercourse of different ethnic and national groups and the participation of political parties, citizen initiatives, and nongovernmental organizations (NGOs). Important in this context is the cultivation by integration institutions of informal structures and forums for promoting such transnational, substate interaction.

The CSCE can be defined as a dynamic process and framework in which CSCE member states are moving away from antagonistic security by consensually adopting informal as well as treaty-anchored principles, norms, and procedures based on common, collective, and comprehensive forms of security.

The four types of security defined above are evident in varying degrees and in different forms in the pan-European and global security landscape today and in the European process of institutional reform. As empirical categories, they illuminate the highly uneven historical and political process in which antagonistic forms of security, particularly those characteristic of the postwar East-West military and ideological conflict, are giving way to experimental, cooperative relationships among states, groups of states, and institutions. Comprehensive security also implies cooperation in different problem areas simultaneously and the consensus that security cannot be exclusively defined in negative terms as the absence of military conflict. It must also be understood positively as a process aiming to achieve political, economic, and cultural well-being through cooperation and the progressive integration of former or potential antagonists into informal and institutionalized relationships of mutually beneficial interaction.

As theoretical categories, the four types of security are "ideal-typical" simplifications for the purpose of analysis. In the real world of international politics, these four types of security coexist, overlap, and interact in a variety of ways. Even forms of antagonistic security, such as the deterrence system of the postwar era, have coexisted and presuppose limited forms of cooperation and "rules of the game" between antagonists, as testified by arms control, confidence building, and East-West nonmilitary detente during the postwar era.[2]

The CSCE Inter-Institutional Landscape

The EAS, composed of the 52 member states of the CSCE, includes the following "security and cooperation areas":

1. The Europe of the 12 that make up the EC;
2. The 16 states belonging to the NATO alliance;
3. The 35 states of the NACC;
4. The 9 states belonging to the WEU;
5. The Europe of the 19 that combines the states of the EC with

those of the European Free Trade Association (EFTA) in the larger European Economic Space (EES);

6. The Europe of the 26 composed of the states in the Council of Europe;

7. The subregional integration networks, such as the Council of Baltic Sea States, the Nordic Council, Central European Initiative (CEI), the Balkan Initiative, and the Economic Cooperation Council.[3]

The above geographic and political units within the CSCE area are at the same time institutions that are engaged in organizing and institutionalizing cooperation that involves all four forms of security discussed in the previous section. Because these changing institutions are still just emerging out of the shell of the postwar era, they are far from finalized. Their political competence, structures, and aims, as well as their relation to each other, continue to change in response to political developments in Eastern Europe; the disintegration of the former Soviet Union; the interethnic conflicts in Yugoslavia, Moldova, and Nagorno-Karabakh (and the effectiveness of current CSCE efforts to resolve these conflicts); and the deepening worldwide recession.

Inter-Institutional Change and the CSCE

With the end of the East-West conflict and the problems left in the wake of the revolutions of 1989, the CSCE has ceased to be merely a forum for building bridges between East and West and has become the framework for constructing an inter-institutional political space in which different cooperation and integration processes are increasingly interfaced. In this context, the CSCE, the EC, EFTA, the Council of Europe, NATO, the NACC, and the WEU have entered into a period of transformation. Cooperation institutions are carrying out the following tasks:[4]

1. Continuing to significantly deepen their informal and formal ties with the reform regimes of Eastern and Central Europe and the CIS republics.

2. Redefining their functions, structures, and goals as institutions.

3. Intensifying their cooperation and competition with one another; and in this process, the traditional division of labor between the military, economic, and human dimension institutions, such as NATO and the WEU on the one hand, and the EC, the CSCE, and the Council of Europe on the other, is being transformed under the shared premise that these different areas interpenetrate and that political conflict prevention and resolution strategies must take account of their interaction.

4. Creating new organs and institutions. In some cases, this is partly to replace political, security-related, or communist-era economic institutions and organizations--such as the WTO and the Council for Mutual Economic Assistance (CMEA)--and other organizations that have dissolved or are in the process of dissolving.

As a result of these trends, the need has increased for a new inter-institutional division of labor that can more effectively meet the pressing demands of Eastern reform under conditions of scarce resources and fill the security vacuums caused or catalyzed by the collapse of the communist order.

The construction of a pan-European security architecture

has been characterized also by greater coordination between global and regional institutions. This includes the expansion of the UN's informal and formal ties with the EC, WEU, NATO, the NACC, and the CSCE.

The CSCE's additional organs and institutions created since 1990 are being shaped to function in an inter-institutional, interdisciplinary way. Important here is the ongoing creation and fleshing out at Helsinki II of coordinating and steering organs at the level of 1) political decision making; 2) expert working groups; and 3) NGOs, citizen groups, and parliaments. Liaisons and checks and balances between these different levels are also essential.

We can distinguish in this context between two dimensions at play in the discussion at the Helsinki meeting: 1) existing or still-to-be created or enlarged CSCE institutions and organs themselves; and 2) the CSCE as a process of interfacing different cooperation and integration institutions of the EAS with support and political input of global institutions, such as the UN, the IMF, the World Bank, and the OECD.

The Progress of Institutionalization

The Second Meeting of the CSCE Council

Because the CSCE Council of Europe Ministers largely set the agenda of Helsinki II at its January 30-31, 1992 meeting in Prague, a brief overview of the meeting is necessary for our analysis. The results of Prague included 1) a major strengthening of the CSCE institutions created by the Charter of Paris; 2) a clearer definition of the function, tasks, and aims of the CSCE in the field of the human dimension and conflict management and resolution; and 3) a substantial building out and specification of the inter-institutional division of labor within the CSCE itself and between the CSCE and other European institutions and international organizations.[5]

In order to improve the coordination of the CSCE process, the Committee of Senior Officials (CSO) will meet regularly every three months and delegate specific tasks to other CSCE institutions and to open-ended ad hoc groups of participating states.

In the area of the human dimension, the Council of Ministers assigned additional functions to the Office for Democratic Institutions and Human Rights (ODIHR), which must be further specified at Helsinki II in order for the ODIHR to become fully operational.[6]

The Prague document on CSCE institutions also reinforced the human rights mechanism, whereby the CSCE Council or the CSO, in order to "safeguard human rights, democracy and the rule of law through peaceful means," can take appropriate action "if necessary in the absence of the consent of the State concerned, in cases of clear, gross and uncorrected violations of relevant CSCE commitments."[7] Such action includes political declarations or other political steps "outside the territory of the State concerned."[8]

The Prague document established on paper a CSCE Economic Forum within the framework of the Committee of Senior Officials. The Forum's main purpose will be to provide political stimulus to the development of free market economies, to offer practical proposals for economic cooperation, and to "encourage activities already underway within organizations, such as the Organization for Economic Cooperation and Development (OECD), the European Investment Bank (EIB), the EBRD, and the United Nations Economic Commission for Europe

(ECE)."[9]

Section 6 of the Prague document, which deals with crisis management and conflict prevention instruments, mandates Helsinki II to further develop the CSCE dispute settlement infrastructure, including the use of good offices, conciliation, and rapporteur missions. The Helsinki delegations are also requested to consider possibilities for CSCE peacekeeping. This section of the document calls for setting up additional instruments to further operationalize decisions by the Council or the CSO. Tasks may be delegated in this context to 1) the Chairman-in-Office of the CSO; 2) the Consultative Committee of the Conflict Prevention Center; or 3) ad hoc groups of participating states.

In order to substantially build out the CPC, the Consultative Committee will, inter alia, serve as a forum in the security field, in which CSCE member states "will conduct comprehensive and regular consultations on security issues with politico-military implications."[10] It will also establish, if necessary, subsidiary working bodies, including open-ended ad hoc groups entrusted with specific tasks.

Section 9 of the Prague document on CSCE institutions reinforces the role of the CSCE in acting as a clearinghouse and coordination center for the work of other institutions with the CSCE network. The Council of Europe, the UN Economic Commission for Europe, NATO, the WEU, the OECD, the EBRD, the European Investment Bank, and other European and transatlantic organizations will make contributions to specialized CSCE meetings and annually inform the Secretariat of their current work and of the resources that would be available to the CSCE.

Section 4 of the meeting's summary of conclusions deals specifically with the crisis in Yugoslavia. In addition to warning against any extension of the conflict and expressing CSCE support for early deployment of UN peacekeeping forces, the Council issued the following list of principles and conditions for settling the conflict:

- respect for international obligations with respect to the rule of law, democracy and human rights;

- guarantees for the rights of ethnic and national communities and minorities, in accordance with the commitments subscribed to in the framework of the CSCE;

- respect for the inviolability of all borders, whether internal or external, which can only be changed by peaceful means and by common agreement;

- commitment to settle by agreement all questions concerning State succession and regional disputes;

- guarantees for the absence of territorial claims towards any neighboring State, including abstention from hostile propaganda activities that would, inter alia, promote such territorial claims.[11]

The above should also be viewed as a set of principles and conditions to be invoked in efforts to bring to an end not only the Yugoslav conflict but other conflicts--such as that between Armenia and Azerbaijan--that have erupted or are likely to erupt in the EAS space in the coming years.

In Section 6 of its summary of conclusions, the ministers stressed that

the CSCE has a prominent role to play in the evolving European architecture and that the challenges facing Europe call for multi-faceted forms of cooperation, and a close relationship among European, trans-Atlantic and other international institutions and organizations, drawing as appropriate upon their respective competence.[12]

Section 7 of the summary of conclusions calls for a broader security dialogue and the establishment of new CSBM negotiations among all CSCE states to commence after the conclusion of Helsinki II. Also mentioned are the importance of the signing of the CFE treaty by all "relevant newly independent States," completing the Opens Skies draft treaty, and the pending accord on limiting military personnel strength within the CFE area also in time for the Helsinki Summit.[13]

The Prague and Helsinki Ministerial Meetings

The Prague Council meeting reaffirmed the CSCE's multisided approach to security and cooperation and, building on the Charter of Paris for a New Europe and the first Council meeting in Berlin, strengthened the institutionalized organs, such as the CSO, the CPC, the Consultative Committee, and ODIHR, which were set up to deal with each of the items on the CSCE's expanding agenda and at the same time emphasized their reintegration into a common, interconnected CSCE-coordinated system.

The Prague Council also committed the CSCE to integrate into its cooperation and regime-building process the work and resources of international, transatlantic, and European organizations. The Prague decisions to establish a more efficient operational internal division of labor placed the CSCE in a better position to work with the unwieldy (current) number of 52 member states.

The Council, the Committee of Senior Officials, and the

Consultative Committee have become, as a result of the Prague Council's decisions, coordination and steering instruments for the transatlantic/pan-European cooperation and integration process as a whole. Yet recent CSCE experience, particularly regarding the problems in dealing with the Yugoslav conflict, has led to a number of proposals at the Helsinki Follow-Up Meeting to streamline the operation of the CSCE to allow it to more expeditiously respond to crises and increase its all-around effectiveness. These proposals include the following:

- A German proposal for a troika that would consist of the present, previous, and future chairman-in-office of the Council. The troika, together with a small number of rotating states, would constitute a "steering committee" that could be upgraded into a CSCE regional "security council" based on Chapter 8 of the United Nations Charter. This body would be able to take binding decisions in certain areas, including the sanctioning of states that grossly violate CSCE principles. These decisions could not be overturned by a CSCE state on the basis of consensus voting.

- A related German proposal for setting up special CSCE blue helmet forces for peacekeeping and green helmet forces to provide humanitarian and other forms of aid in ecological and natural catastrophes. These forces would be under the authority of the proposed security council.

- A NATO proposal for a "security forum" designated as a "Committee on Security Cooperation" (CSC) that would consist of 1) a standing committee for negotiations on arms control, disarmament, and discussion of proposals in nonmilitary security fields for strengthening security cooperation; and 2) the

Consultative Committee in its upgraded form, as already discussed above. The Committee on Security Cooperation and the Consultative Committee would have a common secretariat and both could delegate specific tasks to additional ad hoc groups whose membership would be open to CSCE member states on a voluntary basis.

- A Dutch proposal to create a CSCE High Commissioner for National Minorities to act in an early warning capacity by identifying potential sources of crises and conflict.

- A proposal for applying the "consensus-minus-one" rule now valid in CSCE human rights activity to certain areas of conflict prevention.

The diversity of topics being dealt with at the Helsinki meeting suggests the complexity involved in creating a more efficient, operational division of labor. In this context, we can distinguish between 1) the interrelated issue areas taken up in the CSCE itself; 2) tasks that could be delegated to institutions associated with the CSCE that are considered better equipped to deal with a particular problem, such as economic issues in the case of the EC or the human dimension in the case of the Council of Europe; 3) different EAS institutions acting cooperatively in a particular issue area or in a multi-issue approach to particular problems, such as migration or settling ethno-national conflicts; and 4) all major EAS institutions in a concerted political action, e.g., imposing various types of sanctions and other punitive measures on a state that grossly violates CSCE principles on a scale considered threatening to international peace. Here, the CSCE could act as the main coordinator, or as one of several coordinating institutions, of a collective political response, as has

271

been the case in the Yugoslav crisis, where the main coordination and the convening of the peace conference was delegated by the CSCE to the EC and subsequent peacekeeping operations to the UN. It should be kept in mind that the CSCE with its 52 member states was able to muster an overarching mandate for collective action that no other pan-European institution was capable of matching. In dealing with serious crises, such pan-European legitimacy is indispensable for a genuine collective security response and hindering "go-it-alone" policies at the national or subregional level. Such fragmentation could under certain circumstances become a risk to stability.

Problems of CSCE Institutionalization

The creation of new organs that began with the start of the institutionalization process of the CSCE occurred during a period of political and social revolution and under a variety of global, interstate, and inter-organizational political pressures. This storm of events continues to outpace the ability of the CSCE institutionalization process to adapt and to use its still incomplete machinery to defuse crises before they erupt into military violence. The revolutionary pace of events has pushed the institutionalization process forward, but, at the same time, has not made the mutual adjustment of new CSCE organs to each other an easy task. Because so many different political, economic, and other interests are involved in expanding the CSCE and making it into a major pillar of a pan-European architecture, it was to be expected that delays, bottlenecks, and other problems continue to occur before the crisis prevention and management machinery is fully in place and effectively operational.

A related problem linked to the CSCE's ongoing institutionalization is that new CSCE and non-CSCE organs and institutions that have been created since the Paris summit risk falling into competition with one another in their functions and aims. This risk is evident in the case of the NACC and the CPC. They shared the aim of dealing with crises and conflicts in the former Soviet Union; both decided in early March to take up the conflict between Armenia and Azerbaijan.[14] In addition, the CSCE crisis prevention and management organs are in different locations. This dispersal of work sites has resulted in significant loss of efficiency and could hinder timely responses during crises and the relative effectiveness of CSCE institutions vis-a-vis other institutions.

Emerging Characteristics of the CSCE Process

The emerging Euro-Atlantic system, as roughly blueprinted in Prague and further shaped in Helsinki, is not centralistic but polycentric. The raising of problems and the putting forth of proposals to deal with them can be initiated by the EC, the WEU, NATO, the NACC, etc., or by a combination of these acting together within the CSCE.

The consultations and cooperation between the CSCE, the EC, the WEU, NATO, the UN, and major powers on Yugoslavia broke new ground in forging collective crisis management procedures at the bilateral, regional, and global level and demonstrated the feasibility of a flexible, inter-institutional division of labor. This experience within the CSCE created the legitimacy for the Council's decision at the start of the Helsinki Follow-Up Meeting to send a high-level delegation headed by CSFR Foreign Minister Jiři Dienstbier to Nagorno-Karabakh and to call for a CSCE peace conference in Minsk to discuss the conflict between Armenia and Azerbaijan on the disputed mountain enclave.[15] The decision to convene the conference marked a historic advance of the CSCE with its enhanced powers to intervene in interstate and internal interethnic conflicts. It is likely that the CSCE will assume growing responsibilities in this area, given the fact that central governments in crisis-ridden regions, such as the CIS, are often not in a position to effectively deal with major internal conflicts on their own and for this reason will look to the CSCE for help.

The emerging pattern of delegating tasks to the different institutions can be termed inter-institutional subsidiarity. Euro-Atlantic institutions receive mandates and requests from each other and are obliged to provide ongoing consultation with all major actors involved in a crisis or non-crisis concerted action. The institution or particular organ of an institution best suited for a specific task in crisis prevention, management, or resolution is mandated to carry out that task, but inter-institutional consensus is continuously sought before making any major decisions in a specific crisis.

The act of delegating, mandating, or requesting assistance can be directed to a "higher" global authority, such as the UN, or a "lower" authority, such as a subregional body, a national government, an NGO, or an ad hoc group.

The subsidiarity principle has also been similarly built into the new institutions of the CSCE, whereby the Council, the Committee of Senior Officials, the Conflict Prevention Center, etc., were empowered at the Prague Council meeting to delegate tasks to particular CSCE or non-CSCE institutions or organs for specific commissions in all areas of CSCE activity. The German proposal for a troika within the Council and a security council-type body and the NATO proposal for a Committee of Security Cooperation reflect the need to create a much more efficient operational division of labor based on subsidiarity among an increasing number of CSCE member states, administrative organs, work groups, and inter-institutional activities.

Building out the CSCE process is also linked to the ability and responsibility of pan-European institutional and state actors to develop a qualitatively greater degree of democratic legitimation by responding to the latent demand of European publics for an inter-institutional system based on democracy, accountability, checks and balances, and a qualitatively higher degree of citizen participation than what exists today. This demand is inseparable from greater democratization within the individual institutions, in particular, in the EC and the CSCE. In this context, the work and inter-institutional dialogue, cooperation, and integration of the respective parliamentary assemblies of the EC, the Council of Europe, the CSCE, NATO, and the WEU must be upgraded. This is an area that is receiving insufficient attention at the Helsinki meeting. The failure to generate a high degree of pan-European inter-institutional democratic legitimacy could result in the refusal of national governments and publics to accept the supranational and interstate authority of pan-European institutions.

Military Security and Economic Issues

In the area of military security, Helsinki II has among its many tasks that of formulating the mandate for the future post-Helsinki negotiations on disarmament, arms control, and CSBMs. In contrast to earlier negotiations, the new CSCE negotiating framework is likely to include all CSCE states as equal participants and will have as one of its central tasks harmonizing these three sets of negotiations and integrating the new dimension of cooperative military projects. These include the

275

already extensive cooperative security agendas of NATO and the NACC. Creating a unified CSCE "security forum" or "Forum for Security Cooperation" in which disarmament, arms control, CSBMs, and military cooperation will enhance and reinforce one another also presupposes a corresponding division of labor between NATO, the NACC, the WEU, and with and within the CSCE.

While the end of the East-West conflict has not eliminated the concerns of CSCE states for a specifically military dimension of their security, it has qualitatively changed the future of arms control, disarmament, and confidence-building. The fundamental criteria and goal of parity in armed forces and weapons systems between NATO and the WTO are no longer relevant and have given way to a broader range of considerations. These include the problem of setting national limits on armed forces personnel in states that are characterized by very different defense needs, profiles, and policies, as well as integrating cooperative military dialogue and projects into future CSCE negotiations.

On a more general level, a major challenge for the CSCE process will be how to combine the traditional focus on quantitative reductions of armed forces and weapons systems to remove antagonistic security threats where these exist, while at the same time incorporating qualitative measures into future CSCE negotiations.[16]

Despite its historic advances in European disarmament, the CFE treaty contains a number of serious weaknesses. Because the CFE treaty applies only to the Atlantic-to-the-Urals (ATTU) area, the obligation to destroy military equipment was partly obviated in the early stages of the negotiations by the former Soviet Union, which withdrew more than half its equipment east of the Urals in order to save large amounts of equipment without violating the letter of the accord. The treaty also presupposed the continued existence of the WTO and, more generally, the division between East and West and thus the ability of the WTO to guarantee the unified enforcement of CFE among WTO member states.

With the end of the postwar East-West conflict, the CFE treaty has lost much of its substance as a treaty between NATO, an alliance of equally sovereign states, and a defunct WTO, which dissolved into independent, separate states each responsible for its own security. Similarly, with the breakup of the Soviet Union, the treaty must be ratified by all individual CIS and non-CIS republics that made up the former Soviet Union. Due to the changed environment and the emergence of new types of security risks within the Euro-Atlantic Space, the treaty will have to be extensively modified to achieve its full aims.

Political developments in 1992 have given rise to greater caution in assessing the treaty's future prospects.[17] Tension continued to grow between Ukraine and Russia concerning control over the former Soviet armed forces (including naval units stationed in the Black Sea), the disposition of thousands of tanks and other equipment covered by CFE, and the fate of Soviet nuclear weapons deployed on Ukrainian territory.[18] A major point of contention has been Ukraine's demand for military equality against Russia's insistence on retaining an overwhelming military advantage.[19] Negotiations between Ukraine and Russia were further complicated by the fact that, if CFE were ratified without modification, its implementation would give Ukraine more military equipment than the area of Russian territory west of the Urals, a prospect that Moscow would be hard put to accept.

Eastern Demilitarization and the CSCE's Role

With the breakup of the Soviet Union, the CFE and other agreements of the Paris CSCE Summit became in effect instruments capable of promoting internal stability in the former Soviet Union, assuming, as is likely, that the Baltic states and the CIS republics will ratify the agreement, possibly as early as the closing phase of the Helsinki Follow-Up Meeting. A framework would then be established that would limit the ability of individual CIS republics to wage war against Western states and also potentially discourage inter-republican military rivalry and potential military conflict. The treaty could also help move events in the former Soviet Union in a positive direction by encouraging reform forces that support demilitarizing policies in the individual republics. Accordingly, Russia, Ukraine, and Belarus have been offered Western political, military, and economic incentives to participate in the treaty. Similarly, Western states made their willingness to recognize Ukrainian independence conditional on the new government's adherence to CSCE principles on human rights, rule of law, privatization, democracy, and the signing of the CFE and SALT treaties.[20]

On the other hand, the dissolution of the Soviet Union, the continuing disintegrating tendencies that threaten the CIS, the armed conflict in Nagorno-Karabakh and Moldova, and other potential or manifest interethnic conflicts throughout the CIS could raise serious doubts concerning the commitment and ability of CIS signatory states to faithfully implement the letter and spirit of the CFE treaty once it is ratified.

One of the most serious challenges for Central and Eastern Europe and the CIS republics in moving away from antagonistic to comprehensive security structures is the economic, political, and social problems linked to converting bloated armed forces and military-industrial sectors to nonmilitary use.[21] The sheer size of Eastern military force structures in terms of personnel and equipment means that any effective, combined disarmament and conversion program will necessarily be a long process that must be linked to economic reform supported by considerable Western assistance.[22] The interrelationship between disarmament, conversion, and economic programs in Eastern societies suggests the importance of linking security issues with cooperation in science, economics, technology, and the environment. The implementation of the broader visions of pan-European cooperation and integration in the 1990s will depend to a significant degree on the pace, breadth, and scope of the CSCE disarmament process and security dialogue.

Particularly relevant in this regard is the setting up of pan-European frameworks under the roof of the CSCE for cooperation on environmental and health problems, energy and information networks, scientific and technological norms and standards, technology transfer, long-term programs for demilitarizing technology development, and controls to prevent the transfer of military and dual-use technology.[23] A first step in all these areas would be a declaration of guidelines, long-term aims, and recommendations by the CSCE, which could be progressively translated into policy by CSCE institutions and individual member states.

To this could be added the setting up of ad hoc interdisciplinary policy research teams within the CSCE and in institutions working with the CSCE to establish practical approaches to disarmament, arms control, and CSBMs that could most effectively contribute to stable, social market development.

279

A Euro-Atlantic Collective Security Architecture

Developments since 1989 have made it clear that the future structure of European military security is unlikely to be dominated by one institution, such as NATO, the WEU, the EC, or the CSCE, but is more likely to take the form of a structure of different interfaced institutions with partially overlapping capacities and a flexible division of labor. The reasons a network structure is much more likely than a single dominant institution, on the model of NATO in Western Europe during the postwar era, include 1) the highly heterogeneous security needs of a pan-European approach, due in part to its geographical and political complexity; 2) the broadening of the concept of security, as already discussed; 3) the new possibilities, with the end of the East-West conflict, to develop highly specific and differentiated conflict management and peacekeeping scenarios that can target localized environments; and 4) the fact that existing institutions and organizations, such as NATO and the WEU, are quite willing to revamp themselves in light of new security demands but are not willing, due to various military-security, political, and bureaucratic reasons, to transfer the greater part of their authority to other institutions, much less to a central European security body, if such a body existed.

The compromise between their claims to continue to exist, on the one hand, and their recognition that they must reform themselves, on the other hand, if they are to find a new security role adequate to the challenges of the post-Cold War era, is to accept and work within an inter-institutional network structure. Networking has the advantage of facilitating working together without merging. Institutions such as NATO and the WEU can retain their traditional but changed (diminished or increased) military functions, while being able to take on new functions (such as peacekeeping) in synchronization and through deepened cooperation with other members of Europe's family of institutions. An example of such adjustment is the establishment by NATO of the NACC, which will work with East Central European and CIS states and with the CSCE.

It should also be pointed out, however, that the pan-European diversity of state and institutional actors are still far from having agreed on how exactly an inter-institutional division of labor should look. The rudimentary pan-European structures that now exist are still not in a position to effectively carry out their central task of preventing military conflict.

NATO and the CSCE

The Rome Summit Declaration in November 1991 reflected a stronger consensus among NATO partners that the political and security challenges of the 1990s required greater willingness on the part of NATO to adjust to and support the expansion of the CSCE and other security and integration institutions. The old debate appeared for the most part resolved between the strongly Atlanticist proponents of NATO, who traditionally had been wary of the CSCE, including the US and the UK, and the strong supporters of the CSCE, such as Germany. US Secretary of State James Baker and German Foreign Minister Hans-Dietrich Genscher agreed in May 1991 on a formula whereby both NATO and the CSCE would remain pillars of Europe's future security architecture.[24]

The Rome Summit Declaration on Peace and Cooperation emphasizes that the challenges confronting the nations of the EAS cannot be addressed by one institution acting alone but only in a framework of "interlocking institutions tying together the countries of Europe and North America."[25] NATO, the CSCE, the

EC, the WEU, and the Council of Europe would, according to the authors, complement each other, and their interaction would be essential in preventing instability and divisions that could result from various causes, including economic disparities and violent expressions of nationalism.

While maintaining an "overall strategic balance" and continuing to function as the enduring military security link between Europe and North America, the alliance's new strategic concept would be a broader approach encompassing political, economic, social, and environmental dimensions of security achieved through the mutually reinforcing policy of "dialogue, cooperation, and the maintenance of a collective defense capability."[26]

NATO's military forces, according to the Rome statement, will become smaller and more flexible; conventional forces will be substantially reduced and more mobile. They will be organized for

> flexible build-up, when necessary, for crisis management as well as defense. Multinational formations will play a greater role within the integrated military structure. Nuclear forces committed to NATO will be greatly reduced: the current NATO stockpile of sub-strategic weapons in Europe will be cut by roughly 80 percent.[27]

The building out of a European security identity and defense role and strengthening the European pillar within NATO was accepted in Rome as an essential dimension of NATO reform within the larger European security context. While the alliance would remain the main forum for consultation among the 16 and the venue for agreement on policies bearing on their security and defense commitments, European states, including those who are NATO members, must decide for themselves on working out a common European foreign and security policy and defense role. In this process, arrangements must be made "to ensure the necessary transparency and complementarity between the European security and defense identity as it emerges in the 12 and the WEU, and the Alliance."[28] A reinforced WEU should assume the double role of becoming the defense component of an evolving European union and that of strengthening the European pillar of the Alliance.

The decision of the 1990 NATO summit in London to establish ties of friendship and regular diplomatic liaison with the states of Central and Eastern Europe and the Soviet Union, together with the initiatives of the NATO Copenhagen meeting in June 1991, resulted in an extensive program of high-level visits and exchanges of views, intensified by military contacts, and expert consultations in various fields. These initiatives, according to the Rome Declaration, were to be "broadened, intensified and raised to a qualitatively new level" by launching a "new era of partnership" based on the following activities:[29]

- annual meetings with the North Atlantic Council at the ministerial level in a North Atlantic Cooperation Council that would include the NATO 16 plus the foreign ministers of Eastern Europe, including Lithuania, Latvia, Estonia, and the former Soviet Union;

- periodic meetings within the NACC at the ambassadorial level plus additional meetings at the ministerial or ambassadorial level as circumstances warrant;

- regular meetings with NATO's Political, Economic, and Military Committees.

The purpose of these consultations, according to the Rome Declaration, would be to foster cooperation in areas such as "defense planning, democratic concepts of civilian-military relations, civil-military coordination of air traffic management, and the conversion of defense production to civilian purposes."[30] This section of the document also mentions NATO's scientific and environmental programs.

In recognizing the CSCE at the "only forum that brings together all countries of Europe and Canada and the US under a common code of human rights, fundamental freedoms, rule of law, security, and economic liberty,"[31] the NATO declaration proposed further strengthening of the CSCE institutions created at the Paris summit in order to "ensure full implementation" of the Helsinki Final Act and subsequent CSCE documents and "to permit the CSCE to meet the new challenges which Europe will have to face."

At the inaugural gathering of the NACC in Brussels on December 20, 1991, NATO foreign ministers and the foreign ministers of Bulgaria, the Czech and Slovak Federal Republic, Estonia, Hungary, Latvia, Lithuania, Poland, Romania, and a representative of the Soviet Union pledged to work toward "a new, lasting order of peace in Europe" based on democratic institutions, respect for human rights, and the creation of modern competitive market economies.[32] The document emphasizes the importance of strengthening the role of the CSCE and creating a European security architecture based "on a broad concept that encompasses more than ever political, economic, social and environmental aspects as well as defense and an interlocking network in which institutions such as the CSCE, the Atlantic Alliance, the EC, the WEU and the Council of Europe complement each other."[33] Following proposals of the Rome NATO summit, the NACC agreed to deepen its liaison relations and develop more institutionalized structures of consultation and cooperation exactly as summarized above.

The recent changes in NATO policy reflect the view among NATO policy makers that the Alliance's survival depends on its ability to develop a new political legitimacy firmly rooted in the post-Cold War European and global environment.[34] NATO planners must reckon with significantly reduced financial resources, as US and European political elites and publics are no longer willing to expend large sums to support expensive weapons and deployment programs that no longer appear necessary and that divert resources badly needed for nonmilitary projects. High-ranking NATO circles are also aware that the Alliance will recede in relative importance with the growth of a European defense identity and as pan-European political-security structures linked to NATO, the CSCE, the EC, and the WEU take on a larger role.

Partly in response to this prospect, NATO, while wanting to retain its basic military infrastructures, is moving in the direction of assuming pan-European cooperative security responsibilities vis-a-vis East Central Europe and the CIS republics. These include 1) taking on greater common, collective, and comprehensive-type security responsibilities; and 2) restructuring NATO's military mission along the lines that include, beside building out rapid reaction forces, developing blue and green helmet contingents that could be on call for missions organized under the auspices of the CSCE.

Here it should also be clearly noted that NATO and

European political elites remain sensitive to residual military-type security threats stemming from the legacy of the East-West conflict. The breakup of the Soviet Union; the political and military tensions between and within the CIS republics, including interethnic conflicts; the open military conflict between Azerbaijan and Armenia over Nagorno-Karabakh; the existence of 27,000 nuclear weapons in the former Soviet Union; and the rising incidence of various forms of conventional and nuclear proliferation and hence of nuclear theft and terrorism are relevant in this context and are viewed as reason enough not to reject NATO's specifically military deterrent role. Moreover, the East Central European states and Russia view NATO (and, in particular, Germany's membership) as a prerequisite for European stability.

Recent developments strongly suggest that NATO and the CSCE will cooperate and tend to overlap in areas such as disarmament, CSBMs, cooperative military programs, and support of the Eastern reform regimes. Some of the new functions of NATO that go beyond a traditional military mission that must be harmonized and progressively underpinned with arms control, disarmament, and confidence-building agreements within the CSCE include the following: providing early-warning systems for potential military threats and for nonmilitary political and civil crises; aiding in civil emergency situations, such as ecological or other types of accidents; managing the coordination of civil and military air traffic; East-West demilitarization and cooperation with Eastern armed forces; multilateralizing different forms of technical aid; retaining and reeducating Eastern armed forces that have become superfluous; and encouraging dialogue and cooperation between Eastern parliaments and the North Atlantic Assembly. These initiatives were supplemented and given a potentially common framework with the NATO proposal at the Helsinki conference for a Forum for Security Cooperation.[35]

The tension between NATO as a military organization and its cooperative security agenda poses the question of translating NATO's and the NACC's broad programs into an operational strategy that would be acceptable to the Euro-Atlantic public, political elite, and also to the CSCE, the EC, and individual CSCE member states. While the achievements of the NATO Rome summit and the discussion on the NATO proposals at the Helsinki Follow-Up Meeting on security cooperation, disarmament, etc., reflect a broad general consensus, there remains considerable room for potential disagreement over the various tabled proposals; the task of operationalizing the various blueprints on the table; and working out a division of labor between the CSCE, NATO, the NACC, the WEU, and the WEU Consultation Council.

In its search for a new identity suitable for the post-Cold War era, NATO finds itself today between two contradictory approaches to its future security role in Europe. The net result is an attempt to pursue traditional military preparedness through the building out of rapid reaction forces, etc., together with a set of new programs and initiatives within the framework of the NACC and the CSCE. The problem with this dual approach is the trade-offs it is likely to entail. There are already sufficient indications that the costs and complexity of consolidating Eastern reform regimes exceed present financial and other commitments of the West to this effort. Cooperative forms of security fleshed out at the Helsinki Follow-Up Meeting, including more concerted programs of disarmament, conversion, and economic cooperation, are indispensable for achieving the Eastern and Western goals of consolidating Eastern regimes and providing sensible avenues for

287

building down the military side of NATO's budget to the advantage of NATO's promising cooperative security agenda. If such programs fail, while at the same time resources continue to be stretched thin by high military budgets and expensive weapons projects in the period of depressed international economic growth, the result could be a failure to achieve the critical mass of demilitarizing help necessary for the Eastern democracies to get off the ground and running. The result could be a regression of Eastern and Western countries to anachronistic forms of antagonistic security thinking and policy.

Conflict Prevention and Security

The Human Dimension

The end of the postwar East-West conflict has led to a favorable international political environment for qualitatively expanding international cooperation to resolve interethnic conflicts. Constructing a pan-European architecture for this purpose within the CSCE process and embedding it in an inter-institutional division of labor is one of the most challenging tasks of Helsinki II. Such a system must be designed to deal not only with immediate, burning human dimension political crises, but also with the deeper economic and psycho-social causes and dynamics of interstate and substate ethno-national conflicts.

Under present post-Cold War conditions of weakening national state formations, particularly in Eastern Europe and the former Soviet Union, conflicts often cannot be resolved by national governments or local communities acting alone. Therefore, peaceful conflict prevention, management, and resolution mechanisms at the local and national level must be linked to collectively mandated international monitoring and intervention systems. A division of inter-institutional labor must be established that is able to combine and coordinate emergency aid and development-catalyzing investments with 1) instruments for early warning before confrontation-prone situations escalate into violence; and 2) more expeditious forms of intervening for the purpose of crisis prevention, management, and resolution.[36] A variety of instruments are necessary to help prevent interethnic, nationalist, border, or other types of conflicts from turning autistically into themselves, blocking out the outside world, and escalating into a spiral of violence. These include experimental programs in inter-community and intercultural relations to help educate conflicting ethnic groups in how to recover their ethnic identity in the new international political environment, while at the same time overcoming the psychological dynamics and tragic outcomes of interethnic hatred and violence.[37]

The CSCE agenda for further developing its human dimension and conflict prevention infrastructures include

1. Building out the CSCE codex of minority rights. In this context, the CSCE should also consider existing proposals for upgrading parts of its catalogue of individual and minority rights from their present status as merely politically binding commitments to the status of an international treaty.[38]

2. Improving the effectiveness of monitoring the implementation of individual and minority rights by CSCE members. The ODIHR has a mandate to expand CSCE collaboration with other institutions, particularly the Council of Europe and the European Commission for Democracy through Law (ECDL). Proposals for further deepening CSCE-Council of

Europe collaboration have included participation of CSCE member states who are not members of the Council of Europe in the Council of Europe's more advanced, treaty-based human rights system, which in contrast to the CSCE rights regime, enables states and persons to lodge formal complaints before the European Court of Human Rights.[39] More detailed guidelines for linking the CSCE and the Council of Europe human dimension systems must be agreed on in order to avoid unnecessary duplication and to increase their general effectiveness. Similarly, the ODIHR is mandated to establish contacts with NGOs active in the field of democratic institution building. A detailed plan should be drawn up for institutionalizing cooperation between the CSCE and NGOs and citizen initiatives concerned with human dimension violations in CSCE member states. The participation of NGOs and citizen groups in CSCE bodies must be emphasized, given the limited resources of the CSCE relative to the daunting job of protecting the rights of individuals and minorities in the new Eastern democracies. The application of the CSCE human dimension mechanism, including expert missions, can be effective only if the ODIHR, with the help of a new generation of post-Cold War "Helsinki committees," can, on the local and national level, set up informal human dimension infrastructures and promote a vibrant popular political culture of democratic and human dimension values. In this context, it should be noted that the mandate of the ODIHR that was decided at the Prague Ministerial also included:

- organizing short annual meetings to examine the implementation of CSCE human dimension commitments by member states;

- serving as a clearinghouse for exchanging information on

available technical assistance, expertise, and national and international programs for assisting new democracies in institution building;

- organizing meetings and seminars among all participating states on subjects related to building and revitalizing democratic institutions, including subjects such as migration and free media.

3. Building out mechanisms of dispute mediation and settlement so that the CSCE can use its relatively new inventory of instruments, including the dispute settlement mechanism, to intervene in disputes that could escalate into serious human dimension violations and violent conflicts. The articulation of the ODIHR's future work in this area with existing international institutions, such as the Council of Europe, the International Court of Justice, and the Permanent Court of Arbitration, must be strengthened.

4. Enlarging the CSCE's still quite limited powers for sanctioning states or non-state parties that grossly violate human dimension and other basic principles of the CSCE. The German proposal for a CSCE security council is relevant in this context.

A principal function of a CSCE security council would be to determine whether the peace were broken or a serious threat to peace were at hand.[40] On the basis of Article 40 or 41 of the UN Charter, the CSCE security council could respond initially to a breach of the peace with an economic embargo. If the embargo fails to contain the act of aggression and the economic measures taken prove inadequate, the council can then impose military sanctions along the lines of Article 42 of the UN Charter. The council could also create its own collective security forces, whose functions would include utilization as blue helmets in a peacekeeping and peacemaking capacity; carrying out military sanctions according to Article 42 of the UN Charter; and use as green helmets in ecological and natural catastrophes.

These CSCE forces would be subordinate to a Euro-Atlantic command structure under the authority of a CSCE security council that would assess acute, potential crises, while the command structure would plan and organize interventions.[41] The force could be composed of specially trained troop contingents from NATO, the WEU, and individual CSCE states, according to a treaty resting on the principles of collective security. Such a force would be used only in those cases in which all efforts to settle a dispute peacefully had failed and a military conflict had ensued or threatened to ensue. The deployment of this collective security force would be tightly linked to the evolving CSCE system of peaceful conflict resolution based on the CSCE mechanisms to prevent, regulate, and peacefully settle conflicts, as briefly reviewed above. If collective security were decoupled from the latter, such a force would risk being perverted into a purely military instrument without the political legitimacy that derives from its peacemaking and peacekeeping role.[42] The result would be a type of rapid deployment force serving particular, not collective, interests, and thus contrary to the interests of the CSCE and individual member states.

As an evolving Euro-Atlantic inter-institutional crisis prevention system, such a CSCE would tend to become a more prominent global political actor and project to other regions of the world a model of cooperative security for promoting stability, democratic reform, and development. This would be particularly relevant for the Middle East and for the future of North-South and South-South relations.

The Yugoslav Conflict and a Pan-European Security Order

If the six months of the Yugoslav crisis revealed the glaring structural deficiencies of the then still embryonic pan-European architecture for crisis prevention, it also accelerated the process of building out an inter-institutional division of labor for the purpose of dealing with the conflict. As a result, its potential to spread to neighboring states was contained and the massive assaults by the Serbian-controlled armed forces were largely brought to a halt with a combination of concerted international diplomacy, the CSCE mandate given to the EC to convene the peace conference on Yugoslavia in The Hague, EC sanctions, and the decision by the UN, supported by the EC, the CSCE, NATO, the WEU, and all major powers, to send in UN peacekeeping forces.

It is too early to judge the effectiveness of these measures to pacify the conflicting parties and irregular forces, and to halt the civil war raging in Bosnia-Herzegovina and prevent it from spreading to other disputed areas in post-federation Yugoslavia. Nevertheless, it is important to note, as a provisional conclusion, that this conflict and the danger of other ethno-national conflicts in East Central Europe and the CIS republics has sensitized governments and international publics to the destruction and horrendous loss of life that can result from ethno-national conflicts. This awareness has also accelerated the building out of new crisis prevention and regulation machinery.

The revolt of the Slovenes, Croats, and Macedonians against the Serbian-dominated Yugoslav federation can be viewed as a movement for self-determination, characterized by the striving to preserve or recover ethnic identity in a political environment in the throes of radical transformation. Neither domestic political forces in Yugoslavia nor the international community were able to halt the disintegration of the Yugoslav federation nor restrain Slovenia and Croatia from demanding their full national sovereignty vis-a-vis the Serbian-controlled center. Two key questions underlying the international debate on whether or not to recognize the independence declarations of Slovenia and Croatia were, first of all, whether or not the national states that make up the international community should encourage, or allow, the breakup of existing national state formations by minorities and national groupings wanting to secede in order to form their own states, if their living within the status quo would endanger their human rights and, in some cases, their very existence. The second key question was whether or not minority rights can be sufficiently guaranteed at the national and global level so that nationalities and minorities would not feel constrained to overturn the statist status quo and establish their own separate independent state in order to preserve or recover their identity and to achieve self-determination.

The Yugoslav crisis and the formation of new independent states has not provided clear answers to these questions. New states were formed as a result of the use of military force by all sides. The recognition of the independence of Croatia and Slovenia by the international community opened the way to sending in UN peacekeeping troops and to a possible, but by no means assured, pacification of the conflict. The protection of minorities in the different post-federation republics and prevention of civil war remain very much open questions, both for the Yugoslav republics themselves and the international community.

While the CSCE process enshrined the principle of self-determination of peoples and the universal human rights of the individual, it failed throughout the postwar era to deal squarely with the issue of the fate of suppressed minority and national groups.[43] A fully functioning regime of minority and nationality rights with adequate implementation, monitoring, and conflict resolution machinery, combined with a system of effective international sanctions to enforce such rights and obligations, did not resonate among most Western and Eastern CSCE member states during the postwar era. The majority had traditionally been adverse to politically enfranchising their own national minorities because such a course, in their view, would unacceptably weaken their central authority in domestic and foreign policy.

As a result, minorities did not acquire their rightful place in postwar international law, nor did they enjoy the right of self-determination as political subjects, either in relation to the national state or in international human rights regimes. With the systemic changes in Eastern Europe and the former Soviet Union in the late 1980s, the past neglect of group rights became a nemesis for the architects of a post-Cold War order of peace and security, as the storm of interethnic and nationality-related violent conflicts in the CIS republics, Yugoslavia, and southern Turkey demonstrate. The setting up of a comprehensive minority rights regime has thus become a high priority on the Helsinki II agenda.

On the positive side, the Yugoslav crisis has shown that the evolving Euro-Atlantic security system is capable of applying a policy of collective political containment of military conflicts in order to preempt a regional or global escalation of violence. This tentative and still fragile success was achieved through a combination of concerted diplomacy, a carrot-and-stick EC linkage policy, and the application of peace-promoting instruments. The decision of the CSCE Helsinki Follow-Up Meeting to convene a peace conference on the conflict between Armenia and Azerbaijan over the disputed mountain enclave Nagorno-Karabakh is indeed another historic step, albeit belated and risky, in moving forward the building out of the CSCE system.[44]

Conclusion

Several challenges face the CSCE. Notwithstanding the milestone advances of the CSCE in its overarching and linchpin role in the construction of a Euro-Atlantic security architecture, it faces a number of daunting challenges in the current phase of its institutionalization process. These include the following:

1. As an evolving crisis prevention, management, and resolution system, it may prove too slow in its structural development to be effective in keeping up with the proliferation of major ethnic and other types of conflicts that are likely to increase in number.

2. Beside the problems of structurally building out CSCE institutions, there is also the danger of the CSCE becoming bogged down in lengthy bureaucratic procedures.

3. Similarly, the crystallization of a fully worked-out division of labor within the CSCE and between the CSCE and other institutions is a complex process that is likely to take a number of years to work out and involve a great deal of trial and error

before it will become fully operational and effective.

4. States belonging to the CSCE might be unwilling to recognize and implement expanded rights of self-determination of ethno-national minorities within their borders, despite the fact that events since the end of the East-West conflict strongly suggest that ethno-national strife and minority rights are among the most serious security problems the EAS and the entire world will face in the coming years. These conflicts, moreover, cannot be genuinely resolved by using violence to reassert the power of status quo-bound, centralized states over ethno-national minorities that are determined to claim their self-determination in the post-Cold War world. In this context, there appears to be two options:

- greater recognition of minority rights and self-determination, including a "new deal" between national states and minorities, in which mutual rights and obligations would be enshrined and implemented at the local, national, subregional, regional, and global level; or

- states would tend to close in on themselves, become more narrowly nationalist in outlook and policy, and place greater emphasis on military as opposed to cooperative forms of security. Such a trend would result in reducing the promise and effectiveness of the CSCE and Euro-Atlantic security architecture as a whole and would be a grave risk for international stability.

5. The difficulty of the 52 CSCE member states in achieving agreement among themselves on the highly complex and lengthening agenda of current issues and crises they face should never be underestimated.

While the CSCE and the Euro-Atlantic system as a whole face daunting tasks, there are many reasons to be optimistic concerning the chances for their achieving qualitatively new forms of security in the EAS and globally in the coming years.

Notes

1. In this essay, I will use the term "Euro-Atlantic Space" (EAS) to denote the geographic-political area encompassing the territory of member states of the CSCE extending from Vancouver to Vladivostok. The term "pan-European" is used synonymously unless otherwise stated.

2. Manfred Efinger and Volker Rittberger, "The CSBM Regime in and for Europe: Confidence Building and Peaceful Conflict Management," in *European Security--Towards 2000*, ed. Michael C. Pugh (Manchester and New York: Manchester University Press, 1992), pp. 105-23.

3. The ECO, founded in 1963 and revived by Turkey in February 1992, consists of the coastal states of the Black Sea, including Iran, Pakistan, and the CIS republics of Azerbaijan, Turkmenistan, and Uzbekistan. See Wolf J. Bell, "Strategischer Eckpfeiler und Brücke des Westens zum Orient," *General Anzeiger*, Feb. 20, 1991. The CEI has grown out of the Pentagonale initiative, which became the Hexagonale and then was subsequently renamed the CEI in December 1991. See Jan B. de Weydenthal, "Poland, Rapprochement with the West," *Report on Eastern Europe* 2, no. 51/52 (Dec. 20, 1991), p. 23. A necessary addition to the list of European institutions is the planned WEU Consultation Council, which will have its founding meeting in Mainz, Germany, on May 5, 1992.

4. Michael R. Lucas and Anna Kreikemeyer, "Der Europarat und der gesamteuropäischene Integrationsprozeß," *Südosteuropa* 39, no. 10 (1990), pp. 609-26; Michael R. Lucas and Anna Kreikemeyer, "Pan-European Integration and European Institutions: The New Role of the Council of Europe" (unpublished manuscript, 1992).

5. The Prague Document on Further Development of CSCE Institutions and Structures (Prague, Jan. 30, 1992).

6. Ibid., para. 10. See also later in this chapter.

7. Ibid., section 4, para. 16.

8. Ibid.

9. Ibid., section 5, para. 19. The first meeting of the CSCE Economic Forum will take place in early 1993.

10. Ibid., section 6, para. 27. On the CPC, see Yves Ghebali, "Une institution européene nouvelle: le Centre du CSCE sur la prevention des conflits en l'europe," *Trimestre du Monde*, no. 13 (1991), pp. 122-29.

11. Section 4, Summary of Conclusions, Meeting of the CSCE Council of Ministers, Prague, Jan. 30-31, 1992.

12. Ibid., section 6.

13. Ibid., section 7.

14. See in this context the interview with Dr. Manfred Wörner, NATO General Secretary, on the North Atlantic Cooperation Council, BBC, "The World Tonight," March 9, 1992.

15. Summary of Conclusions of the Helsinki Additional Meeting of the CSCE, March 24, 1992. Reprinted in *US Policy, Information and Texts* (henceforth *USPIT*), March 24, 1992. The participants of the conference were Armenia, Azerbaijan, Belarus, the Czech and Slovak Federal Republic, Germany, Sweden, Italy, the United States, the Russian Federation, Turkey, and France.

16. Günther Altenburg, "Von der Rüstungskontrolle zum Sicherheitsforum," *Berichte des Bundesinstituts für Ostwissenschaftliche und Internationale Studien*, no. 43 (1991).

17. Rick Marshall, "CFE Treaty Seen as Hedge Against Remilitarization," *USPIT*, Nov. 13, 1991.

18. On the Soviet nuclear arsenal, see Kurt M. Campbell, Ashton B. Cantor, Steven E. Miller, and Charles A. Zraket, *Soviet Nuclear Fission: Control of the Nuclear Arsenal in a Disintegrating Soviet Union* (Cambridge, MA: Center for Science and International Affairs [CSIA], 1991).

19. "CFE Treaty Endangered," *RFE/RL Report* 1, no. 8, (Feb. 21, 1992), p. 53.

20. Rick Marshall, "CFE Treaty Seen as Hedge Against Remilitarization."

21. Daniel N. Nelson, "The Costs of Demilitarization in the USSR and Eastern Europe," *Survival* 28, no. 4 (July/August 1991), pp. 312-26. See also in this context Hans-Georg Ehrhart, Anna Kreikemeyer, Ursel Schlichting, "Die Sowjetunion in Europa. Beiträge zur sowjetische Frage," *Hamburger Beiträge*, no. 54 (May 1991).

22. In 1990, Soviet security specialist Alexei Arbatov estimated that 40 billion rubles would be needed by the end of 1995 to finance Soviet conversion (as cited by Nelson, "The Costs of Demilitarization in the USSR and Eastern Europe").

23. See in this context Michael R. Lucas, "The Abolition of COCOM and the Establishment of a Technology Disarmament and Transfer Agency in the CSCE," *Bulletin of Peace Proposals* 21, no. 2 (1990), pp. 219-25.1

24. The Baker-Genscher statement is reprinted in "Baker, Genscher Issue Statement on NATO, CSCE," *USPIT*, May 13, 1991.

25. "Rome Declaration on Peace and Cooperation," reprinted in *USPIT*, Nov. 8, 1991; "The Alliance's New Strategic Concept," reprinted in *USPIT*, Nov. 7, 1991.

26. "The Alliance's New Strategic Concept."

27. Ibid.

28. Ibid., para. 6.

29. Ibid., para. 9.

30. Ibid., para. 12.

31. Ibid., para. 13.

32. "Security, Economic Issues Top European Agenda," NACC communique, reprinted in *USPIT*, Dec. 20, 1991.

33. Ibid.

34. Manfred Wörner, "Die Atlantische Allianz und die europäische Sicherheit," *Europa-Archiv* 47, no. 1, pp. 1-6.

35. See also in this context the NATO communique of the meeting of defense ministers in Brussels, April 1, 1992. Reprinted in "NATO Statement on Defense Ministers Meeting," *USPIT*, April 1, 1992.

36. Dieter Senghaas, "Therapeutische Konflikintervention in Europa, Eskalation und Deeskalation ethnonationalistische Konflikte," Research Report, Stiftung Wissenschaft und Politik, June 1991. See also Dieter S. Lutz, *Sicherheit 2000* (Baden-Baden: Nomos Verlagsgesellschaft, 1991).

37. Senghass, "Therapeutische Konflikintervention in Europa."

38. For a critique of the decalogue principles, see Luigi Vittorio Ferraris, "Réflexions critiques sur le Décalogue de la CSCE," *Trimestre du Monde*, no. 1 (1992), pp. 203-10.

39. Lucas and Kreikemeyer, "Der Europarat und der gesamteuropäischene Integrationsprozess."

40. For a discussion of a CSCE security council, see Eric Remacle, "L'esquisse pour une nouvelle paysage européene," in UNIDIR, *Travaux de recherche* (October 1991).

41. This model is largely based on Senghaas, "Therapeutische Konflikintervention in Europa.

42. Ibid.

43. On human rights in the CSCE during the postwar era, see Michael R. Lucas, "The Conference on Security and Cooperation in Europe and the Post-Cold War Era," *Hamburger Beiträge*, Heft 48, September 1990.

44. "KSZE-Minister einig über Kaukasus-Konferenz," *General Anzeiger*, March 24, 1992.

List of Participants

Conference on "Redefining the CSCE: Challenges and
Opportunities in the New Europe"
Helsinki, May 21-22, 1992

Martti Ahtisaari
Secretary of State
Finnish Ministry for Foreign Affairs

Adam Smith Albion
Research Associate
IEWS European Studies Center

Jaakko Blomberg
Director General
Finnish Ministry for Foreign Affairs

Oleg N. Bykov
Deputy Director
Institute of World Economy and International Relations

Fraser Cameron
Foreign Policy Advisor
Secretariat General of the European Commission

Henning Christopherson
Vice President
Commission of the European Community

Andrej Cima
CSFR Ministry for Foreign Affairs

Ian M. Cuthbertson
Director of the Security Program
Institute for EastWest Studies

Nils Eliasson
Director
CSCE Secretariat

Lily Gardner Feldman
Research Director
American Institute for Contemporary German Studies

Felice Gaer
Executive Director, European Programs
United Nations Association of the USA

Heinz Gärtner
Researcher
Austrian Institute for International Affairs

Magarditsch Hatschikjan
Research Associate
Konrad Adenauer Stiftung

Jyrki Iivonen
Special Research Fellow
Finnish Institute of International Affairs

Andrzej Karkoszka
Research Fellow
Polish Institute of International Affairs

Patrick Keatinge
Associate Professor of Political Science
Trinity College, Dublin

Charles W. Kegley, Jr.
Pearce Professor of International Relations
University of South Carolina

Jean Klein
Senior Research Fellow
Institute Francais des Relations Internationales

Jaakko Laajava
Deputy Director General
Finnish Ministry for Foreign Affairs

James Macintosh
Senior Research Associate
York Centre for International and Strategic Studies

Margarita Mathiopoulos
Guest Professor of International Relations
Humboldt University

Kari Möttölä
Special Advisor
Finnish Ministry for Foreign Affairs

Richard Müller
Former Finnish Ambassador to the United States

Juhani Paakkinen
Colonel
Finnish Frontier Guard

Risto Penttilä
Special Advisor
Finnish Ministry of Defense

Weijo Pitkänen
Special Research Fellow
Finnish Institute of International Affairs

Adam Daniel Rotfeld
Director
Stockholm International Peace Research Institute

Alpo Rusi
Director of Nordic and Other Western States Affairs
Political Department
Finnish Ministry for Foreign Affairs

Tapani Vaahtoranta
Director
Finnish Institute of International Affairs

Paavo Väyrynen
Minister for Foreign Affairs of Finland

Raimo Väyrynen
Professor
University of Helsinki

Rauno Viemärö
Ambassador
Finnish Ministry for Foreign Affairs

Janne Virkkunen
Editor in Chief
Sanoma Corporation

Jarmo Virmavirta
Chairman
Board of the Foundation for Foreign Policy Research

Radovan Vukadinovič
Head of Department for International Relations
Institute of Political Sciences
Zagreb University

About the Authors

Adam Smith Albion has been a research associate at the IEWS European Studies Center since 1991. He specializes in issues relating to East Central European militaries, ethnicity and nationalism, and peacekeeping.

Oleg N. Bykov is Deputy Director of the Institute of World Economy and International Relations (IMEMO) in Moscow. He is also a corresponding member of the Russian Academy of Sciences and a former member of the UN Advisory Board on Disarmament Studies and the UN Group of Governmental Experts on Confidence-Building Measures.

Fraser Cameron has been a foreign policy advisor in the Secretariat General of the European Commission since September 1990. From 1975-1989 he was a member of the British Diplomatic Service.

Andrej Cima has been a member of the Czechoslovak presidency of the CSCE Secretariat since January 1992. He has participated in the recent CSCE monitor missions to Armenia and Azerbaijan and was a member of the Czechoslovak delegation at the meetings of the CSCE Committee of Senior Officials in Prague and Helsinki between September 1991 and May 1992.

Ian M. Cuthbertson currently works as the Director of the Security Program at the Institute for EastWest Studies. He was previously a senior research officer in the Arms Control and Disarmament Research Unit of the British Foreign and Commonwealth Office.

Heinz Gärtner has been a researcher at the Austrian Institute for International Affairs since 1979. He also serves as a member of the Expert Group on Arms Control of the Austrian Ministry for Foreign Affairs.

Andrzej Karkoszka has been a Research Fellow at the Polish Institute of International Affairs since 1969. He also worked as a researcher at the Stockholm International Peace Research Institute and served on UNIDIR Expert Groups on Outer Space and on Verification of Disarmament.

Charles W. Kegley, Jr. is Pearce Professor of International Relations at the University of South Carolina. He is President-Elect of the International Studies Association, and has held visiting appointments at Rutgers University and the University of Texas.

Michael R. Lucas is a Senior Research Fellow at the World Policy Institute in New York. He has recently served as a Visiting Scholar at the Institut für Friedensforschung und Sicherheitspolitik at Hamburg University.

Margarita Mathiopoulos has been a Guest Professor of International Relations at Berlin's Humboldt University since 1990. She has also served as Associate Director of the ASPEN Institute Berlin and worked as a journalist for German and Greek newspapers since 1974.

Adam Daniel Rotfeld has been Director of the Stockholm International Peace Research Institute (SIPRI) since 1991. He has participated in CSCE negotiations since 1973 and has published extensively on European security and arms control.

Alpo Rusi is currently the Director of Nordic and Other Western States Affairs in the Political Department of the Ministry for Foreign Affairs of Finland. He is also an adjunct professor at Tampere University and has served with the Finnish Mission to the United Nations.

Institute for EastWest Studies
BOARD OF DIRECTORS